D1485510

Working with
Parents of
Anxious Children

A Norton Professional Book

Working with Parents of Anxious Children

*Therapeutic Strategies
for Encouraging
Communication, Coping, & Change*

CHRISTOPHER McCURRY

W.W. Norton & Company
New York • London

For information about permission to reproduce selections from this book, write to
Permissions, W. W. Norton & Company, Inc., 500 Fifth Avenue, New York, NY 10110

For information about special discounts for bulk purchases, please contact
W. W. Norton Special Sales at specialsales@wwnorton.com or 800-233-4830

Manufacturing by Maple Press
Production manager: Christine Critelli

ISBN: 978-0-393-73401-0

W. W. Norton & Company, Inc., 500 Fifth Avenue, New York, NY 10110
www.wwnorton.com

W. W. Norton & Company Ltd., Castle House, 75/76 Wells Street, London W1T 3QT

1 2 3 4 5 6 7 8 9 0

For Ian
Being your dad will be the
best part of my life.

CONTENTS

Part Three:
Sustaining the Dance—and the Dancers

Working with
Parents of
Anxious Children

ACKNOWLEDGMENTS

It's been said that if you steal an idea from a person, it's plagiarism; but if you steal lots of ideas from lots of people, it's research. This is a very well-researched book. I have done my best to cite everyone whose work has informed this book, and their publications can be found in the References section. I want to specifically acknowledge the important clinical/research work and writings of David Barlow, Timothy Cavell, Bruce Chorpita, Jean Dumas, Jill Ehrenreich-May, David Rettew, and Robert Wahler.

I am also indebted to the local heroes from whom I have learned so much: Steve Engelberg, Laura Kastner, Travis Osborne, and Matt Speltz. I would like to acknowledge Dr. Rich Adler for his mentorship and teaching me about The Referral Path. I want to thank D. I. for the metaphor of adjusting to the loss of an important chess piece.

To everyone at W. W. Norton, especially Andrea Dawson, Ben Yarling, Katie Moyer, and Sara Peterson. Thank you for your faith in this project and for your deep well of patience from beginning to end. I would also like to express my gratitude to Jean Blomquist, freelance editor extraordinaire.

To all my partners at Associates in Behavior and Child Development, Inc.; thank you for your comradeship every day. It would be so much harder to do this work without your support and good humor.

For all they have taught me, I would like to convey my gratitude to the many families I have had the privilege of working with over the years.

Finally, and with deep appreciation, I want to acknowledge the loving support of my wife, Sue, and my son, Ian.

INTRODUCTION

I handed Sara the box of tissues and, between sobs, she recounted recent events. Every school morning Sara and Wyatt, her ten-year-old son, would go through the same highly predictable routine. Sara woke Wyatt at 6:30, the time they'd agreed to the night before. She'd rub his back and tell him what a great day this would be and how she would prepare his favorite breakfast. "Remember, we had an agreement," she'd say lightly. But the nervousness and strain in Sara's voice revealed her lack of confidence and resolve.

Wyatt would then moan and curl himself into his blankets. Sara would leave him there for ten minutes, coming back to let him know breakfast was on the table. Wyatt would then complain of a stomachache, a headache, and a lack of clean underwear. Sara would calmly reassure him about his stomach and head and point out the generous supply of underwear in his top drawer. "But that underwear feels weird and it's baby underwear," Wyatt would cry. Sara would state, with growing agitation, that the underwear was perfectly fine and breakfast was getting cold. Wyatt's protests would grow louder and more desperate, "You don't understand. I can't do this. I hate you. Why don't you just kill me?"

At this point Dan, Wyatt's father, would burst into the room demanding Wyatt get out of bed or lose all screen time ("no T.V., no video games, no computer—*nothing*") for the next month. Sara would try to get Dan out of the room saying, "This isn't helping." Dan and Sara would retreat to the hallway where they would argue, each accusing the other of mishandling the situation, until Dan angrily left for work.

"I just can't force him to go to school when he feels that way," sighed Sara. Then she adds with conviction, "I won't force him. I have anxiety. I know what it's like and it just breaks my heart." Wyatt had not been to school in two weeks.

If you're a clinician—psychologist, clinical social worker, mental health counselor, psychiatrist—working with anxious children as I am, this scenario undoubtedly sounds all too familiar. And, if you work with anxious children, then you also work with their parents, "officially" or not. In this book, we'll explore the role that parents and other caregivers play in the life of the anxious child. Together we'll look at the complex parent-child "dance" that is childhood anxiety. The emphasis will be not on casting blame, but on how parents can foster getting through daily life in spite of the strong emotions and thoughts that inevitably arise in challenging situations, such as the one involving Wyatt and his parents.

But before we look at how we can work more effectively with parents of anxious children, I want to lay some necessary groundwork by describing the landscape of child anxiety, starting with differing perspectives on diagnosis. After some brief general information on childhood anxiety, I will first look at child anxiety from the traditional diagnostic system of the *Diagnostic and Statistical Manual of Mental Disorders,* fifth edition (DSM 5) published by the American Psychiatric Association (2013). I will then discuss complementary diagnostic approaches to childhood anxiety that will be familiar to many of you and perhaps be somewhat new to others. These models—functional analysis and transdiagnostic assessment/treatment—are derived from behavioral theory and have received a great deal of attention lately, especially in the mindfulness and acceptance-based therapies, such as dialectical behavior therapy and acceptance and commitment therapy. As I'll point out, these latter approaches to diagnosis and treatment are less symptom focused than the DSM and more interested in the *function* of the anxious or fearful child's *behavior* in context. For our purposes, then, the most developmentally significant context for evoking and maintaining a child's behavior is the parent-child relationship. The parent-child relationship is also the first and most important context for encouraging communication, coping, and change.

But before we get to the heart of this chapter, let me say that if you're a busy clinician like me, you pick up books like this one and start reading with a "just tell me what to do" mindset. You may be tempted to skip ahead to chapters X and Y where the "real action"— the "tools"—await you. Please resist this temptation. Read through the entire book. Although you are likely familiar with much of the information in Part One, I strongly assert that a big part of helping parents of anxious children involves psychoeducation, offered early and often in the treatment process. In fact, change—in the form of shaping a parent's thinking about "the problem"—starts with your understanding of how the child has come to you, how your first questions are posed, and other aspects of the assessment phase.

As you know, and as I will describe, parents often come into your office with patterns of feeling, thinking, and behavior (reacting) that have become rigid and habitual with months or years of "practice." They may carry misinformation about child development, the brain, parenting, psychotherapy, or any number of topics relevant to your work. In Part One, you will find nuggets that can be conveyed to parents to help organize their thinking in more flexible, compassionate, and productive ways, so please don't skip that section!

ANXIETY DISORDERS IN CHILDREN

Anxiety disorders are among the most common presenting problems in the typical child psychology or counseling practice. Transient, episodic fear and anxiety occur in virtually all children. However, between 10 and 20 percent of children will experience significant anxiety that interferes with everyday life and qualifies them for one or more anxiety disorders (Costello & Angold, 1995).

Childhood anxiety in particular can be quite persistent with significant impairment continuing into adulthood. Additionally, anxiety in childhood sets the stage for depression later in adolescence and adulthood, especially for girls (Garber & Weersing 2010). Overall, half of the mental health issues adults experience began before their fourteenth birthday (Kessler, Gruber, Hettema, Hwang, Sampson, & Yonkers, 2008).

Worries and fears can be quite distracting and children with an anxiety disorder are often described as having an attention deficit disorder as well. Anxiety can also affect sleep, and poor sleep hygiene is related to both attentional and behavioral problems in children (Virring, Lambek, Jennum, Møller, & Thomsen, 2014). Vicious cycles can then develop that are difficult to break.

Internalizing and Externalizing Disorders

Within the DSM system, anxiety is considered one of the internalizing disorders. *Internalizing disorders*, such as anxiety and depression, are marked by the individual's propensity to express distress inward (Cosgrove et al., 2011). This is in contrast to the so-called *externalizing disorders*, such as attention-deficit/hyperactivity disorder (ADHD) and oppositional defiant disorder (ODD), which are marked by the child's expressing distress through outward behaviors and which often create distress and problems for others in the immediate vicinity. But as you know from experience, and as I will explore, childhood anxiety often manifests as outward behavior—behavior that is often difficult to distinguish from ADHD and ODD symptoms.

Anxiety and Others

Childhood anxiety does not affect only the child. Virtually all children reside within a system—for example, a family system or the classroom—and the child's ongoing moods and behaviors will affect those around him. Other family members may share in the anxiety, become frustrated or annoyed by it, despair, retreat, or display any number of other reactions. Clinical research has explored the interpersonal nature of child anxiety, both in terms of its effect on those around the anxious child and in terms of how anxiety develops "within" the individual as a product of biology, experience, and socialization.

Anxiety and Context

Then there is the influence of *context*. Recall the painful morning endured by Sara, Wyatt, and Dan from the beginning of this chapter. Every parent, and every clinician, knows that certain times of day or certain tasks may be especially challenging for a child, fraught with anxious arousal and its accompanying behaviors. As a clinician working with anxious children, you have heard the stories about the dreaded "transition times": getting ready for school in the morning, returning home and having to leave again for soccer practice or gymnastics, starting homework, getting ready for bed, and so on. Identifying the relevant anxiety-provoking situations or contexts is an important part of the assessment process.

Anxiety also has a social context. Children, especially young children, are rarely alone for any length of time, and, as I will emphasize, anxiety almost always involves a parent or other adult, such as a teacher or nanny, attempting to manage the child's fears, anxieties, and accompanying behaviors. Assessing these interpersonal components of childhood anxiety is central to understanding how to help not just the child, but the involved, and likely distressed, adults as well.

DIAGNOSIS IN CHILD ANXIETY: THE DSM SYSTEM AND CATEGORIES

Changes are occurring in the world of mental health diagnosis. It's a little hard to keep up. In 2013, the American Psychiatric Association published its fifth edition of the *Diagnostic and Statistical Manual of Mental Disorders*, or DSM 5. Even before it saw the light of day, this revision was a lightning rod for criticism from many quarters. Space here does not permit a full critique of this manual nor is that necessary for our purposes. Some comments below will serve to illustrate issues relevant to our work. By the time you read this, we may all be using diagnostic codes from the tenth edition of the *International Classification of Diseases*, or ICD–10 (World Health Organization, 1992).

The DSM 5 represents what is known as a "formal" diagnostic system; it looks at the "form" or the topography of the individual's symptoms. Thoughts, feelings, and behaviors observed in or reported by the individual are noted and compared to a standard set of thoughts, feelings, and behaviors believed to hang together in the form of a syndrome or a template. If the description of the presenting problems matches the description of the standard syndrome to a sufficient degree, you "have" the disorder—ADHD, separation anxiety, and so on.

The DSM system is relatively silent on the etiology, or cause, of the vast majority of its disorders. This is probably a good thing—which theoretical model should be used? Instead, a formal or syndromal diagnostic system often gives us rather circular reasoning:

- Why does Freya exhibit "clinically significant anxiety provoked by exposure to certain types of social or performance situations, often leading to avoidance behavior"?
- Because she has social phobia.
- Why does Freya have social phobia?
- Because she exhibits "clinically significant anxiety provoked by exposure to certain types of social or performance situations, often leading to avoidance behavior."

Also, it is clear to everyone in this field, and to parents as well, that these categories are also *dimensional* or on a continuum. There can be mild manifestations of anxiety as well as severe presentations.

THE MANY FACES OF ANXIETY: THE MORE COMMON DSM 5 ANXIETY DIAGNOSTIC CATEGORIES

Unless otherwise noted, the source for these descriptions is the DSM 5 itself.

Separation Anxiety Disorder

Separation anxiety is the most common form of anxiety found in children. It manifests as anxious arousal and worries associated with separation from a primary caregiver or simply from the home. Because anxiety at separation is fairly common in children, to obtain the diagnosis the child's distress must exceed what might be expected for his developmental level. Estimated six- to twelve-month prevalence is about 4 percent of children, with declining prevalence from childhood to adolescence. Separation anxiety disorder rarely develops after puberty (Costello et al., 2004). Like most childhood anxiety disorders, separation anxiety affects females somewhat more than males.

Common presentations include general distress, worries about harm to oneself or to the caregiver, poor concentration (for example, at school), difficulty sleeping, somatic complaints, nightmares, and avoidance of situations requiring separation (school, sleepovers, sleep-away camp).

Selective Mutism

This category includes consistent failure to speak (initiate or respond) in common social situations, such as school. The child may have little or no difficulty speaking at home or to immediate family members. The condition is rather rare, found in only about 0.03 to 1 percent of the population. It tends to appear about the time a child enters school, around age five. Selective mutism does not appear to favor one gender over the other.

This condition must be distinguished from autism spectrum disorders or mere shyness. It can be difficult to tease apart selective mutism from social anxiety or separation anxiety.

Specific Phobia

Specific phobias are persistent and unusually severe fear responses to particular situations or objects: animals and insects, wind and thunder, elevators, the dark, clowns, almost anything. Overall anxious distress and physiological arousal (fight-or-flight response) along with avoidance of or attempts at escape from fearful situations are the most common behavioral symptoms of specific phobia. Additionally, we might see reassurance seeking and attempts at controlling situations—for example, not allowing windows to be open in the house or car for fear of insects flying in.

The one-year prevalence rate for specific phobia is approximately 5 percent in children and 16 percent in adolescents. The average age of onset is six, but the syndrome can appear at almost any age (Costello et al., 2004). Females are involved at roughly twice the rate as males.

Social Anxiety Disorder

Social anxiety or social phobia involves anxious thoughts about being in social situations and receiving negative or critical feedback or attention. Per the DSM 5, the child's worry must be related to peer interactions and not simply the scrutiny and judgment of adults (for example, teachers). Social situations are avoided altogether or endured with considerable distress. The twelve-month U.S. prevalence rate is approximately 7 percent, with equal numbers of males and females at younger ages, but with increasingly more girls represented among adolescents and young adults. The median age of onset is thirteen.

Panic Disorder

Panic disorder is defined as recurring, abrupt, uncued panic attacks: extreme anxiety, sweating, racing heart, trembling, chest pain, shortness of breath, dizziness, and other unpleasantness. Episodes last five to twenty minutes. Panic disorder can be quite debilitating and lead to anxiety over possible panic in the future and to avoidance of potential triggers (real or imagined) or situations associated with panic attacks in the past.

Panic disorder rarely emerges before adolescence, with the median age of onset somewhere between ages twenty and twenty-four. Panic disorder affects approximately 2 to 3 percent of the population.

Agoraphobia

Agoraphobia is a combination of fear/anxiety about situations that often include thoughts of feeling trapped or being unable to escape or to get help if anxiety/panic occurs. These situations include modes of transportation (especially public transportation), large open spaces, enclosed places (stores, theaters), crowds, or simply being away from home alone. Avoidance of these situations, or needing a companion present to tolerate these situations, is a hallmark of this disorder. The full disorder is fairly rare (under 1.7 percent of adolescents and adults) and rarer still in younger children, although it is not unheard of. Females are twice as likely to experience agoraphobia as males.

It is not that unusual for a child to want a safe person to accompany him to new or challenging situations; a friend going to the same sleep-away camp can make all the difference. Problems arise when the avoidance starts to interfere with developmentally important tasks and the child's arc toward independence.

Generalized Anxiety Disorder (GAD)

Generalized anxiety disorder (GAD) is your basic, classic worry diagnosis. The diagnostic criteria state that *excessive* anxiety and worry must be present more days than not for a minimum of six months. The worries must concern several areas in the child's life (for example, home, friendships, and school). The child must perceive that the worries are difficult to control. Additionally, the worries must be associated with one or more additional symptoms, such as irritability, headaches, difficulty concentrating, or sleep disturbance. Typical age of onset is ten and older (Beidel & Turner, 2005). Again, avoidance of important activities and places is a common behavioral component.

Obsessive-Compulsive Disorder (OCD)

One significant change in the DSM 5 was moving obsessive-compulsive disorder out of the anxiety disorders altogether and placing it in a new category, Obsessive-Compulsive and Related Disorders. The diagnostic criteria remain much the same. An *obsession* is a recurrent, persistent, and intrusive thought, urge, or image that evokes some anxiety or distress that the individual attempts to eliminate or neutralize through some action (the compulsion). A *compulsion* is then the repetitive outward behavior or mental act that will ward off some negative event and/or reduce the anxiety associated with the obsession.

The average age of onset is ten (Beidel & Turner, 2005), but children as young as preschool age can develop symptoms as well. Obsessions in children may include thoughts about death or injury to self or others (which can lead to separation anxiety), aggression or sexual issues, germs and other contamination, or fires and burglars, to name a few. Common compulsions include hand washing, checking, and ordering.

Some compulsions involving order or symmetry may be thought of as "just so" compulsions. Some children with these "just so" compulsions report no anxiety associated with the thoughts or behaviors. These children may simply state that they just like things to be that way. Whether there is an underlying anxiety or fear these children can't recognize or articulate is a matter of speculation.

It should be noted, however, that many children, and some adults, indulge in all sorts of superstitions and magical thinking. Additionally, children tend to like and need structure and predictability. It is sometimes hard to draw the line between a favored good-night routine and a compulsive ritual.

Illness Anxiety Disorder

Another fairly common syndrome in children that is somewhat related to OCD is illness anxiety disorder, which is found in DSM 5 under the category of Somatic Symptoms and Related Disorders. Here the preoccupations are with having or acquiring a serious illness. This syndrome may also be thought of as "health anxiety," somatization disorder, or hypochondriasis. Outward behaviors include avoiding perceived sources of threat, seeking reassurance, and repeatedly asking questions about illness and threats.

COMORBIDITY

A child (or adult) with one diagnosable anxiety disorder often meets criteria for another. Separation anxiety disorder, for example, is highly comorbid with generalized anxiety disorder. Selective mutism is most commonly associated with social anxiety, as well as with separation anxiety and specific phobia. You've no doubt seen this in your practice.

Anxiety disorders in children also have significant co-occurrences with a number of other syndromes. These include attention-deficit/hyperactivity disorder, oppositional defiant disorder, depression, and substance abuse in adolescents. Typically, anxiety shows up in childhood and then depression emerges in adolescence (Garber & Weersing, 2010).

Anxiety and aggressive/oppositional behaviors are common comorbidities. If one thinks of anxiety as involving the fight-or-flight response, with an emphasis on "fight," then this would make sense. In Chapter 1 I describe research into selective attention to threat cues in anxious individuals that likely contributes to this unpleasant combination of syndromes.

Anxiety is also a common condition in children with intellectual disabilities and those on the autism spectrum, especially the mild end with conditions such as Asperger's syndrome (Gobrial & Raghavan, 2012). Finally, the presence of a learning disability greatly increases the risk for anxiety, especially social anxiety, compared to children without learning issues (Cowden, 2010).

TWO IMPORTANT LIMITATIONS OF DSM DIAGNOSIS

Since its inception in 1952, the DSM, and the sort of diagnostic system it represents, has had its critics. Again, it is not my purpose to give a full and balanced critique of the DSM. But I would like to point out two limitations in relying *solely* on DSM-type categorical, symptom-based diagnosis.

First, the DSM, and other systems based on cataloging symptoms, give us "the false impression that anxiety disorders are more different from one another than they really are" (Eifert & Forsyth, 2005, p. 4). At the level of diagnostic specificity, how does one distinguish between social anxiety, generalized anxiety, and separation anxiety if outwardly the child is distressed and avoiding school? An older child may offer a reason: critical peers, an upcoming test, thoughts of harm coming to a parent. But often the reason-giving is vague, cuts across multiple domains, or seems like "backfilling" (to be discussed later).

Second, and more important for our purposes, a symptom-based diagnostic system focuses treatment efforts on reducing, if not eliminating, the symptoms themselves. This makes sense. If you have a splinter in your finger, you pull it out. However, you may have discovered that trying to eliminate anxiety symptoms is quite difficult. Classic cognitive behavioral therapy (CBT) has concerned itself with attempts at altering the content of a client's cognitions or in some way reducing the "negative" thoughts or increasing the "positive" ones. Among many other treatment strategies, clients are challenged on the validity or likelihood of a worry, encouraged to think a certain number of positive thoughts for every negative thought, asked to give themselves positive affirmations, or instructed to set aside a limited amount of "worry time" every day. Each of these techniques has its value in psychotherapy, depending on the person and the person's unique situation.

However, distraction and thought suppression are subject to *rebound affects*, whereby the unwanted thoughts and feelings return with greater strength under the very conditions the individual most wants to not have them (Wegner, 2011). Almost by definition, worries and fears are not rational. Every clinician, while trying to reason with an anxious client, has experienced the "Yes, but what if. . ." response. As I tell clients, "The 'what ifs' always win the argument." But that doesn't have to be a problem.

FROM SYMPTOMS TO COMMON PROCESSES: A FUNCTIONAL APPROACH TO DIAGNOSIS

Look again at the struggle involving Wyatt, his mother, and his father. What exactly is *the problem* in this situation? Yes, there is a great deal of distressing emotion and thinking going on for everyone involved: worry, tension, frustration, anger, discouragement, to name a few. But is Wyatt's mother bringing him to see you, the clinician, because he's anxious and she's frustrated? Somewhat. But the real issue seems to be that Wyatt *is not going to school and the family is fighting about it every morning.*

Likewise, in the coming pages, we'll see that Mycroft has tantrums at almost every transition, Grace exhausts herself and everyone around her by trying to control every moving part in her world, and Brayden takes ten minutes to pick a shirt from his closet. Along with these problematic child behaviors, parents are distressed by their own behavior: pleading and cajoling, angry yelling, giving in to the child's demands just to avoid unpleasantness, avoiding important places and activities out of fear of the child's likely emotions and behaviors, and many other negative and largely ineffective parent *reactions* brought out by these situations. If what the parent and child were *doing* was working, they wouldn't be coming to see you, regardless of how everyone was *feeling.*

THE HAIRBALL MODEL OF PSYCHOPATHOLOGY

Many parents, and even some clinicians, subscribe to what I call the "hairball model of psychopathology." This is the idea that a troublesome thought, feeling, or memory is literally inside our bodies somewhere as a physical entity and must be hacked up, expelled in some way, in order for the person to feel better and thereby function well. Anger is the most common hairball. Children will claim that they must get their anger "out" by hitting someone or something. But hitting some *thing,* while preferable to hitting some *one*, only reinforces the connection between anger and hitting. I will suggest throughout this book that not only is it extremely difficult to purge one's "bad" thoughts and feelings, but such efforts often backfire and actually increase the prevalence of those inner events, as mentioned earlier (Wegner, 2011). But, as I will emphasize, getting rid of negative thoughts and feelings is unnecessary for a vital and effective life. After all, being brave means feeling anxious *and* doing what needs to be done anyway.

FUNCTIONAL CLASSIFICATION SYSTEMS: ANTECEDENTS, BEHAVIORS, AND CONSEQUENCES

In contrast to the symptom-based DSM system, a *functional* classification system is interested less in the *what* of behavior than in the *what for*—that is, what does this set of child behaviors reliably obtain for the child? In other words, what need is the child trying to meet through this pattern of behavior? The purpose of functional classification is to look at the *processes* that organize a particular set of behaviors for a particular individual. Importantly, these processes describe the various contexts in which behavior occurs and how those behaviors are encouraged or discouraged through feedback from the environment.

The ultimate goal is to identify important and potentially controllable variables in the form of antecedent conditions (also thought of as "activators" or triggers) and subsequent consequences (the feedback), with the behaviors in question sandwiched in between. With this information, I can begin to understand what causes and, more importantly, what *maintains* the anxious behavior pattern. I then may be able to influence these variables in order to change the pattern of behavior. With behavior change we can expect some changes in thinking and feeling.

Most graduate training in clinical psychology and psychotherapy involves some exposure to functional analysis, the assessment technique for determining these antecedents and consequences and how they hang together and provide feedback loops and contingencies that keep the dance going. This diagnostic technique helps us, the clinicians, better understand the function of the child behaviors in various contexts. Additionally, this is a powerful tool for helping parents understand the bigger picture surrounding and maintaining the problematic behavior patterns—their child's and their own. (In Chapter 4, I will describe using functional analysis to examine the behaviors of anxious children and their parents.)

TRANSDIAGNOSTIC APPROACHES

A fairly new approach to assessment and treatment—some would call it a paradigm shift—is gaining traction in the world of psychotherapy research and practice. The *transdiagnostic approach* stems from a theoretical model that explains different behavioral presentations by describing common psychological and behavioral processes (Barlow, Allen, & Choate, 2004, Norton & Barrera, 2012). The goal is parsimony: to describe and explain psychological conditions using the smallest number of "key mechanisms" or processes.

Transdiagnostic models are based on "lumping" psychological conditions according to the processes involved, as opposed to the DSM approach of "splitting" diagnoses into finer and finer supposedly distinct entities. As a quick aside, given the new DSM 5 criteria for posttraumatic stress disorder, Galatzer-Levy and Bryant (2013) have determined that, with a requirement that the individual have a *minimum* of eight out of nineteen possible symptoms across four categories (for example, alterations in arousal and reactivity, avoidance), there are 636,120 different combinations of symptoms that would meet full criteria for a PTSD diagnosis.

Instead of slicing behavior into finer entities, with the presumption that each diagnostic entity requires its own distinct treatment protocol, the emphasis here is on understanding mechanisms and processes that will adequately describe the problem. And importantly, this understanding should suggest treatment strategies that will lead to changing those mechanisms or processes and thereby alleviate suffering and dysfunction.

In particular, I am interested in *maintaining* processes. Like homeostatic mechanisms in biological systems, certain intrapersonal (psychological) and interpersonal (social) mechanisms serve to keep behavior patterns in place and resistant to change. As I'm sure you've experienced, the origins of worry or fear, and the onset of the associated behavior patterns, may be obscure. But even if the origins of the problem were well known—the dog attack, the year of being bullied at school—we would still want to know why the maladaptive patterns of thinking and behavior have persisted and are so resistant to change. We will explore these maintaining processes, in their many manifestations, throughout this book. (For those of you wishing to delve deeper into this model, see *Transdiagnostic Treatments for Children and Adolescents: Principles and Practice*, edited by Jill Ehrenreich-May and Brian C. Chu [2014]).

TWO COMMON PROCESSES, WRAPPED IN A THIRD, NESTED IN A FOURTH

As you will see in all of the case examples I present, four common processes, or themes, are found in childhood anxiety. Let's take a closer look at each of them.

The First Process: Avoidance/Escape

The first process is *avoidance/escape*. Wanting to avoid things that disturb, distress, and frighten us is understandable. And, in fact, there are many situations (high-voltage power lines, piranha) that probably should be avoided if we wish to have a long and healthy life.

Avoiding situations that cause anxiety can be useful. I will *never* bungee jump off some railroad trestle. It's just not my idea of fun. But then, I don't need to bungee jump off a railroad trestle to have a vital life. I do need to fly on airplanes, however, even though flying invites a raft of uncomfortable thoughts and feelings. The children you work with may not need to try out for the school play or go off the high dive, but it's likely they cannot afford to avoid school, playdates, or being in one room of the house while the parent is in another room.

Repeatedly avoiding challenging situations that are nonetheless important or necessary can have a serious and negative impact on the quality of our lives in the present and make it difficult to acquire and develop important skills and experiences for the future. For example, it would not surprise you to learn that Wyatt has had some difficulties academically and socially. School has always been a challenging place. Now, the more Wyatt avoids going to school, the further he falls behind academically and socially, which only fuels his anxiety about showing up and looking inadequate, which invites more avoidance. If he's not showing up, reasonable exposure to anxiety and fearful stimuli cannot occur. Then Wyatt, or any child, cannot habituate to the situation both psychologically and physiologically. In fact, prematurely truncated exposure can lead to the individual becoming *more* sensitized to the situation.

As such, avoidance interferes with emotional processing and learning—for example, the individual is deprived of the opportunity to disconfirm negative beliefs. Additionally, avoidance of the challenges robs Wyatt of opportunities to successfully manage anxiety-provoking situations and to develop new and more realistic appraisals of these situations and his own competence.

Escape is simply bailing out of anxiety-provoking situations. Again, sometimes this is the right thing to do. But the powerful contingency of *negative reinforcement* is at work here. Often confused with *punishment*, it is an important concept for parents to understand. Negative reinforcement occurs when a behavior serves to avoid or escape from an aversive situation. That behavior will then be more likely occur in the future in similar situations. This is an extremely common and powerful process in the anxiety behavior patterns we encounter as clinicians. The case examples I will present later in this book will describe this process in its various forms.

In short, avoidance and escape can become a vicious cycle, preventing necessary experiences for growth and change. Creating experiences that promote growth and change is what we do as clinicians. Among our most powerful tools is exposure/response prevention. This technique lies at the heart of much therapy, whether it's going out and touching doorknobs or simply talking about some emotion-rich topic. Exposure/response prevention is the antithesis of avoidance and escape.

The Second Process: Control

A second common process is control; the anxious or fearful child's behaviors are often in the service of attempts at controlling the anxiety-provoking situation in an attempt to feel better or to avoid/escape the situation altogether. Compulsive behaviors are a classic example of attempts at control: "If I count backward from one hundred, the lightening won't hit our house"; "If I cry and plead, I can get Mom to take me home from the birthday party" (control combined with escape). Defiance and aggression may serve the same function.

Here, too, control by itself may not be the problem. Appropriate control strategies—wearing a bike helmet, arranging to be at a summer camp when friends will be there—can keep us safe and allow us to try new things. As with avoidance and escape, the problem, as we'll see, lies in applying excessive and overly general control behaviors at the expense of realistically appraising and managing situations. Additionally, controlling behaviors can have a significant social cost if the anxious child is being controlling and antagonistic with peers and adults.

The Third (Meta)Process: The Anxiety Dance

Third, in my experience, the process of childhood anxiety very often involves others, typically the parents and often a particular parent. Avoidance and control occur within the context, or metaprocess, of the parent-child interaction. Others may witness and be involved in a child's anxiety, but it is the parents (and, as I said, often a particular parent) who find themselves engaged in a frustrating and ultimately unhelpful "dance" with their anxious child.

The change strategies I describe in the coming chapters center on this metaphor of the parent-child anxiety dance. There are many dances parents have with their children, many small routines and procedures that give lives structure and predictability and that can be very efficient in getting things done. But when these routines are fraught with tension, miscommunication, and maladaptive reactions, life is not good. And, being overpracticed and automatic, these maladaptive dances are very difficult to change (Dumas, 2005).

The Fourth Process: Context

Context may not seem so much a process as a situation or set of variables. But to the extent that context *transacts* with (that is, influences bidirectionally) other processes, I include it here. In *real* medicine, a person tends to have a disease twenty-four hours a day, seven days a week, and anywhere she happens to be. The person *has* the disease, although it may wax and wane depending on any number of variables. Clinicians and parents know that children think and feel and behave anxiously in certain circumstances or contexts: before leaving the house, on Sunday evening while contemplating returning to school, during thunderstorms, or only in the presence of dogs. At times, it is reported that the child only exhibits anxiety in the presence of one parent but not the other.

Context is vital to behavior change. In fact, it is a basic tenet of acceptance-based therapy that behavior can change *only* as a result of changes in the individual's contextual field—that is, through feedback from the environment. Daniel Pine states that, in children, "behavior changes quite dramatically in the short-term through the influence of context, and in the long-term, through the influence of development" (2010, p. 533). Development, too, transacts with context, especially the social environment.

TRANSDIAGNOSTIC TREATMENTS

Several psychotherapies fit the *transdiagnostic* model, and research suggests they can be quite effective for treating child anxiety and its impact on family life. The idea is that, rather than have many, many treatment manuals and protocols for all of the hundreds of psychological disorders described by the DSM, we might identify the basic targets of intervention and the basic strategies or treatment components for achieving improved functioning across a range of topographically different, but functionally similar, emotional and behavioral disorders. I will describe these treatment models and their specific strategies related to working with the parents of anxious children in more detail throughout this book, especially in Chapter 6. Here is a brief overview.

Cognitive Behavioral Therapy

At this time, two general categories of well-researched transdiagnostic therapies are recognized (Craske, 2012). First are the generic or unified *cognitive behavioral therapy* (CBT) protocols (Barlow, Allen, & Choate, 2004; Kendall et al., 2014). Employing treatment strategies developed over the last several decades, these approaches identify maladaptive patterns of thinking and behavior and attempt to change these patterns through psychoeducation, cognitive reappraisal, exposure/response prevention, and tolerance of physical sensations through relaxation and other stress reduction techniques. (We will use some of these strategies and tactics in Chapter 6.)

Barlow and colleagues (2004) have reduced the effective components of psychotherapy to three:

1. Cognitive reappraisal
2. Preventing emotional avoidance
3. Promoting courageous behaviors

Cognitive reappraisal is also known in older writings as *cognitive restructuring,* or learning to think about things differently. But I will suggest that cognitive reappraisal is mainly a *consequence* of having engaged the world in a new and more effective manner, as opposed to an a priori decision to change one's thinking about a situation ahead of experience. As such, this may be the last of Barlow's three components to come about. First, one must engage the world, if only in very small and manageable steps. Exposure/response prevention (ERP) is the classic strategy for preventing *emotional avoidance* (the unhelpful avoiding of unpleasant or unwanted feelings and thoughts) and engineering successful contact with life through courageous behaviors. Courageous behaviors are the mirror image of avoidance. Strategies for cuing and encouraging these "positive opposite" behaviors will be important to our work.

Acceptance and Mindfulness Approaches

A second category of transdiagnostic treatments is found in a newer extended family of therapies variously known as acceptance-based or mindfulness-based treatments. Of these, dialectical behavior therapy, acceptance and commitment therapy, mindfulness-based stress reduction, and mindfulness-based cognitive therapy are the best known and have the most empirical support. Stated simply, what these treatments have in common is a concern less with symptom reduction and more with (1) increasing adaptive awareness (mindfulness) of one's experiences and (2) an intentional direction of attention toward good functioning or taking "values-driven action." This change in attention and action occurs in spite of, without having to alter or get rid of, the "negative" thoughts and feelings that are part of the present circumstances. This is the *acceptance* part: the recognition that true change can occur only with a full and realistic (accepting) appraisal of the current situation, as opposed to expending time and energy wishing things were otherwise—that is, denying or fighting reality.

This does not mean people passively receive whatever happens to them without efforts to protect themselves from harm or change things for the better. But like theologian Reinhold Niebuhr's message in the Serenity Prayer—"God, grant me the serenity to accept the things I cannot change, the courage to change the things I can, and wisdom to know the difference"—we need to help parents discern what can be changed and what must be met with equanimity and coping. The therapeutic goals in acceptance and mindfulness therapies are to encourage more flexible and effective patterns or processes in terms of cognitions (private behavior) and acting in and upon the world (public behavior). For our purposes, the latter category would include interpersonal functioning (social or dyadic behavior), specifically the parent-child interaction or dance. Mindfulness-based treatment strategies are used with other, more traditional child treatment interventions such as contingency management (for example, reward programs) and skill building. I will borrow extensively from this family of treatments in the coming pages.

Parent Management Training

Parent management training, or parent behavioral training, has been shown to be an effective treatment for a variety of childhood externalizing problems (McMahon & Forehand, 2003). Based on operant and social learning principles, the basics of parent training include increasing the parent's accurate monitoring of the child's behavior, manipulating antecedent situational variables (discussed at length in Chapter 4), and providing contingent delivery of rewards and punishments. More recently, attention has been given to the use of these techniques for internalizing disorders such as childhood depression and anxiety (Barrett & Farrell, 2007).

Parent-Child Interaction Therapy

Parent-child interaction therapy, or PCIT, has a long and fruitful track record for helping treat disruptive or externalizing disorders and for encouraging positive social interactions in young children (Eyberg & Boggs, 1998). Variations of this basic technique are known as floor time (Greenspan, & Wieder, 2006), child-directed play, and child's game, among others.

The basic approach is based on the play-therapy model: Through the medium of play, the parent and child redefine and recalibrate their relationship away from tension, rigidity, and coercive control and toward mutual sensitivity, warmth, support, and trust. Recently, this model has been applied to internalizing child problems such as anxiety (Puliafico, Comer, & Pincus, 2012). I will present my variation on this model in Chapter 4.

A LOOK AHEAD

In some ways, the structure of this book models the themes of the Serenity Prayer: learning to accept what cannot be changed, changing what can be changed, and discerning when to do what. Chapters 1 and 2 focus on helping parents increase their awareness, and even acceptance of their child's biologically based temperament and problematic reactions to life's demands. Along with fostering this new appreciation of the *child's* automatic, habitual behavior patterns of feeling, thinking, and behaving, I describe methods for increasing the *parents'* awareness of their own helpful and less than optimal contributions to how anxiety develops and is played out in the family. I conclude with a survey of the clinical research into the ways in which parents are involved in the origins and maintenance of their child's behavior patterns, those associated with anxiety as well as with adaptive and growth-oriented behaviors.

Chapters 3 through 7 present change strategies, with an emphasis on promoting courageous behaviors in the face of fear and worry. Chapters 8 and 9 offer ways to help parents find the wisdom to pick their battles well and suggestions for maintaining resilience—both the parents' and the clinician's—in order to sustain the efforts required.

Six case examples will illustrate a number of common anxiety presentations and family dynamics. I provide a variety of strategies and tactics (the distinction will be made later) for children who represent a range of DSM anxiety disorders: separation anxiety, obsessive-compulsive disorder, and phobic reactions, among others. Additionally, as so often happens in a clinical practice, these children will present with comorbidities commonly found in anxious children. Chief among these comorbidities are oppositional behaviors. Interesting and important family dynamics include marital difficulties, sibling issues, school issues, parent psychopathology, parent (and grandparent) overinvolvement, and parent underinvolvement.

There are obviously many, many ways families can present in terms of family composition, ethnicities, socioeconomic status, community size, and available resources, to name a few variables. Space here does not permit an extensive survey of all these important factors in a manageable set of case examples. My goal is to have these children and their parents, composites of many families I have seen over the years, feel real to you and for the situations and behaviors to reflect what you contend with in your daily clinical practice. I want these cases to reflect the messiness and frustration inherent in the work we do, but also to convey the curiosity, passion, and empathy.

Spoiler alert: No one gets cured before the end of this book. I wanted to describe treatment at the early stages—when concerns and behavior patterns are identified and conceptualized, when treatment goals are selected, and when the treatment contract, or *frame*, is established. For me, this is a crucial phase in the work we do; the treatment going forward will rest on these foundational understandings and mutual expectations.

NOTES:

A quick comment about pronouns. Dealing with gender pronouns in writing is always tricky and can lead to cumbersome wording. In this book, I describe several fictional children and their parents as case examples. When I mention individuals by name, I, of course, refer to them as "he" and "she," as appropriate. In talking more generally about children and an individual parent, I alternate gender by chapter: female child/male parent for the introduction and even-numbered chapters and male child/female parent for the odd-numbered chapters.

All of the case examples in this book are composites of many individuals and represent no particular individuals. They have been created for the purpose of illustrating key concepts and treatment strategies. Any resemblance to actual individuals is coincidental and perhaps evidence of how common these clinical concerns and situations we see every day are.

Part One

*Understanding
the Anxiety Dance*

CHAPTER 1

Biology, Temperament, and Adaptability

It is often helpful to engage the parent, and the anxious child, in a bit of psychoeducation concerning the nature of anxiety in order to make the fearful and anxious experiences somewhat more "normal" and more expectable, even as we attempt to change things for the better. It's not that we're going to revel in our anxiety; rather, as I mentioned in the Introduction, change begins with a certain acceptance of what is in the moment. This kind of acceptance starts with the acknowledgment that anxiety *will* show up in certain situations and often in situations of great importance. Anxiety is a fact of life—at least a life that is vital and moving forward—and it is important to acknowledge that biology and temperament play a critical role in it.

So, how do we begin with the necessary psychoeducation for our clients? A good place to start is with the biology of anxiety.

THE BIOLOGY OF ANXIETY, OR WE ARE ALL DESCENDANTS OF THE PARANOID PEOPLE

For many tens of thousands of years, human beings survived and even flourished in harsh and unforgiving environments. Our abstract thinking, time concepts, and imagination gave us an edge for survival. Humans could anticipate the future and prepare for it; we set aside food for the winter, avoided dangerous animals and places, and kept an eye on the children lest they came to harm. We learned from experience (or the experience of some unlucky or careless member of the tribe) and passed that learning on to others through language. Life was brutal and short. Complacent and unobservant early humans didn't make it. We are all the descendants of these paranoid people, and we are here because of the highly valuable fight-or-flight mechanisms that evolved over eons. These mechanisms are still very much in place and ready to go, as we see in the lives of the children who are our clients.

The Fight-Flight-Freeze-or-Freak-Out Reaction

Children often come to me, for example, with intense fears of fire alarms and fire drills at school. They find that these events, or even the idea of these events, provoke very unpleasant arousal and a strong motivation to escape the situation or avoid school altogether. This can lead to school refusal or simply to being miserable and distracted in class. As the child tell his story, I look for an opportunity to point out that fire alarms, like smoke detectors at home, are *meant to be alarming.* The whole point of alarms is to alert us to possible danger and motivate us to take action. It would indeed be a very ineffective, and even dangerous, smoke detector that played a quiet and soothing lullaby!

Likewise, fear and anxiety are meant to be alarming. The human race would have died out long ago if danger, or perceived danger, evoked warm and pleasant feelings. A smoke detector is supposed to be obnoxious. And so is the so-called fight-or-flight response. Some add *freeze, freak-out,* or even *submit* to the description—all are appropriate. The fight-or-flight response involves twenty-plus all-or-nothing physiological reactions that we have no control over, all of them serving to prepare us for battle or escape. All other matters are a distant second. This is basic, adaptive biology—that is, those who survive get to reproduce. And that adaptive biology includes a tendency to be highly attuned to threats in our environment.

Genetic Factors in Anxiety

In addition to attentional bias toward threats, genetics plays an important role in anxiety. Children of anxious parents are two to seven times more likely to develop an anxiety disorder than are children of nonanxious parents (Capps, Sigman, Sena, & Henker, 1996). Overall, heritability may account for 40 to 50 percent of anxiety symptoms in children (Thapar & McGuffin, 1995).

Although anxiety disorders tend to run in families, there is little evidence of direct transmission of anxiety disorders per se. For example, parents don't pass down separation anxiety disorder or siderodromophobia (Google it) to their offspring. Instead, it appears that *risk* for anxiety, and mood disorders quite generally is what we see transmitted from one generation to the next. As I tell parents, this risk can be mitigated by many factors, many of which are under our control—good sleep hygiene being just one example.

Now that we've very briefly explored the biological basics of anxiety, let's take a closer look at temperament. Although also biologically based, temperament provides a slightly different avenue of psychoeducation for both child and parents.

TEMPERAMENT AND BIOLOGY: TENDENCY, NOT DESTINY

The parents you see may have some familiarity with the term *temperament*. They might think of it as analogous to one's personality but perhaps a little more basic and biological. For our purposes as clinicians, we don't need to make temperament scholars out of the parents or the older children we see. Rather, our talk of temperament is just another aspect of the general discussion of anxiety's biological basis and its adaptive nature—along with the predictability of anxiety in the lives of children, especially some children. And, perhaps most important, our goal is to convey that temperament and other biological factors are not destiny but *tendencies* (Rettew, 2013). Along with this, we want to convey the powerful idea that tendencies can be shaped at the level of behavior so that thoughts, emotions, memories, and bodily sensations don't have to be a problem to be solved at the expense of living a vital life.

Temperament is exceedingly important for understanding the channels child behavior may follow. Space here does not permit an extensive review of this area. For a book-length treatment of temperament and its relationship to treating childhood emotional and behavioral disorders, I recommend David Rettew's excellent *Child Temperament: New Thinking About the Boundary Between Traits and Illness* (2013).

Defining Temperament

There are various definitions and conceptualizations of temperament and many research methods—from behavioral observations to questionnaires—for studying it. Common among these definitions are features such as temperament's biological basis and therefore presence early in life. Most definitions of temperament recognize a relationship to certain patterns of behavior in response to the environment and specifically to default emotional and cognitive states, adaptation, and self-regulation. Kagan and Snidman (2004) define temperament as "an inherited physiology that is preferentially linked to an envelope of behaviors and emotions." I like this definition because it conveys the idea that temperament is not a rigid, straight line from biology to particular behaviors; instead there are probabilities associated with a range or "envelope" of sensations, emotions, and behaviors. This is an important message to give to parents: temperament is not destiny, but it can be a vulnerability. It is just one factor, albeit an important factor, in the development and maintenance of anxiety.

Finding ways to mitigate the impact of the child's vulnerabilities and improve important self-regulation skills is the treatment goal. Presenting anxiety from a temperament perspective gives the parents a way to think about how their child's anxiety has come about that does not blame them and their parenting, that does not blame the child, or that does not single out any one factor in the child's life as the culprit. As we'll see, and as you might convey to parents, these are complex interactions, *transactions* really, between the child's biology and the world. I like using the term parent-child *transactions,* after the work of Arnold Sameroff (2009). This term conveys an appreciation of the bidirectional influences passing between organism and environment. And as I stated in the Introduction, the most important environmental factor in the child's ecosystem is the parent. And for many parents the child is the most salient feature of their environment much of the time.

Thomas, Chess, and Birch: Nine Dimensions of Temperament

Most clinicians are familiar with the work of Thomas, Chess, and Birch (Thomas, Chess, Birch, Hertzig, & Korn, 1963). Their early observational research and parent questionnaires yielded nine dimensions of temperament, and children were described as being high or low on these dimensions:

- activity level
- rhythmicity or regularity
- approach/withdrawal
- adaptability
- threshold of response or sensitivity
- intensity of reactions
- quality of mood
- distractibility
- attention span or persistence

In addition to these nine dimensions, Chess and Thomas described children who fell into three categories made up of combinations of temperamental traits. These included the famous, or infamous, *difficult child* (low regularity, low or negative quality of mood, withdrawal, high intensity, and low adaptability) as well as the *easy child* and the *slow-to-warm-up child.* These discrete categories, however, have not held up well upon further study. Fully one-third of children observed in subsequent studies did not fit into one of these three groups. More important, children identified as fitting into one of the three groups displayed very different behaviors depending on the situation. The same is true for individual dimensions. This research showed what every parent knows: A child can be sensitive to some aspects of the environment and relatively insensitive to others—for example, the sounds of one's brother eating breakfast and the loud cacophony of a video game, respectively.

Dimensions and Predicting Behavior

Also important for our purposes was the discovery that a child's temperament, even a "difficult" one, did not itself predict later behavior problems (Thomas & Chess, 1977; Rettew, Stanger, McKee, Doyle, & Hudziak, 2006). Research suggested that it is the parent's ability to adapt to the child's temperament and work with the whole constellation of that child's traits that determines the course of the parent-child relationship and subsequent child functioning (see "Biology and Temperament Meet Society: Parent-Child Attunement" later in this chapter). This is the so-called "goodness-of-fit" model. The boisterous child born into a family of mellow parents and older siblings may generate confusion, dismay, and awkward handling. Similarly, the quiet, withdrawn child who finds himself in a family of passionate extraverts may feel overwhelmed and set up a pattern of awkward interactions, reactions, and maladaptive coping patterns. As I will describe and emphasize throughout these pages, biology *transacts* (bidirectional influence) with the very earliest social experiences.

Other Important Descriptions of Temperament

Other descriptions—negative affectivity, extraversion, and behavior inhibition, in particular—add important and helpful information to our understanding of temperament. Again, conveying this material nonjudgmentally to parents can help them gain insight into their child and their interactions with him.

Negative Affectivity

A common finding in temperament research is the trait or predisposition to negative emotions, such as anxiety, anger, or sadness. This trait has been variously labeled *negative affectivity*, emotionality, neuroticism, or harm avoidance. Two subtypes of this tendency to negative affect have been described (Rothbart et al., 2001). One subtype manifests as feelings of frustration and even rage when the child's autonomy is threatened or limits placed on his behavior. The second subtype is the more classic shyness or aversion to novel situations and manifests as fearfulness or withdrawal. Both subtypes of negative affectivity may be seen in the anxious child.

Interestingly, negative affectivity is a nonspecific factor for anxiety disorders. In other words, negative affectivity is not correlated with any particular DSM anxiety disorder. Instead, this trait appears to predispose children for both anxiety and depression. It is lack of *positive* affectivity that is specifically associated with depression. Lack of positive affectivity is not associated with any DSM anxiety disorders except for social anxiety.

Extraversion and Behavioral Inhibition

Extraversion is the tendency toward approaching novel situations. This trait can manifest as sociability, spontaneity, and exuberance or as impulsivity and poor delay of gratification. This trait can be found in about 10 to 15 percent of the population.

Jerome Kagan (1994a) has researched the opposite of extraversion, introversion or *behavioral inhibition,* which is found in another 10 to 15 percent of the population. Often noted simply as BI, behavioral inhibition describes the tendency to anxious avoidance of novel situations. This style is characterized by shyness, reticence, and withdrawal behaviors along with a variety of physiological indicators, such as increased muscle tension and increased heart rate. Behavioral inhibition can be distinguished from simple shyness, which is "the tendency to be timid, withdrawn, and uncomfortable in social situations." BI, however, is "the tendency to show restraint and fear when presented with novel situations or people" (Rettew, 2013, p. 27).

Here too, variability is evident. On the one hand, the behavioral manifestations of BI (reticence, withdrawal, and so on) commonly show up as a reaction to novel stimuli, unfamiliar events, and new situations. On the other hand, many of the children designated as high on BI may be quite relaxed and skilled in familiar situations— for example, among family members and certain peers. Some children may be restrained in the face of novel situations but not novel people, or the reverse. Social anxiety is a combination of shyness and reticence, despite wanting to be around people. The comorbidity of social anxiety and depression is high, as both involve negative affectivity and introversion.

Following up on children labeled as behaviorally inhibited, as well as a group of uninhibited children, it has been observed that the uninhibited children are likely to remain in that classification over time (Kagan, 1994b). Behaviorally inhibited children at the extreme end are more likely to move toward the mean than to become more inhibited over time. This is likely due to the pressures of social demands for engagement as children enter school (Lonigan & Phillips, 2001).

In spite of these moderating influences on the child by the social environment, behavioral inhibition in early childhood remains highly predictive of anxiety in later years. Adults with anxiety disorders retrospectively report exhibiting characteristics of behavioral inhibition in their childhood.

Whereas negative affectivity is not a *specific* predictor of anxiety symptoms, BI appears to have some associations with particular DSM anxiety disorders. Children of parents with panic disorder are more likely to show characteristics of behavioral inhibition than children of parents with any other DSM 5 anxiety diagnosis. Conversely, parents of inhibited children are significantly more likely to meet criteria for current or past anxiety problems. Thus, children at most risk for anxiety disorders are those who both meet criteria for behavioral inhibition and have parents who themselves have an anxiety disorder.

Most children with BI do not have anxiety disorders. However, as they move into adolescence, they have an increased risk specifically for social anxiety (Schwartz, Snidman, & Kagan, 1999). Social anxiety appears to stem from a combination of shyness and reticence, despite wanting to be around people. We will see how some of these issues play out in the lives of Freya and Wyatt.

Freya

A fifteen-year-old female, Freya is the daughter of Jack and Celeste. She has a history of behavioral inhibition, along with a touch of negative affectivity and low positive mood. Celeste describes Freya as a "glass half empty" sort of person ever since infancy. She was reasonably successful in a small, private, religious K–8 school, where she exhibited moderate social anxiety and low confidence but decent academics. She had one or two close friends who were very accepting of her shyness and introversion. They helped her navigate social situations. But recently, Jack lost his job at the paper mill and Freya was unable to follow her friends into the private high school she had expected to attend after eighth grade. Now she is in the ninth grade in a new school, struggling to find friends and her place in a large and overwhelming setting. The stress of her father's job loss pervades the family.

To add to this mix, Freya's older brother, J. J. (Jack Jr.) had just been deployed to the Middle East with his Army unit. Freya and J. J. have always been close. His positive affect and extraversion had always buoyed up the family's moods.

Freya's family is experiencing a perfect storm of stressful events: the father's job loss, Freya's change to a new school and social environment, her brother's deployment overseas, and Celeste taking on the burden of being the sole bread winner in the family, which adds to Jack's discouragement, given their long-standing traditional gender roles. The family has fragmented into several individuals who are preoccupied by, and lost in, their feelings and thoughts. The environmental supports that had allowed Freya to function reasonably well have gone, almost overnight.

Freya is suddenly without a buffer against her temperament with its envelope of emotions (negativity) and behaviors (with-

drawal). The danger is that Freya will drift in a pattern of avoidance that will only exacerbate her isolation and negative thinking
and feeling. Lack of engagement with the world, even a stressful
world, will result in the erosion of her adaptive skills and rob her
of possible positive experiences. We'll return to Freya later in this
book. Finding a way to navigate these profound changes and losses
and remain afloat will be the work ahead. Finding a way to prevail
in spite of her temperament-based tendencies is Freya's challenge
and will require renewed energy and support from her family and
her clinician.

Wyatt

We met Wyatt at the beginning of the Introduction. A careful
assessment might reveal that Wyatt's temperament is marked
by fairly consistent shyness unless he is with family members or
close friends. Then he can be quite rambunctious and disinhib-
ited. When frustrated, which is a frequent event, Wyatt can exhibit
great bursts of negative affectivity.

It is not a surprise to find that Sara, Wyatt's mother, has had
a life-long struggle with anxiety. She recalls being very shy as a
child, a condition that was exacerbated by a loud, unpredictable
alcoholic mother. As an adult, Sara experiences bouts of sudden,
intense anxious arousal, almost panic. She can deeply empathize
with Wyatt's "anxiety attacks."

Wyatt's father, Dan, however, prides himself on his steady, calm,
and unflappable nature. Until Dan became a parent, he had yet to
meet a problem that could not be solved through reason and calm
discourse. Not only has this tried-and-true approach to problem
solving failed him in his parenting, but also, to his dismay, Dan has
realized he has a "button" that Wyatt can easily, even artfully push
and send Dan into a towering rage. "I've never acted like that with
anyone else in my life," he says with a mixture of bewilderment
and alarm.

Here we have an example of the "goodness-of-fit" model of temperament and its impact on parent-child transactions. For some

reason, for all the years they've been married, Sara's emotionality and reactivity have not been a problem for Dan. He saw her as exciting and passionate, and a welcomed balance to his own style. They complemented each other. But Dan is perplexed by Wyatt's "attitude" and finds all this upset very strange and even frightening. He is profoundly discouraged and sad. On the other hand, he is determined that he can make Wyatt "understand" that he, Wyatt, simply needs to do these things, such as go to school. You don't have to like it; it's just expected, like paying taxes.

Sara's temperament, however, fits Wyatt's like hand in glove. She "totally gets" Wyatt and is frustrated when others, especially Dan, do not totally get Wyatt. To her, Wyatt has a disability that is biologically based. (As an aside, Wyatt has been on several medications, but not on any of them for more than a week or so due to unpleasant side effects.) Anxiety is something he has had all his life and will have for the rest of his life, and managing it has been and will be a central feature of their lives.

We will be seeing Wyatt, Sara, and Dan again soon. Here the work will include some psychoeducation about what's possible to achieve clinically even in the face of strong, biologically *influenced* behaviors. What could help to create some cohesiveness between the parents is a change in orientation to one that acknowledges the biological but also directs attention and effort toward behavior in context, especially the influence of contingencies (rewards and punishments) on subsequent choices and decisions.

INTERLUDE: EFFORTFUL CONTROL AND BRAIN DEVELOPMENT

Before we continue our discussion of temperament, I want to touch briefly on two important related topics: effortful control and brain development.

Effortful Control

As I mentioned earlier, a treatment goal for children with anxiety is to improve their self-regulation skills. *Effortful control* is the ability to regulate affect and, in turn, behavior, through the management of attention and other related cognitive processes. Although it is as much a skill as it is a trait, effortful control is often included in discussions of temperament. I include it here because it is a fundamental self-management process that is vital to coping with anxiety, frustration, boredom, and other stressors that threaten to derail us from pursuing our goals. One way to think of effortful control is persistence or determination in the face of competing ideas or distracting emotions. Put another way, it is the key to the difference between the *experience* of an emotion (fear) and the *expression* of that emotion (clinging, crying, escape). It is a concept and a set of adaptive behaviors that throughout this book will be central to our discussion of treatment of anxiety in children and the engagement of parents in that process.

Effortful control is part of the "executive system" of the brain. It shares features with many of the so-called executive skills or functions currently being discussed in clinical and educational settings. These skills or functions include, among others, goal-directed persistence, flexibility, metacognition, and working memory. As with these other executive skills, effortful control appears to be dependent on the development of brain systems associated with attention.

Like behavioral inhibition and the other more "classic" temperamental traits, effortful control, at least in rudimentary form, can be observed in infancy. It can be seen quite early when a very young infant will turn away from an aversive stimulus such as a loud noise or an overly intrusive adult. As I'll describe later, all of the temperament traits transact with the environment, especially the social environment, almost as soon as the child hits the world. This bidirectional, mutual shaping process between child and the world goes on for the child's entire developmental period. Individuals with low effortful control tend to be highly reactive in aversive situations (externalizing behaviors, withdrawing, poor impulse control), as is typical for a preschool-age child or for any of us when stress evokes the four-year-old within. Where effortful control may differ from the other aspects of temperament is in its strong relationship to brain development. The executive/attentional/self-regulation systems are quite primitive until about age five, when the development of these systems takes off.

Brain Development in Children

Now, I want to say something about young brains that relates to, but goes beyond, the development of effortful control. Very young brains, say up to about age five when the executive functions start coming into their own, behave in certain characteristic ways that will be familiar to anyone who has spent time around a four-year-old. These functions include egocentricity, binary mindset (all-or-nothing thinking), inflexibility, fusion, and literalism. Let's take a quick look at each of these characteristics.

Egocentricity

It's all about them. A typical four-year-old has a profound lack of perspective taking, empathy, or recognition that others have needs, desires, feelings, and so on. The psychodynamic folks refer to this as a lack of "subjectivity"—that is, "Everyone besides me is merely an 'object.'" This restricted view also includes difficulty seeing beyond the present moment; at this stage, children are unable to properly envision future events or to draw on past experience.

This ability to think beyond the present circumstances leads to what are known as "self-states," another analytic concept. You and I, as mature adults, know that we remain who we are, retaining the same sense of self, regardless of our emotional or cognitive state at the moment. My "angry self" is the same as my "happy self." My outward behavior may be different given my state, but I remain consistently who I am.

Young children are still working on that capacity to integrate their different emotional self-states and to recognize that it's all just them *experiencing* different emotions at different times. Instead of being integrated, young children may have important emotionally charged events split off from one another, almost as if the events happened to someone else. I want to emphasize *almost*. I am not saying this is dissociative identity disorder. This is more akin to state-specific learning. It is simply the recognition that it is difficult for some children to dredge up an accurate recollection of a powerful feeling state when they are no longer in that state. Add to this a certain amount of shame or guilt-based reticence to talk about what happened last week and you have a very long fifty-minute hour ahead of you.

The Binary Mindset—All-or-Nothing Thinking

Young children can be very black-and-white, all-or-none in their thinking: "I never get to . . .," "You always . . .," "This is the best day," "You're the worst Mommy," and so on. Everything is a huge deal. Less often spoken aloud is the child turning this mindset on himself, either as "I'm the best" and therefore wonderfully wonderful, or "I'm the worst" and therefore unlovable and hopelessly so, forever. What we observe as perfectionism or unwillingness to try new things like learning to ride a bike or swim can in part be attributed to this binary mindset: "Unless I can do this thing perfectly well immediately, I'm not even going to try." As Homer Simpson says, "Trying is the first step toward failure." This also leads to a great deal of chronic stress, with the child always feeling that he's on the knife edge of total success or total failure.

Inflexibility

Along with, and related to, the binary mindset comes inflexibility. If the situation is seen as all-or-nothing, when we can't see any alternatives or other perspectives, we tend to be pretty rigid. Adapting, coping, redirecting attention, or moving on become next to impossible.

Fusion

Children make connections all the time: cause and effect, what goes with what. At times, connections get made that seem idiosyncratic or downright odd. Ask a four-year-old how to cook something, and you may get this recipe: to cook a chicken, put the chicken in the oven, go to church, come home, and eat the chicken. For this child, "going to church" is inextricably bound or "fused" with "cooking a chicken." Sometimes called "verbal rules," these connections, assumptions, or expectations influence our behavior every day. And many of the rules we operate under may be outside of our conscious awareness. If a young child has only known round waffles that come from a box in the freezer, then the square things arriving in front of him at the restaurant (brunch with Grandma and Grandpa) may elicit alarm and resistance: "These aren't waffles!" A very unpleasant scene may then unfold.

One form of fusion combines thoughts and feelings with behaviors. For example, a child may be operating under the "rule" of "If I'm angry, I must hit someone or something" or "If I see a bee, I have to run away." This has been called "emotion-action fusion" or "thought-action fusion." Disconnecting and reconnecting these "dots" is an important part of psychotherapy. In classic CBT, this would be called "cognitive restructuring." Later in the book, I will refer to the various techniques for doing this as "defusion" exercises. A first step toward defusion is simply helping the child (or parent) articulate important "rules" and to then examine the usefulness of those rules or how they might be more flexibly applied.

Literalism

For very young children, their thinking is equivalent to reality. Thoughts are not simply "ideas," they are "facts." The psychoanalytic folks call this *psychic equivalence*. If a typical four-year-old thinks there are popsicles in the freezer, there *are* popsicles in the freezer. When he goes there and finds no popsicles, reality has been violated. This violation is cause for a reaction that adults consider out of proportion. This is why, when plans must change ("We can't go to the park because it's raining"), children will say things like "You're mean" and "You lied." With maturity comes flexibility, more or less (see the next section on "The Regressed Brain"), so it's hard for adults to imagine how chronically stressful it must be to have reality chronically messed with. We don't remember having gone through this ourselves (perhaps a dim memory or two). But this literal stance toward one's thoughts can be very powerful. It is therefore not surprising that children are so often anxious and reactive.

The opposite of psychic equivalence is *mentalizing* (Allen, Fonagy, & Bateman, 2008), which combines the executive skills of metacognition and perspective taking. Mentalizing is the ability to step back and think about, wonder about, one's own thinking as well as that of another person. It includes the ability to consider alternative ideas and other possibilities: "Maybe he's scowling because he's having a bad day generally and not because of something I've done." As you can imagine, this is a hugely important executive skill and a developmental achievement. I will have more to say about mentalizing in the chapters ahead when I describe treatment strategies.

The Regressed Brain

With maturation and brain development, these more rigid and reactive characteristics of the young brain are overridden or overwritten by new capacities for flexibility, nuance, possibility, attentional control, and perspective taking. These new capacities are very adaptive and beneficial, both for dealing with other people and for effective self-regulation.

Now, you may recognize some of the characteristics of the young brain—for example, egocentricity, all-or-nothing thinking, inflexibility—as sounding familiar. You may associate them at times with some adults you know or, perhaps if you're honest, with yourself. While brain development allows for more perspective taking, attentional control, and flexibility, even the most mature brains can regress, with stress, back to this more rigid and reactive thinking style. The circuitry is still there in our brains, ready to be activated under the right conditions. For me, all that's required is air travel or a computer malfunction and I am for all intents and purposes a three-year-old. I do my best to keep him contained.

This fact of regression is important because it occurs with the older children you work with and it is provoked in their parents as well. It describes important elements of the mutual reactivity we see in the anxiety dance between parent and child. Recognizing and extricating oneself from this regressed mindset is a challenge, but it is a vital part of the treatment plan I will describe later in this book. But now, to see regression at work, let's hear more about Mycroft, whom I briefly mentioned in the introduction.

Mycroft

In mid-November, Mycroft comes to you. He is in all-day kindergarten, having turned five in August, so relative to his classmates, he's fairly young. But his young, single mother, Elena, really needed him to start kindergarten at the local public school, in part because she couldn't afford preschool tuition any longer and in part because she hoped the school staff would find a solution to his "outbursts" and other behavior problems.

Mycroft has always been boisterous and daring. He displays periods of wild, silly behavior that is resistant to containment. Mycroft has significant difficulty with transitions—for example, the school-day morning routine, drop-off at school, and pick up from the after-school program. Mycroft will melt down the moment Elena arrives to collect him from aftercare a few minutes before 6:00. The teacher will invariably say, "I don't understand. He was fine till you got here." Bedtime is an especially long, drawn-out, and difficult ordeal with resistance to the required activities, such as tooth brushing. Mycroft demands more story time and many "curtain calls" when he requests a drink of water or shares worries about ghosts, monsters, and robbers. From beginning to end, this may require two hours.

Mycroft has frequent and powerful tantrums if his expectations are violated, the schedule is changed, a different route is taken from home to school or from school to home, rain cancels a picnic, illness cancels a playdate, or there are no popsicles in the freezer. Mycroft asks questions "constantly": "What are we doing today?" "Who's going to pick me up today?" "Are we going to have a fire drill today?" He has a host of rotating worries and phobias—bees, the dark, monsters, ghosts—that come and go and come back again. Mycroft has burned through three nannies in the past six months due to his uncontrollable behavior.

Mycroft has a lot going on. As his clinician, you would see that he is burdened with behavioral disinhibition, very low effortful control, a low threshold for anxious arousal, a more-or-less typical five-year-old brain (rigid, egocentric, literal), with a vulnerability to instant regression to a three-year-old brain (even more rigid, egocentric, and literal). You would also be wondering about attunement (discussed later in this chapter), given that Mycroft was adopted at eighteen months from an Eastern European orphanage and Elena is currently quite stressed.

I introduce Mycroft here to illustrate how anxiety can manifest itself in very young children, an often neglected cohort in the literature. Clearly, Mycroft will not be a good candidate for individual psychotherapy. Some clinicians might use play therapy to good effect in this situation. When we meet up again with Elena and Mycroft in the chapters to come, my emphasis will be on using the parent-child "dance" itself as the medium of change. The goal will be changing the choreography from rigidity and reactivity to flexibility and responsiveness.

Now, with effortful control in mind and brain development to consider, let's return to our discussion of temperament. In particular, let's explore the durability of temperament and its relation to behavior, especially to the behaviors making up the complex parent-child dance.

TEMPERAMENT IS DURABLE—MORE OR LESS

Much research has gone into showing what many parents already know: Temperament is quite stable, or "durable," over time (Rothbart, 2011). What does change over the course of development, however, is how temperament manifests itself through behavior. For example, the preschool child may resist going to some place new by clinging to a parent or by crying and pleading not to go. In adolescence, the same traits of shyness and inhibition may present through sullen silence and isolation.

One further complication is the situational quality of temperament—and, for that matter, most behavior patterns. For example, parents, usually fathers, will state that their child can't possibly have ADHD because he can be quite focused for long stretches if the activity is the latest Lego project or a video game. It is true: The "trait" of effortful control is highly dependent on the activity in question. An activity that is interesting and enjoyable will elicit more focus and persistence than an activity that is boring or challenging, or both. In fact, any of the temperament features we've discussed can show great variability, depending on contextual factors. As with the "difficult child" designation described earlier, children may show high variability in the display of any number of sets of behaviors based on setting (home versus school) or the presence of another (one parent versus the other or a different adult altogether). I will have more to say about these contextual factors, and how to address and even utilize them in the coming chapters.

Grace

A seven-year-old female, Grace is a tiny thing with delicate features. She has long, straight hair and a permanent scowl. She is a gifted artist and creates delicate and lifelike drawings of flowers and the cute creatures from a Web-based cartoon world she enjoys. Unfortunately, Grace wishes to do nothing else but draw and visit the cartoon website. She reacts with intense anger when teachers try to get her to initiate school tasks, to then finish the tasks once time is up, and to work cooperatively with her peers, a prominent value at her high-end private school.

Grace struggles with a great deal of negative affectivity. Effortful control is low in that Grace lacks the capacity to smoothly and rapidly shift her attention and behavior to meet the demands of the situation. Her "go-to" coping strategies are avoidance and control, mostly control. She has many "just so" compulsions in the form of needing to arrange her school materials in certain ways (leading to her inability to start work) or insisting that her parents perform actions (for example, the bedtime routine) in a certain order. If they don't, she demands they start over.

Grace's mother, Holly, was anxious as a child but has "overcome it." Grace and Holly spend a great deal of time talking about and trying to manage anxiety and upset so that Grace might overcome it as well. Alistair, Grace's father, is rather passive and states that his childhood was "unremarkable" and that he cannot recall feeling anxious as a child.

As with most children, the behaviors and predispositions associated with Grace's temperament can be influenced by context. For example, when the family is on vacation and staying in a hotel, Grace is not nearly so insistent that the bedtime ritual be performed exactly, or even at all if she is tired from the day's activities. Also, Grace may be quite deliberate about taking out and arranging her drawing materials at home before she begins an art project of her own. But this task is met with significantly greater efficiency and speed than initiating her work at school.

Context or environment influence behavior, even quite rigid and long-practiced behavior patterns. Again, social aspects of the environment rank as some of the most important influences on behavior. Even the absence of a person, as in separation anxiety, can have a significant impact on a child's behavior. This social component of temperament and behavior will be discussed next.

BIOLOGY AND TEMPERAMENT MEET SOCIETY: PARENT-CHILD ATTUNEMENT

As the child develops from infancy through toddlerhood and into the preschool age and beyond, the expression of temperament is increasingly influenced by transactions with the environment, especially the social environment (Kiff, Lengua, & Zalewski, 2011). The parents, of course, are part of the child's social environment, and the quality of parent-child attunement will influence the child's experience of, and expression of, anxiety and fear.

Although a comprehensive look at parent-child attachment or attunement is beyond the scope of this book, you no doubt have at least a passing familiarity with the basic ideas behind attachment theory: Infants and young children appear to be hardwired to behave in ways that will regulate caregiver proximity and obtain help when the child is distressed. The caregiver will respond, or not respond, in characteristic and predictable ways, for better or for worse. The child then develops internal working models (*schema*), or rules about the world and himself that are largely unconscious and will influence subsequent interactions with the caregiver and perhaps other important persons throughout his life. For example: "I will be heard and responded to in a reasonable amount of time. Therefore, I can wait patiently for a certain amount of time, and then I'm going to really start wailing." These schema, laid down within the first year of life, will endure into later childhood and even into adulthood with *potential* influence on future social relations, for better or for worse. Note the emphasis on "potential"; like temperament traits themselves, the influence of attachment history is a matter of probabilities, not certainties.

The quality of the parent-child relationship appears to greatly influence the development of behavior problems in children. I am defining anxiety as a behavior problem to the extent that, as we've seen, the presenting problems of children we work with and the children in this book tend to be less the child's anxiety per se and more the child's *behavior when anxious*. I find it helpful to emphasize anxiety *behavior* over the more typical, DSM symptom-based approach to thinking about anxiety. The behaviors the child, and parent, habitually express when anxious are the actual problem. This approach helps distinguish mere anxious feelings and ideas from "disordered anxiety" (Eifert & Forsyth, 2004). Upon inspection, it seems to be the case that most often these anxiety-related behaviors are an attempt at regulating the parent's proximity and obtaining rescue. As such, it would be surprising if the behaviors seen in Mycroft, or Grace, Wyatt, or even Freya did not have their origins in the earliest caregiver-child experiences.

When talking with parents about the shaping of temperament through parent-child transactions, it's vitally important to *not* convey to the parents that their child has an attachment disorder, or that they in some way caused their child to be anxious, or that attachment is set in concrete after the first year of life and can never to be modified. We have, in fact, the concept of "earned secure attachment" whereby a person, even years later, can receive and metabolize warmth, acceptance, and esteem. Internal working models are difficult—but not impossible—to change.

For these reasons, I prefer the term *attunement* over *attachment*. Additionally, *attachment* connotes barnacles adhering to a boat hull and does not convey the reality of a complex and often subtle dance between parent and child. Attunement connotes the sensitivity and mutual engagement that mark good parent-child transactions, whether it's getting through the morning routine, managing a crisis, or baking cookies together. What these and many other common situations require for success is good communication, broadly defined.

As I'll describe in more detail in Chapters 3 and 4, the anxiety dance goes bad when communication goes bad; typically, important messages are either unclear or freighted with other material (side issues, strong emotions, accusations, historical references, and so on), which makes problem solving or coping impossible. Good communication requires the skill of effortful control (self-regulation). It also requires a certain level of perspective taking. Both effortful control and perspective taking are sorely lacking in young children or in any of us at times when we are stressed and regressed.

The ability to use a skill such as perspective taking, even when one is stressed, relates to the idea of *capacity*. I may have the skill, but do I have the capacity, the psychological stability and resilience (some might say "ego strength"), to draw out this skill even when it's difficult to do so, which is exactly when I need it most? At this time I want to take a look at attunement as it relates to the development of these skills and capacities.

The Development of Self-Regulation: Moving from Physical to Verbal Tools

Over the course of first six years or so of life, the child should develop and evolve strategies or tools for regulating (we can call it "manipulating") the parent into coming to his aid. We would expect to see a decrease in physical control and the need for help in the form of a parent's physical presence. A child's clinging, hitting, crying, and so on should be gradually, if inconsistently, replaced by the use of words. The child, when distressed, will also move developmentally toward being soothed and regulated by a parent's words or simply by a mental image of the parent. The inability to move from physical to verbal control and "mentalizing" is often why parents bring their children to see us.

Similarly, parents should be able to rely less on physical control of their growing children and instead utilize verbal commands and cues, discussion and negotiation, and setting of rules and expectations with an underlying trust that these rules will more or less be followed, even when the parent is not present. As I will describe in more detail in the next chapter, overly harsh or restrictive psychological control by the parent can contribute to anxiety and/or the lack of psychological growth, skill building, and autonomy in the child.

Parental Internal Working Models

Another factor in attunement is the internal working models by which the parents live. All of us, parents included, have internal working models or semiconscious verbal rules that influence us: "I am a good person, even if I mess up sometimes"; "Seatbelts are for wimps." Many were forged during our earliest years with our own caregivers, who were—or were not—attuned to us and our needs. For most of us, it was a mix of variable attunement and we emerged from childhood with a stock of both useful and not-so-useful internal working models. Over the years, the many transactions we have with teachers, coaches, bosses, coworkers, and others continue to shape our models in various ways. Some of these later encounters and experiences will improve a person's flexibility and adaptability. This better-late-than-never experience of attunement is sometimes referred to as "earned secure attachment." Other individuals in our lives may elicit and reinforce old patterns of rigidity and reactivity. As we'll see, parents may respond to their anxious child less out of a sensitive and contingent stance toward *this* child at *this* moment and more out of obedience to hidden rules distilled from previous or even other current relationships.

Since their inception in the 1960s, what has driven basic parenting therapies such as Behavior Parent Training is an operant model with differential reinforcement of positive behaviors and mild punishment, such as time-out or privilege loss, for misbehavior. This sort of contingency management works very well for moving behavior around, and I will describe strategies for doing so in the chapters ahead. But not all families succeed with this type of intervention. Also, treatment gains are not always maintained over significant periods of time. Recently, clinicians and researchers have looked more closely at the assumption that contingencies alone will move behavior in a positive direction and maintain those improvements over time.

Two aspects of parent-child interactions may undermine attempts to change those interactions effectively and for the long term. First, there is the growing awareness that much of what we do every day in our routine interactions with the world or with others is on autopilot. Think of a typical morning: getting ready for work, getting the kids ready for school, commuting to work. Often we're multitasking, moving from one task to another, thinking about something other than what we're doing or what's in front of us: taking the right exit, getting off at the right stop. We do this without a lot of conscious awareness unless something truly novel appears and alerts us via a mild poke at our fight-or-flight response system.

This "automaticity" makes life efficient, but it also makes behavior patterns difficult to change (Dumas, 2005). It is very hard to change something you're not aware of. Therefore, the first step in changing these highly routinized anxious parent-child interactions (recall

Wyatt and his parents in the morning) will be to make everyone just a little more aware of—or attuned to—what they are, in fact, doing.

This strategy of increasing awareness has been used successfully to change unhealthy behavior patterns in adults. Smokers who carry a little notebook and merely write down the time and their intention to have a cigarette find their smoking decreases. Keeping a food diary for a few days will result in healthier dietary choices. Awareness helps increase our contact with the choices we're making, and they can become actual choices as opposed to habits.

The second issue is this: Simply being contingent may not be enough. Doling out the rewards and punishments in a timely and consistent manner is necessary, but it is not sufficient. Recall Harry Harlow's attachment experiments with wire and cloth "mother" monkeys. Something more is needed to grow healthy children and to have healthy relationships.

Responsive parenting is not merely the consistent and timely application of consequences (or being "contingent," the term I used earlier). And it is not necessarily being positive all the time. Research shows that mothers of compliant children do not consistently provide positive attention for compliance and that positive maternal attention is not an especially effective reinforcer for compliance in children with a history of defiance (Wahler & Meginnis, 1997). In short, this means that doling out praise and punishment does not fully explain child behavior patterns. Something else must be at work here. That something else is the parent's capacity for warmth and sensitivity, of which I will have more to say. All of the many parenting behaviors that reflect warmth and sensitivity create the framework for the relationship, the field on which the relationship can play itself out with a balance of acceptance and expectations.

ADAPTABILITY: BIOLOGY, TEMPERAMENT, AND THE POSSIBILITY OF CHANGE

In the process of offering psychoeducation about biology, temperament, and anxiety, I make the case to the parents that anxiety makes sense and is even adaptive. It is not necessarily a "problem to be solved," given our biology as humans generally and as individuals with certain traits or predispositions, or what we've been calling temperament.

As mentioned, behavioral inhibition is associated with anxiety disorders, especially social anxiety. The pattern of avoiding novel and edgy situations, while somewhat adaptive, can lead to lack of experience with these situations and poor development of subsequent coping skills and the experience of "Well, that turned out okay" that allows further exploration and more adaptive skill building.

So, adaptation can cut two ways: We could consider fight-or-flight to be adaptive if it allows the individual to survive a truly dangerous, threatening situation. But for so many of us in modern society, although sadly not everyone, our lives do not pose a great deal of genuine, unavoidable danger. On a typical day a fairly modest amount of caution and good judgment will get us safely back in our beds at night. A balanced adaptation to life would involve reasonable caution and judgment alongside a willingness to explore the possibilities and even take some reasonable risks. Do wear the seatbelt.

Achieving that balance of caution and risk is necessary for a vital life. Further it is a developmental achievement no less fundamental than learning to walk or read. And as with most developmental achievements there is a social component in terms of passing on knowledge from the caregiver to the child, encouraging the child, and supporting the child's efforts, especially when growth is hard. An important aspect of the parents' encouraging adaptation and growth is their own modeling of adaptability and growth when things are challenging. To do so, they must at times override some deeply engrained biological tendencies and behavior patterns and then teach the child how to do this for himself. This process will require a summoning up of one's effortful control, the temperamental trait related to attention and will. This results in good adaptation, thoughtful adaptation, and will subsequently lead to positive experiences even within difficult situations.

As I'll describe more fully in Chapter 4, when I talk to parents about managing difficult situations, I like to make a distinction between *reacting* and *responding*. Children with low effortful control tend to be reactors; they are impulsive, going with the emotion or idea that's "loudest" in their mind. They're not considering the whole situation, not considering what's novel and what's familiar, not drawing on past experience. They may be thinking about the future, but they're not *anticipating;* they're not imagining the potential consequences of their actions nor coming up with an accurate "vision" or prediction about the near future. As we saw with Mycroft, this results in the anxious question asking—"When are we leaving?" "Who will be there?"—that comes up even for the most routine events.

Good effortful control results in actions that are more in tune with the facts of the situation. This comes with consciously or unconsciously asking questions like this: "How is this situation similar to ones I've been in?" "How is it different?" "What might be the consequences of this or that response?" "What help is available?" And most important, "What should I be focusing on?" Anxiety and attention are closely related. As such, any measures that help strengthen attentional control can be enormously helpful in working with children and adults with anxiety. In the coming chapters, I will describe more connections between improving attention and improving overall functioning in the face of anxiety.

The point I want to stress throughout these pages is this: if anxiety is seen as invariably, inherently wrong or bad, or as evidence that something in the world is truly wrong and bad and dangerous, or that there is something wrong with the child, then the suffering of both parents and child is compounded and the probability that they will resort to frantic and desperate coping measures increases. In such situations, the parents and the child will likely seek "solutions" to the "problem" of anxiety—for example, escape, avoidance, and control—that are unhelpful in both the short run and the long run. If, however, we can provide informative and effective psychoeducation, we may be able to convey a very different message to parents: Your child is, in many ways, built to act this way, but we can help you and your child nonetheless.

WHY WE DO WHAT WE DO

We are in this business because we believe people can adapt and change. And we see adaptation and change resulting from our work. Temperament is not destiny. Temperament is tendency. And tendencies can be shaped by the environment from the earliest months of life. And tendencies can be overridden by conscious decisions and behavioral habits.

What is important to remember, and to convey to parents, is that temperament is real and durable and it will always be a force to reckon with in your work with a family. This leads to the inevitable "three steps forward and two steps back" that we so often experience in treatment. It also explains why treatment progress can become stalled. I've found that about three to four months into treatment temperament stubbornly reasserts itself in spite of everyone's best efforts. At those times it's important to acknowledge everyone's frustration and then examine the situation for possible adjustments to the treatment plan. But frequently, the plan is sound but the hoped for quick fix is nowhere in sight. Discouragement can set in. Chapter 9 will cover how parents, children, and we ourselves as clinicians can maintain our resilience in the face of this challenging work.

THE ACTUAL ORIGINS OF ANXIETY

I imagine the Creation Design Team. They're sitting around a large celestial conference table. Coffee cups and pizza boxes are strewn about. It's late Friday night. They've had a busy week. Separated the light from the dark. Check. Separated the land from the water. Check. Plants, creatures of the air and those that crawl upon the earth. Check, check, check.

Now, all they have left to do is the "humans" if they're going to get Sunday off. But at the moment they stare in weary disappointment at the model before them. They've used up their supply of exoskeletons, fur, fangs, and claws in creating the other animals and so this thing, this human, looks quite naked, soft, and vulnerable. It's never going to survive long enough to reproduce. The CEO will not be happy.

Finally, one of the engineers lifts her head from the table and says, "Hey, let's give them "thinking." Then they can *anticipate* dangers and that will help keep them out of trouble." "Good enough," they all reply. The final design was approved by the CEO with only minor reservations and the team got its well-deserved day off. We got anxiety.

Biology itself is all about survival and adaptation. Too hot, start sweating. Too cold, start shivering. Got a foreign invader, crank up the internal furnace to kill it off. Unfortunately, adaptive responses such as fevers can cause damage and even death. And danger signals such as the fight-or-flight response can ruin lives as well, depending on how they are handled. Somehow, everyone must learn to use the particular danger-anticipation system humans are born with. For our clients, and their parents, it is enormously helpful to begin our journey with them by normalizing these biologically based reactions and to frame the problem as one of learning to cope with the system we've got, recognize when the signals are in fact useful information, and to ultimately put our energies into adapting to what life gives us and living large in spite of the stressors.

A LOOK AHEAD

I hope I have made the case that it is useful to begin your work with anxious children and their parents by providing a biological framework for these distressing experiences. This will hopefully get everyone on the same page regarding the origins of the child's anxious thoughts and feelings as well as preparing everyone for the challenges ahead. Part of the challenge in working with parents of anxious children is that one or more parents often have their own significant history with anxiety. Thus, situations that provoke anxiety in the child may ignite anxiety in the parent. Or the child's apparent fear and anxiety itself may, through contagion, elicit similar feelings and behavioral reactions in the parent. If a parent does not particularly struggle with anxiety, his or her reaction to the situation may be one of frustration or impatience. How parents respond or react to the child's anxiety and fear, from the earliest months of life, sets up future parent-child transactions and can define the boundaries of a child's resilience, competence, and self-concepts. No pressure there.

In the next chapter I describe what we know about the role of parents in the development and maintenance of child anxiety and fear. My intention is *not* to blame parents for their child's anxiety. Rather, I want to help parents see which parenting behaviors help, or don't help, their child act with courage, self-regulation, good communication, and self-efficacy. Parenting behaviors that help attain these important developmental goals include rewarding coping behaviors, discouraging unhelpful anxiety-related behaviors, modeling distress tolerance, developing good family communication and problem-solving skills, using an authoritative parenting style, and expressing warmth and acceptance.

Summary of Key Ideas

- Anxiety is a fact of life.
- We are here because of the fight-or-flight mechanisms that evolved over eons.
- Temperament and other biological factors are not destiny but tendencies.
- Finding ways to mitigate the impact of the child's vulnerabilities and improve important self-regulation skills is the treatment goal.
- It is the parent's ability to adapt to the child's temperament and work with the whole constellation of that child's traits that determines the course of the parent-child relationship and subsequent child functioning.
- Even the most mature brains can regress, with stress, back to a more rigid and reactive thinking style.
- Temperament is not destiny. Because temperament is a tendency, it can be overridden by conscious decisions and behavioral habits.
- The children at most risk for anxiety disorders are those who both meet criteria for behavioral inhibition and have parents who themselves have an anxiety order.
- While the behaviors and predispositions associated with temperament can be quite durable, they are also influenced by context. Stability is not synonymous with intractability.
- Parents may respond to their anxious child less out of a sensitive and contingent stance toward this child at this moment and more out of obedience to hidden rules distilled from previous or even other current relationships.
- Decades of research have shown the efficacy of treatment models that address the relationship between parent and child.

CHAPTER 2

The Role of Parents in Child Anxiety

The muscles along Elena's jaw line twitch as she describes Mycroft, her five-year-old, and the typical morning routine:

> I've read tons of books. I know what to do; everything's very predictable, very routine. I move things along by interspersing little rewarding activities after Mycroft completes some portion of the routine. We cuddle on the couch for five minutes *after* he gets out of bed. He can watch a twenty-minute video *after* he eats all his breakfast and gets dressed. I'm very careful about what he watches, because he can get freaked out by almost anything—Disney cartoons, Muppets. He's very sensitive that way.
>
> Anyway, it's all very predictable, the morning is, and it's set up to move him through the routine so that we can get out of the house on time. I can't be late for work. But at some point, the questions begin: "Am I going to extended day today?" Yes, Mycroft. You go to extended day every day except Tuesday when Carla (she's the new nanny) picks you up from school. "When are you going to pick me up from extended day today?" Same time I always pick you up, Mycroft. Between 5:30 and 5:45. It goes on and on. Same questions. Same answers. Every day.
>
> Then, right as we're ready to head out the door, he starts

becoming frantic about something. My mother's a retired psychiatric nurse, and she's convinced he has OCD. Can five-year-olds have OCD? Anyway, he just starts obsessing about something. The straps on his backpack don't feel right or his shoelace lengths aren't even or he needs to put on a different shirt, usually one that's in the laundry. He starts demanding that I fix this stuff, and he gets hysterical: "You're the worst Mommy ever"; "I'm so stupid." And then I'm arguing with him about all that. There's just no time and it shouldn't matter. It just shouldn't matter. Mycroft has to get to school and I have to get to work.

From our experience as clinicians, we know that parents play a crucial role in child anxiety—in its treatment and, unfortunately, in its development and maintenance. In the process of treating the child, by default we often also "treat" the parents. Clinical studies support the involvement of parents in the treatment of child anxiety (e.g., Barmish & Kendall, 2005). Throughout this book, I will describe two somewhat overlapping ways in which parents can be involved in treating child anxiety. First, parents can be engaged as "co-clinicians" who will support the treatment efforts outside your office and in the world where the anxious thoughts and feelings occur and then elicit the accompanying *anxiety behaviors*. Second, parents may be "co-clients," which means you must respectfully address *their* thoughts, feelings, and behavior patterns which may occur in the context of their child's anxiety and fear. To the extent that parent behaviors influence the emotions, cognitions, and behaviors of their children, it's important to recognize and understand the contributions of the parent and larger family systems to the overall presenting problem. This is an explicit and agreed upon component of treatment as I will discuss in the next chapter under the topic of establishing the therapeutic "frame."

UNDERSTANDING THE PARENTS' ROLE IN CHILD ANXIETY: CHARACTERISTICS AND BEHAVIOR

As I mentioned in the previous chapter, genetics appear to play a role in child anxiety (Capps et al., 1996, Thapar & McGuffin, 1995). However, genetics is only tendency, not certainty, and a number of family processes are considered important in the final common pathway of how anxiety and fear may be expressed in a particular child.

If as clinicians we are to affect child anxiety, we must recognize and address the processes relevant to anxiety that are manifested in the parent-child anxiety dance. To do this work, we need to recognize and understand the common processes that I introduced in the introduction: avoidance/escape, control, parent-child transactions, and context. It's important to use effective communication tools to convey this information to the parents in a nonpunitive, supportive way (see Chapter 3). Finally, we need treatment strategies to promote healthy engagement between parent and child in situations marked by anxiety and fear.

Studies have described a number of parent characteristics and behavior patterns that are correlated with anxiety in children: overprotectiveness, overcontrol and intrusiveness, anxious interpretation of events, tolerance or encouragement of escape and avoidance, and high family conflict (Ginsburg & Schlossberg, 2002; McLeod, Wood, & Weisz, 2007). I'll describe these briefly now and provide more detail with the case examples in the coming chapters. It should be stressed that these observed correlations between parental behaviors (fathers are woefully underrepresented in these studies) and child anxiety are far from perfect. These are complex, dynamic, and bidirectional systems; it's often hard to know what is *cause* and what is *effect*.

That said, in your assessment phase you should be on the lookout for unhelpful parent behaviors but at the same time keep a compassionate and open mind regarding how these behavior patterns have come about, how they contribute to the overall picture you're being asked to deal with, and how you can use the gathered information to develop an effective course of treatment. These parenting behaviors of concern fall into two loose and somewhat overlapping categories: parental modeling of unhelpful coping strategies and parent behaviors that interfere with the child's developing coping and self-regulation skills (Wood & McLeod, 2008).

Overprotectiveness

It's hard to define with any precision when a parent is *overprotective*; this will depend on the individual child, her development stage, and the relevant circumstances. Research studies have used a variety of operational definitions for terms such as *overprotectiveness* or *overcontrol*, one being that it applies to parents who use "excessive caution and restrict and/or protect their children in the absence of a cause or reason" (Ginsburg & Schlossberg, 2002, p. 145). Still rather subjective. But in any clinical practice, a clinician comes across parents who, as a general approach to parenting, are quite limiting in the opportunities they afford their child for taking reasonable risks, facing anxiety-provoking situations, or persisting toward valued goals when anxiety or frustration is running high.

The clear problem is that overprotecting, however defined, can deprive a child of opportunities to learn that she is resilient and capable and that common anxiety-provoking situations are manageable. Without opportunities to learn to manage anxiety-provoking situations, the child can't develop new, realistic reappraisals of those situations. The damage is twofold: (1) the child's self-efficacy cannot develop, and (2) the natural habituation to novel and feared situations is impeded. Interestingly, parental overprotectiveness is specifically associated with social phobia (Leib et al., 2000).

Overcontrol and Intrusiveness

Parental *overcontrol* has been defined as "intrusive behavior, granting minimal autonomy to their child, constraining their child's individuality, use of excessive commands or instructions, and restriction of their child's behavior during a task" (Ginsburg & Schlossberg,

2002, p. 146). Parental *intrusiveness* is generally thought of as high psychological control and low autonomy granting. Both of these sets of parenting behaviors have been implicated in the development of childhood anxiety and in its maintenance (Dadds & Roth, 2001).

Like overprotectiveness, overcontrol and intrusiveness interfere with a child's developing autonomy and coping skills along with the ability to acquire experiences that provide honest feedback about the world and her capabilities. Grace, whom we met in the previous chapter, can take *forever* to get dressed in the morning. moving as if she's underwater. It is a strong temptation on her parents' part to step in and just dress her in the service of getting to school and work on time. In doing so, Grace's parents may be denying her, and themselves, an opportunity to understand the nature of her difficulty with this age-appropriate task and to come up with an alternative response to the overall situation. In Chapter 8, I will have more to say about how parents might decide when to *lean in* and when to *hang back* at these times.

Clearly, parents need to exert some control and even intrusiveness into the life of their child. Elena is not going to allow Mycroft to carve the Thanksgiving turkey. *And*, one has to allow some age-appropriate risk taking if the child is going to develop tolerance for strong emotions and to manage challenges. It's a difficult balancing act.

Parents who are controlling and intrusive send a message to their child that (1) the world is a dangerous and unpredictable place, and (2) the child is not mature enough or competent enough to handle it. This may lead to increased anxiety and decreased confidence. Confidence is a matter of importance because classic anxiety, in the form of worries, often involves a two-part cognition: (1) I have the idea of an impending negative event, and (2) I have the companion idea that I am not going to be able to handle it well. If, on the other hand, a child "has" the confidence that she can handle the upcoming situation (for example, a birthday party with a lot of children she doesn't know), she is less likely to experience anxiety in relation to that event. I put "has" in quotes in that last sentence because we can't really talk about constructs like "confidence" or "motivation" as *things* people have or don't have; they are essentially *stories* we tell ourselves about situations. If this child can focus on her "I can do this" story (and take steps to actually *do this,* whatever that might mean) rather than focusing on her "this is going to be bad" story, she will likely be successful at the party.

If, however, a parent is stoking the "this is going to be bad" story through his own anxious behavior (modeling), the child's focus of attention will readily swing toward the anxious aspects of the situation (the attentional bias I described in the last chapter). The parent may also be sending messages that the child is incapable ("Are you sure you're going to be okay if I'm not there?") or trying to micromanage the child's behavior and emotions while at the party ("Why don't you go and talk to Suzie? She's someone you know."). Talking to Suzie may be just the ticket, but too often parent moves of this kind serve to short-circuit the child's ability to gain experience and develop stress management skills such as self-soothing or shifting attention.

Finally, there are times when overcontrol and intrusiveness takes the form of a parent pushing the child into anxiety-provoking situations when and where the child is simply not able to be successful. This may present to you as one parent taking a stance of insisting the child engage in difficult tasks with insufficient support, a "sink-or-swim" approach, while the other parent takes the opposite stance of overprotecting. This state of affairs is often born of frustration with an ongoing, stressful situation and basic difficulties in effective co-parenting. Some work on your part will be necessary to find a "third way." This can be done in the context of setting up some thoughtful exposure exercises, as I will describe in Chapter 6. Each parent will be able to feel heard in terms of "Yes, we're going to get her out there meeting some challenges" and "Yes, we're going to be careful about how we do that so that we don't overwhelm her."

Anxious Interpretation of Events

Parents may tend to overprotect and overcontrol because they themselves see the world as threatening. A considerable body of research shows that individuals with anxiety disorders, both children and adults, demonstrate an attentional bias toward threats, or perceived threats, in the environment (Bar-Hiam et al., 2007; Puliafico & Kendall, 2006). In a study by Barrett and colleagues (Barrett, Rapee, Dadds, & Ryan, 1996), groups of anxious children and aggressive children, along with their parents, were presented with various common scenarios in which there was some ambiguity about what is happening. For example, a vignette might describe hearing a noise in the hall when you're in your bed at night or "you are approaching a group of boys at recess and you notice they are looking at you and laughing." The children and parents were then asked to interpret, or make sense of, these situations. Both the anxious and aggressive children *and their parents* made a relatively high number of threat interpretations in response to these ambiguous situations when compared with nonclinical children and parents. In the recess scenario for example, "The boys are making some joke about how I look" or "They're thinking I'm stupid."

What appears to be important in the contagion of anxiety from parent to child is the parents' heightened sensitivity to threat and conveying their own fear and anxiety to the child along with "lessons" about how dangerous the world is. And, as I've mentioned before, it may be one parent (rather than both) who conveys fear and anxiety to the child. Sadly, though, we humans will tend to err on the side of the anxious story; better safe than sorry.

Tolerance or Encouragement of Escape and Avoidance

The study by Barrett and colleagues went further and asked the children and parents how they would likely respond in these ambiguous situations. While both the anxious and the aggressive children and their parents gave interpretations of events that leaned heavily toward threat, the two groups provided quite different hypothetical responses. Aggressive children, *and their parents,* came up with aggressive "solutions" to these situations—e.g., some sort of "comeback" remark or aggressive response. On the other hand, the anxious children and their parents mainly chose avoidance as the solution—

e.g., steering clear of the group of boys. This "solution" might help reduce the child's anxiety or other distress in the moment, but it would not allow for an actual engagement with the situation that could potentially reveal that the situation is in fact benign.

This illustrates the classic and powerful *negative reinforcement* paradigm described in the Introduction—that is, the likelihood of a behavior in the future is increased if that behavior has served to avoid or escape from an aversive situation. As I will describe in the coming chapters, negative reinforcement operates on the child *and* the parent, thus contributing to a dance of mutually reinforcing avoidance and escape. For example, a child and parent, both prone to anxious arousal, enter a loud, chaotic birthday party scene. The child becomes whiny and clingy. It is highly probable that both child and parent will be looking to escape the situation. If they leave the party prematurely, they will likely both feel great relief and such parties will likely be avoided altogether in the future.

Of course, there are many situations, dangerous or noxious, in which avoidance or escape is appropriate and adaptive, or at least benign. Not everyone has to go off the high dive, try out for the lead in the school play, take up alligator wrestling, or accept an invitation to a birthday party at Chuck E. Cheese. But to the extent that avoiding or escaping from anxiety-provoking situations interferes with learning about the world and developing coping skills and a self-image of competence, it's a problem.

High Family Conflict and Criticism

By definition, families marked by high conflict experience more than their fair share of arguing, fighting, coercive behaviors, rejection, criticism, and ineffective problem-solving skills. Family conflict, per se, appears to be less a specific factor in the development and maintenance of anxiety in children and more a general contributor to a broad range of negative states, including anxiety and depression. Parents who criticize or minimize their child's "negative" feelings do not provide a safe space in which to explore, understand, and tolerate anxious emotions and thoughts. The result, once again, is the inability to develop distress tolerance through appropriate coping and help-seeking behaviors.

Families such as Wyatt's may have one parent, in this case the father, who is critical of and impatient with the child's anxiety, while another parent tries to "balance" the situation by being perhaps too yielding on the chronic avoidance and control. One parent sees the other as too harsh on the child and in turn is seen as too indulging of the child.

Of course, as I mentioned earlier, it's hard to know what is the chicken and what is the egg. Parents trying to manage daily life with an anxious child will certainly find themselves frustrated, short-tempered, and depleted by all the work involved in the simplest family routines. One might expect some criticism or dismissing of the child's feelings and ideas at times. The dance is always bidirectional. However, when criticism and negativity in general become a major component of the parent-child anxiety dance, no one is happy and it will be harder to get everyone unstuck and moving toward good communication, courageous behaviors, new experiences, and new ideas about oneself and the world. The final chapter of this book will discuss parent (and clinician) resilience and strategies for staying buoyant in the face of these challenges.

An important theme throughout this book is the clinician's acknowledging and validating each parent's, or extended caregiver's, experience of the child and their own distressing thoughts and feelings as they do their best to be the best parent they know how to be. But addressing these anxious thoughts and feelings, in either the parent or the child, is tricky, and some commonsense approaches, such as *reassurance,* in fact don't work very well. As my mother likes to say, "Common sense tells us the earth is flat."

PARENT BEHAVIORS THAT HELP

Thankfully, there are parent behaviors that are correlated with resilience in the face of anxiety (Ginsburg & Schlossberg, 2002). The chapters that follow will provide strategies and tactics (I'll make the distinction in Chapter 6) for promoting these helpful parent behaviors and traits. These positive behaviors include rewarding coping behaviors, discouraging unhelpful anxiety-related behaviors, modeling distress tolerance, developing good family communication and problem-solving skills, using an authoritative parenting style, and expressing warmth and acceptance. Let's take a brief look at each of these behavior sets now.

Rewarding Coping Behavior

In successful families, parents encourage brave behavior in the face of challenges. This encouragement could be in the form of a structured reward program such as a marble jar, sticker chart, and the like. In Chapter 6 I'll describe the use of these tools for encouraging positive behaviors. More typically, we are talking about simple, in-the-moment recognition of when the child is doing what needs to be done *even though* she is feeling anxiety or experiencing worried thoughts. This is, after all, the very definition of being brave.

In terms of the functional, transdiagnostic, process model, our treatment goals will emphasize increasing brave behaviors over the reduction or elimination of the anxious thoughts and feelings. To that end it will be important for parents to recognize these behaviors ("Ah, you're doing X now"), show positive regard for them ("I'm so happy you're doing X"), and make the connection between the behavior and a successful outcome ("Doing X got you Y, which I know you really wanted").

Persistence and effort are recognized and valued even when, or especially when, the outcome is less than perfect. As I described in Chapter 1, we all have a tendency to become more all-or-none in our thinking when under stress. Children are especially prone to this regression, and it can affect their experience of their ideas and feelings in the moment ("This *is* the worst . . ."), and retrospectively ("It *was* the worst . . ."). At bedtime, when all is cozy and safe and the day is being recounted with a parent, it's easy for the few negative events to come to the surface and the general "okay-ness" of the day as a whole to be submerged. The anxious children we work with have a difficult time walking the "messy middle," as my valued colleague Seattle psychologist Laura Kastner likes to describe so much of life. At these times parents can gently inquire about or point out the merely okay and then recognize and value partial successes and the efforts behind them. The middle is messy precisely because *coping* does not necessarily mean that the situation will turn out perfectly well. And some days coping and "okay-ness" are as good as it gets.

Discouraging Unhelpful Anxiety-Related Behaviors

As mentioned in the Introduction, the two primary behavioral processes in the anxiety dance are *inappropriate control efforts* and *avoidance*. There are occasions when control and avoidance are effective and appropriate responses to anxiety-provoking situations. Often, however, it is these two classes of behaviors (essentially two sides of the same coin) that define the child's anxiety problem and have led the family to your office door. Mycroft and Grace are trying to control their immediate environments at the expense of moving forward with necessary tasks. Wyatt, and other children we will meet, are avoiding important situations and the uncomfortable thoughts and feelings these situations provoke. It is these control and avoidance behaviors we want to gently discourage and replace with more effective problem-solving or coping strategies.

Parents of competent children refrain from giving undue attention to anxious behaviors, especially those coercive behaviors anxious children can display when they become desperate for rescue. Wyatt, in his rising distress about having to face his day, goes for the verbal artillery that he knows, through experience, will get his mother to vacillate in her efforts to get him out of bed and heading to school. For his father, Wyatt's words and tone are waving the red flag that gets Dan angry and charging in. None of this is working especially well.

I will have more to say about dealing with defiance and other coercive, anxiety-related child behaviors when we get to Chapter 8. For now, I would like to emphasize that this is a particularly challenging area for parents: *not* giving attention to the child's anxious behavior.

But the transdiagnostic model will allow us to reframe the expectation a bit, and this can be an opportunity to shift the dance a little. Rather than *ignore* the child when she is distressed (we're not cruel here and, more important, that would probably not be effective) we will emphasize attending to the *process* at work in the moment and the *meaning* of the child's behavior over getting caught up in particular content such as "I hate you. Why don't you just kill me?"

Modeling Distress Tolerance

Along with discouraging unhelpful child control and avoidance behaviors, parents of resilient and competent children model and teach competence through their own actions, when there is anxiety and stress under the skin. As I'll describe in the chapters ahead, instead of giving centrality to their own anxious emotions and thoughts ("Oh #8%!, traffic's a mess and we're going to be late"), effective parents consciously and publicly (thinking out loud) model shifting attention toward actionable goals, be they problem-solving goals or simply coping: "Oh dear, traffic's a mess and now I'm thinking we're going to be late. *Deep breath.* I wonder if we can safely turn here and take another route?"

Developing Good Family Communication and Problem-Solving Skills

Families are complex, dynamic systems and there is always a lot going on. Accurate and timely communication among the players is necessary for everyday functioning. Good communication does not mean that everything is conveyed and received perfectly. Good communication in families means that information, about events or about persons, can flow back and forth in spite of the inevitable *mis*communication or unexpected event. In Chapter 5, I will talk about communication skills related to child anxiety, and the importance of these strategies and tactics will be stressed throughout this book.

As briefly illustrated in the previous section, communication in the service of helping the anxious child includes parents' "letting the child in on" how we can make things work when anxiety and fear are part of the picture. Parents encourage discussion and exchanges of information about one another's experiences. These experiences are validated and respected, if not completely shared. Problem solving is great, *when there's a problem to be solved.* I'll describe how at times, however, the anxious situation at hand calls more for adaptation and coping than for problem solving. Making this distinction is critical for picking our battles, directing our attention and efforts, and preserving our energies.

Using an *Authoritative* Parenting Style

Based largely on the work of Diana Baumrind (1968), an *authoritative* parenting style is one marked by balance among the competing demands of setting limits on the child's behavior with flexibility, bidirectional communication, and granting autonomy when appropriate, offering choices, emphasizing personal responsibility, and using punishment sparingly. This is in contrast to an *authoritarian* parenting style, associated with strict control of the child's behavior, limited and rule-governed opportunities for freedom and autonomy, and harsh discipline. The *permissive* parenting style, on the other hand, is one with few demands or expectations for the child and leaves the development of self-regulation up to the child to figure out.

Needless to say, the *authoritative* style of parenting is associated with increased child competence and reduced levels of anxiety (Stark, Humphrey, Laurent, Livingston, & Christopher, 1993). It is easy to see how families stressed by an anxious child might drift into some unhelpful patterns of either too much control of the child or avoidance of parental responsibilities for managing the child's world while teaching her how to deal with it. The authoritarian and permissive (also known as *laissez-faire*) parenting styles embody the reactions of control and avoidance, respectively, on the part of the parent. They are just two of the more extreme forms the parent-child anxiety dance can take.

More often than not, you will see a combination of parenting styles within any one family, shifting day to day or even minute to minute.

The parents' particular reactions and responses will be influenced in any given moment by many, many factors both external (circumstances) and internal (thoughts, feelings, memories). I will describe some of these factors when we talk about *antecedent* or *activator conditions* and *setting events* in the context of functional analysis in Chapter 4.

Expressing Warmth and Acceptance

Among the attributes describing authoritative parenting are warmth and acceptance. Parental *warmth* is a broad category of behaviors including positive affect when around the child (laughing, smiling), expressing affection and positive regard, and so on. Children, especially young children, often take their cues for how to think, feel, and act from the adults around them. Parents who model warmth and positive behaviors in the face of anxiety, their own or the child's, will provide a safe space for the child to experience and effectively manage distress.

Acceptance is defined as parental behaviors that signal understanding and acceptance of, and a measure of tolerance for, a child's thoughts and feelings. Active listening, patience, and validation (see Chapter 5) are prime examples of parent behaviors that convey warmth and acceptance. Acceptance is conveyed most often through patience with and understanding of the full range of a child's emotions. It is through the parent's empathy and acceptance that the child can begin to understand, tolerate, and manage "negative" emotions such as anxiety.

I will have more to say about acceptance in the coming chapters. For now, I want to emphasize that the definition of acceptance used here is not a passive resignation or somehow trying to be happy with unhappy circumstances. It does not mean that every *behavior*, parent's or child's, is acceptable. I will talk about an acceptance that denotes courageously facing present reality as it is and serves as the starting point from which change can occur. In my clinical experience, acceptance of what is in the moment is the *only* place from which one can begin the process of real change; you can only get *there* from *here*.

ENLISTING PARENTS' HELP: CONVEYING THE TRANSDIAGNOSTIC APPROACH

As I mentioned at the beginning of the chapter, parents can be "co-clinicians" who assist with the treatment process out in the world. One way of enlisting their help is to present the transdiagnostic approach in a way that is credible, understandable, and doable. A transdiagnostic or functional/process model of conceptualizing childhood psychological issues will not, and should not, replace categorical descriptions such as DSM 5 or ICD–10. As I'll describe in Chapter 4, doing a functional assessment is time consuming, although it's worth the time and effort, in large part because it is a golden opportunity to increase the parents' awareness of how their habitual processes actually play out.

Certainly, checklists such as the Achenbach Child Behavior Checklist and the related Teacher Report Form (Achenbach, 1991) can provide useful information regarding symptoms and other concerns. These tools can be used to efficiently obtain important information, especially for teachers and others whom you want to weigh in on the child's functioning. Diagnostic categories can be useful shorthand when talking to teachers, pediatricians, and others. Plus, the reality is that we need to have a billing diagnosis in order to submit claims to insurance companies.

But there are several advantages to providing parents with a "big picture," developmental, and process-driven view of their child's situation. First, a view of "the problem" that integrates biology and social-emotional development helps "normalize" some of what's going on with the child, and to some extent, with the parent. It helps reduce that wariness that parents sometimes bring into your office as they gird themselves for the possibility that they will be blamed for their child's problems.

Second, this process-oriented conceptualization gets everyone away from the symptom-driven view of anxiety and the narrowing of treatment goals to eliminating or reducing anxiety and fear. This allows for a broader, and I think more realistic, range of possible treatment outcomes based on the child's functioning in the world. Instead of "My child won't be anxious anymore," the treatment goal might be something along the lines of "My child will be able to get to school in the morning without undue fussing and conflict."

Third, I will describe how this process-oriented approach can help reduce parental anxiety stemming from the commonly held idea that there are certain tools or scripts that must be applied to specific situations. Unfortunately, many parenting books and programs are quite specific and prescriptive in their recommendations. Parents develop the idea that if they were to just say or do "this" and don't say or do "that," all will be well. But when this "recipe" approach to parenting doesn't work well, or the gains are not sustained, parents can become discouraged or cynical about the advice of professionals. Instead of having parents follow some recipe or script, the approach set out in this book will help you teach and coach parents to utilize some basic strategies and techniques in creative, supple (strong yet flexible) ways, much like an experienced baker knows how to create an almost infinite variety of combinations of flour, sugar, liquid, and butter.

A LOOK AHEAD

A number of years ago Stanley Turecki, author of the classic book on child temperament *The Difficult Child,* spoke here in Seattle. I had the privilege of introducing Dr. Turecki to the audience of about 1,500 parents who'd come out on a rainy Tuesday evening to hear him speak. Dr. Turecki took the lecture hall stage, waved a hand over the audience and said, "You are the best-informed generation of parents in the history of the world. And you're the most neurotic!" Everyone laughed, albeit nervously. He went on to say that parents these days may have too much parenting information to consider, much of it contradictory, and there is tremendous pressure to do parenting "right." His most succinct advice to the parents that evening was "Relax."

The foregoing description of the role of parents in the development and maintenance of child anxiety is not meant to add to that pressure. As I will describe in Part Two, and in Chapter 4 in particular, the behavior patterns that I call the parent-child anxiety dance have come about as a product of everyone just trying to survive, to get their needs met, and everyone is assumed to be doing the best they can with the information and experiences they have. It is vital to maintain and to convey a compassionate stance toward these families.

How can you help both the parents and the anxious child without adding to the everyday stress? How can you support all these players/dancers without appearing to "take sides" or to assign blame? The same way porcupines make love—very carefully, but not timidly either.

In Part Two, "Creating a New Dance," I provide strategies and tactics based both on the extensive research that has been conducted on anxiety and children and on my many years of clinical experience working with families of anxious children. What is important to remember is that this interplay, or *transaction,* between the person and the environment, especially the social environment, is both the source of disordered anxiety and one of the best avenues for realizing real and lasting, positive change.

Now, please turn the page to Chapter 3, where we look at how to begin the process of creating a new dance. There I describe the assessment process and how you can shape the conversation about a child's fear and anxiety in a way that leads to a productive narrative and a good working alliance with the parents. Introducing the metaphor of the parent-child "anxiety dance" helps parents make sense of the difficult and sometimes bewildering interactions between themselves and their anxious child. This new understanding helps empower the parents to turn these struggles into opportunities for growth and change.

Summary of Key Ideas

- Parents play a crucial role in child anxiety. In the process of treating the child, by default we often also "treat" the parents.

- Overprotecting children can deprive them of opportunities to learn that they are resilient and capable and that common anxiety-provoking situations are manageable.

- Overcontrol and intrusiveness interfere with a child's developing autonomy and coping skills and with her ability to acquire experiences that provide honest feedback about the world and her capabilities.

- Helpful parent behaviors include rewarding coping behaviors, discouraging unhelpful anxiety-related behaviors, modeling distress tolerance, developing good family communication and problem-solving skills, using an authoritative parenting style, and expressing warmth and acceptance.

Part Two

Creating a New Dance

CHAPTER 3

Talking to Parents About Anxiety

Salma sighed, "It was a long week. An exhausting week." Her husband, Geoff, looked uncomfortable and checked his phone again. Salma glanced at him, but continued. "Brayden was full of energy that week. Just couldn't be still for a moment. Geoff was in China for a business trip that came up at the last minute. We'd had a tough few days before he left, talking about the uncertainty of Geoff's job and how we might have to move somewhere like China or Raleigh-Durham, or maybe if the project didn't work out, Geoff would be looking for a new job. Brayden is quite mature for a fifth grader. He handles these things very well. But he sure had a lot of energy that week."

I asked, "What was he doing with all that energy?"

"The usual stuff—starting then stopping little Lego projects, organizing and reorganizing his Pokemon cards, repeating everything four times."

"Can you tell me more about the repeating?" I asked.

Salma thought for a moment. "I guess that would be repeating everything three times, right? The first one not being a repeat. So, having to say everything four times total. It could be anything, but mostly questions, like, 'What's for dinner?' or 'What time is it in China right now?' And then I would have to repeat my answer four times, or three times, I guess. If I didn't, Brayden would get very angry and insistent. Like I said, it was exhausting and it makes me tired now just thinking about it. It was an awful week. The week Geoff was in China."

How do we begin to talk with parents like Salma and Geoff about their child's anxiety? How do we engage parents in the treatment process in a way that is as nonjudgmental as humanly possible and that affirms the importance of the parents in the life of their child? In this chapter, we'll find the answers to these questions and more as we explore rationales and strategies for talking with parents and making them an essential part of treating their child. A good working alliance with parents is important to the success of psychotherapy with children. The quality of our relationship with the parents and the child mitigates against premature termination and promotes treatment satisfaction and symptom reduction (Hawley & Weisz, 2005).

THE REFERRAL PATH: HOW HAS THE CHILD COME TO YOU?

Before beginning your assessment, it is vital that you understand how this child has come to you. (And, of course, the parents have come with the child.) This is known as the *referral path*. I am indebted to one of my former supervisors, Rich Adler, MD, for teaching me about the importance of the referral path. Clinicians working with adults tend to see clients who are self-referred. They are, after all, adults and can make decisions more or less for themselves. Some clients may come to you at the urging of a spouse or friend. Some may even be court ordered. But by and large, they come into your office of their own free will, and generally, they seek therapy because they are themselves distressed, concerned, or simply curious about their situation. Sometimes we say that they themselves "own" the problem.

It's different with children. They rarely self-refer. Perhaps the occasional relatively mature adolescent might do so, but the vast majority of the clients you and I see in our offices are there because some adult thought they should be there.

Know the referral path before you begin, or make it among the first of your inquiries during the intake session. How did this child come to you? Whose idea was it to seek out an evaluation? There are several possibilities. It could be the parents' idea, solidly in agreement about the issues and the need for assessment and possibly treatment. However, it may be that one parent is quite concerned and the other less so. One parent may even be antagonistic toward the idea of a psychological evaluation. For example, there may be an underlying fear that this referral is an indictment of her parenting and she fully expects to be blamed for her child's distress and behavior.

A substantial minority of the cases I receive have been referred at the urging of the school or one particular teacher. Sometimes the parents are in agreement with the school that an assessment should occur. Sometimes, though, parents are taken aback by this recommendation, or even demand, by the school. These parents may be confused or feel blind-sided: "They said everything was fine at the October parent-teacher conference. Now two months later they're saying it's been a problem all year." Parents may be angry and see problems, if there are any, as residing somewhere outside their child: "If the teacher and principal would step up and solve the bullying problem, my son wouldn't be so anxious about going to school."

Other possible referral paths include the pediatrician who sees something outside the norm. Parents may accept this recommendation, or they may be unsure that it's necessary: "Teddy was very tired and clingy that day, and Dr. Ward really only spent fifteen minutes with him. But she was very insistent we get in to see you. She seems to think there's something to be concerned about." At times, a relative, such as a grandparent, leans on the parents to have the assessment done. Such parents may come in feeling resentful or guilty.

The referral path is important because it defines your early work with the parents: allowing their own concerns to be heard apart from the concerns of others, discovering what all this means for them as parents, and exploring who "owns the problem." The issue of problem ownership relates directly to who among all these players, or *dancers,* is motivated to engage in the treatment process. If there is any question of problem ownership, you will need to spend some time sorting that question out and addressing any discrepancies to the extent possible.

WHAT'S THE MEANING OF ALL THIS?

The *meaning* of the child's symptoms and behavior is another area to gently explore. This includes the parents' (or teacher's or grand-parent's) ideas about what's causing the anxious thoughts, feelings, and behaviors; biology, bullies, their own parenting, their partner's parenting, and so on. Some of these factors may very well have importance in understanding the child and his pattern of anxious behaviors. Typically, though, parents recognize that these are com-plex situations involving a combination of factors, from temperament to situational variables. But I will often look for an opportunity, while discussing the dynamics and complexities of the anxious situations, to mention that it is often not possible to single out one causal agent that we can be confident holds the key to all that is going on.

I also let parents know very early in the assessment process that I *always* include parents in the treatment, to some degree, regardless of the child's age. Stating this expectation early in the process and framing parent involvement as a matter of routine procedure helps take the edge off any thoughts that I might blame one or both par-ents for their child's situation. As emphasized throughout this book, the child's anxious behaviors have meaning in terms of seeking res-cue from overwhelming situations. We're all just trying to get our needs met. We'd all be doing better if we knew how and were sup-ported in those better behaviors.

Meeting with Grace's Parents: An Initial Conversation

We met Grace in Chapter 2. Her pattern of behavioral inhibi-tion, rigidity, and angry, controlling behaviors has prompted the school to "strongly encourage" her parents to seek an evaluation.

Now Holly and Alistair sit before you, clearly unhappy. "They said 'strongly encouraged,' but we heard 'demanded,'" says Holly, flinging the words in your direction.

"Yes," continues Holly, "Grace can be a handful at home. But she's the girl—we expected her to be the easy one. The twins are still in preschool, and they certainly leave little room for indulging Grace's drama. But I expect the school to be able to deal with these things. They're the professionals. That's why she's in a private school." Alistair looks up and says, "They're also saying Grace's falling behind academically because of all the trips she makes to the nurse's office with stomachaches—that and her inability to get started on her work or get through it in a timely manner."

Holly continues, "My real concern is what this is doing to her socially. The other kids either avoid her or use her fears to tease her, saying, 'Ooh, is that a spider behind you?' and watching her do her freak-out thing. It's bullying, and the school needs to treat it as such. She no longer gets invited to birthday parties. None of the other parents will meet my eye at school. It's embarrassing. I was anxious as I child. I understand, to a degree. But I, at some point, had to just get over it. She needs to get over it, too. The sooner, the better."

FACILITATED LISTENING: THE FIRST STEP IN TALKING TO PARENTS

Where do you begin when you meet parents like Holly and Alistair? Clearly, the first step in talking to parents about their child's anxiety is to *listen* to them. *Facilitated listening* is "a form of communication fostering understanding and nonjudgmental acceptance of thoughts, feelings, and actions—our own and those of others" (Dumas, 2005, p. 783). Getting the parents to tell their story (not obsessively, relentlessly, or by just cataloging their complaints) is partly an art form, but it is also involves technique.

One technique is to ask questions that move from the general to the specific: more open-ended questions ("How's this last week been going?") followed by more specific questions to fill in details and to "unpack" larger descriptions and ideas ("Tell me more about the meltdown"). This inquiry goes beyond what, when, where, duration, frequency, and intensity. Important as those basics are, we also want to understand the parents' *stance* toward the presenting problems or to understand how the problem *is being held*. By this I mean, what is the parents' posture or attitude toward the behaviors and emotions that bring them to see you? Is it one of irritation and impatience, confusion and distress, sadness and discouragement, compassion and love? There are many, sometimes contradictory possibilities. Is this reminiscent of experiences in the past? Perhaps an older sibling went through this. How are they doing now? What are the parents' anxieties about their child's future?

Frequently, it is this "crust" of secondary emotions (frustration, anger, dread), theories, commentary, and other "head talk" that makes the original problem so difficult to address and so difficult to bear. As I'll show, these secondary and tertiary parental thoughts and feelings, wrapped around the original problem, can be addressed effectively through acceptance and mindfulness approaches in coordination with traditional CBT strategies for moving the child's behavior forward.

The Clinician's Stance: Nonjudgmental and Accepting

Jean Dumas also states that the clinician should present as "attentive, nonjudgmental, and sincerely interested in the challenges" the parent (and child) faces (2005, p. 783). Another important feature or objective of facilitated listening is modeled in the clinician's accepting stance. By "accepting," I do not mean that you suggest that all of the child's or parents' behaviors are okay and not a concern, or that there are no corrective actions that need to be taken. Rather, this initial nonjudgmental and accepting attitude is meant to help the parents loosen their grip, if only for a few moments, on the critical, anxious, frustrated "We have to fix this *now*" feelings and thoughts they have been living with. These feelings and thoughts not only make parents unhappy but may also interfere with finding real solutions to the presenting problems, as we'll see.

Additionally, you will make comments and observations of the kind generally known as reflecting, mirroring, or validating. This class of responses will play heavily in our work over the course of these chapters. Finally, you will ask the sorts of questions—sometimes in the form of "I wonder . . . "—that lead to clarifying and "opening up" the parent's story and thereby expanding the possibilities it contains.

Here is a sample of a discussion that might take place between you, the clinician, and Grace's mother. Note the italicized words; their importance will be described below.

CLINICIAN: You mentioned that Grace gets out of control. Can you describe that for me?

HOLLY: Yes, sometimes she's just completely beside herself.

CLINICIAN (*wincing*): *Sounds intense.* I'm wondering . . . if I were there, a fly on the wall, what *exactly* would I see her *doing*?

HOLLY: She'd be shrieking.

CLINICIAN: Words?

HOLLY: Yes, "Get away from me" mostly. But then when I try to leave, she gets even more upset.

CLINICIAN: Same angry upset or does it change to something else like fear or sadness?

HOLLY: It's still anger, but there is some fear mixed in. She's frantic.

CLINICIAN: And I'm guessing that trying to comfort her or problem solve doesn't help *in those moments*.

HOLLY: Absolutely, just more drama.

CLINICIAN: So, your only option *at that time* is what a friend of mine calls 'don't just do something, stand there.

HOLLY (*laughs*): I feel completely helpless. It's not much fun.

CLINICIAN: No, not at all. There you are, *both feeling helpless.*

The clinician's italicized words introduce certain ideas or possibilities to the narrative. The *wincing* and the *sounds intense* are meant to validate Holly's distressing experience, both nonverbally and verbally. (Validation will be covered in more detail in Chapter 5.) The word *exactly* is meant to elicit specificity in the description while *doing* gets at concrete, observable behavior, which is what we want to understand and eventually change. *In those moments* and *at that time* convey the idea that these behaviors are time bound, even if they feel like an eternity while they're happening. They are time-limited situations that show up for reasons that are potentially understandable and changeable.

To say *at that time* suggests that at some time in the future there may be other options. In the same way, as I'll describe in more detail later, I have parents put a "time stamp" on *their* validation messages: "Ah, you're having those worried thoughts *now*." Even to use the trope "As a friend of mine says . . ." is to suggest to the parent that she is not alone in this experience. To mention that Grace, too, is *feeling helpless* in that situation may help Holly feel some empathy for her child *in those moments*.

The Importance of Conveying Empathy and Modeling Patience with the Process

The empathic listening and questions eliciting clarification guide Holly (the parent or parents) toward an understanding of what *is* in those moments, the reality she and the child are dealing with, in as much detail and nuance as possible while maintaining a good pace to the discussion. It is only from this understanding of what *is* that parents can begin to see what might be changeable in the short run, what might be changeable in the long term, and what, perhaps, cannot be changed (for example, a divorce).

Because parents live in high problem-solving mode every day, they may believe that anxiety and other emotions are also problems that can and should be *fixed*. This expectation leads to considerable parental frustration and criticism, of both the child and of themselves, when these emotional "problems" do not yield to conventional problem-solving techniques. I will have more to say about the difference between *problems* and *conditions* in Chapter 4.

All this is conveyed to the parents with respect and empathy. But it can be a hard sell. Most parents come to you for solutions, and quick ones at that. They might say, "We're not here to talk about us." But in my experience, most parents will settle down and actually appreciate the opportunity to tell their story to someone who really listens and doesn't rush in with solutions before getting to know the child and the situation in all its complexity.

I once heard a radio ad for a car dealership. They were touting the interpersonal skills of their sales staff saying, "People don't care how much you know until they know how much you care." My first reaction was "Oh, please!" But the more I thought about it, car sales aside, the more true it seemed to me. Parents need to know you're able and willing to invest the time to really understand what their experience is so that you can truly help them and their child. This is true regardless of who owns the problem.

What Does Facilitated Listening Accomplish?

Sometime long ago—I cannot remember the source—I read that "interpersonal experiences become intrapersonal structures." In other words, the internal working models or rules that I described in Chapter 1 develop out of our early interpersonal experiences. These rules become the mental structures, down to the level of the physical architecture of the brain, that define our reality and define the limits of what we think is important and possible. How other people talked to us and guided us in our earliest years is how we end up talking to and guiding ourselves. Scary thought. Fortunately, these structures are malleable.

Facilitated listening is more than just data gathering. It is, or can be, an interpersonal experience, one that can help soften and shape a child's, or a parent's, internal working models and rules. This experience of facilitated listening can help parents talk to themselves in ways that are more specific, flexible, accepting, and patient just when they need these qualities the most.

TALKING ABOUT "IT" AS EXPOSURE

For children and parents telling one's anxiety story, describing the distressing events, actually saying the feared words or expressing the anxious worries aloud, is like saying *Voldemort* ("he who must not be named," in the Harry Potter series). Heaven knows what horror may be conjured up and made real if "it" is expressed. We often hear the child say, "I don't want to talk about it" as he shows visible discomfort just approaching certain thoughts and feelings. At other times—often at bedtime or when the child is strapped in the backseat of the car—the words come pouring out.

Words do have power. As you read the word *lemon* here, do you find yourself salivating just a bit? Does the name Pavlov ring a bell? Our experiences have created intricate neural networks corresponding to the schema and rules I described in Chapter 1. Connections have been made, like a spider's web, and words (or smells or a fragment of a song) can evoke feelings, memories, and bodily sensations.

Speaking the words is the beginning of many exposure exercises, big and small. We speak the words and nothing bad happens. We feel the shiver of fear or the dull weight of discouragement, but we remain right here, intact, safe, and in control. We redirect our attention to some useful action. We evaluate the experience. Then, perhaps, connections are reexamined, parts of the web are rearranged, and at the level of neural circuits we have the potential for new thoughts, feelings, and behavior. This process, however, is rarely a comfortable one.

Being Comfortable About Being Uncomfortable

This is often my treatment goal in a nutshell: to be comfortable with being uncomfortable, in the service of a worthy goal. It's not difficult to see how this applies to the child being brought to you. Even talking about these events evokes thoughts and feelings connected to anxious arousal. This is the nature of *exposure*. The point, however, is to keep one's eye on the prize, the worthy goal of staying all night at the sleepover or getting through the homework without a lot of time-consuming ritual behaviors.

But exposure is also part of the parents' journey in learning to better support their anxious child. The whole range of unwelcomed thoughts, feelings, and reactions that define the anxiety dance will be provoked by these discussions and by the change strategies you all will employ. Perhaps even some new thoughts and feelings will emerge. That would be interesting.

The clinician both creates a safe place to talk about these difficult topics and models for the parents how one might manage uncertainty, risk, and anxiety as it shows up in the therapy room. The clinician's stance is one of *interest in* and curiosity about the child, the parents, and the challenging situations. The stance is also one of patience with the process, including the inevitable setbacks. The clinician models being okay with not having to know everything right away. Providing the parents with this *holding environment,* another term from the early days of object relations and attachment theory, will help the parents do the same for the child. Let's see how this might play out in a therapy session.

Mycroft: A Little Monster

You will recall Mycroft from Chapter 1. He is five years old and is the adopted child of a single working mother, Elena. He is quite dysregulated at home and at school, and he has had numerous episodes of anxious arousal and accompanying controlling and avoidance behaviors.

CLINICIAN: So, tell me about Mycroft. Before we get into the history of everything, I like to start with a little snapshot of how he's doing now, maybe the last week or so.

ELENA: Well, it's actually been okay lately. But for the last couple of years, it's been awful. He's just been a monster. I was actually going to say he's been a little shit [laughs]. This is so embarrassing. I am the worst mother ever.

[*Note that Elena jumps quickly to a much bigger time frame, her descriptions of Mycroft and the situation are vague and unfocused, and her self-judgment is very black and white.*]

CLINICIAN: This room *has held* a lot of feelings, a lot of embarrassment for sure, my own included. I appreciate your courage in stepping onto this path. The parenting load must feel quite heavy, even if, as you said, it's actually going okay right now. I imagine all kinds of thoughts and feelings are showing up for you as you talk about this. [*pause*] So, things have been *especially challenging* for the last couple of years, since about age two or two and a half?

[*Going for more specificity regarding the time frame. Did something important happen a couple of years ago? You might pursue that or continue to talk about the present.*]

ELENA: Yes, although he's always been difficult.

CLINICIAN: I'm going to want to come back to what was going on then, when things escalated. But for now, tell me what Mycroft is doing, or not doing, that concerns you today?

The remainder of the interview will be an attempt to gain very specific information from Elena regarding Mycroft's behaviors of concern. I will probe for specificity where there is vagueness. I'll be looking for exceptions to the common pattern: school days compared to weekends, morning compared to evening, and any other contextual factors that may be important. In Chapter 4, I will describe a specific technique, the functional analysis, that will get at a number of these questions about what, when, and where.

THE IMPORTANCE OF SETTING THE FRAME

After you've determined the primary issues and concerns from listening to the parents, you can proceed to setting up the frame. We don't hear about "the frame" in psychotherapy much outside psychoanalytic circles. The term was introduced by the analyst Robert Langs. The *frame* is pretty much what it sounds like: the set of rules and expectations that form the boundaries or container for the therapeutic work ahead. It is the contract between clinician and client and establishes the basics of time, place, fees and payment, and any other elements that structure the therapy going forward. This aspect of the treatment process typically occurs after the assessment has been completed and the clinician is providing a summary of her findings to the family and making treatment recommendations. It is a natural thing for us to do, but in being so commonplace, to us, we may not be giving the frame the proper attention.

The frame is important because it creates a set of expectations for how assessment and treatment will be conducted, the various roles and responsibilities of the individuals involved, and the "deliverables" treatment will provide. It makes the treatment process clear, predictable, and stable. Like any contract, it can be referred to if and when misunderstandings arise.

Sometimes, as you know, things can get wonky over even a brief course of treatment. Appointments are missed, new issues come up. The parents may suddenly want to talk about a sibling, or the state of the marriage, or a major life change. All these issues and more can arise and threaten to take you far away from the original presenting problem. You will of course address these deviations and side trips. But having a clear frame will provide you with a structure within which to define the boundaries of the original treatment plan mission and then make, or not make, changes to that mission, as you and the parents deem appropriate. There will always be some need for ongoing reminders or minor adjustments to the frame.

Clarification of Expectations

As I mentioned earlier in terms of clarifying the referral path, I let parents know that their own involvement will be a key part of the therapy and a key expectation within the frame. I tell parents that I do not subscribe to the "dry cleaning" model of psychotherapy whereby the parent drops the child off and comes back an hour later to find him cleaned, pressed, in a bag, and good for another trouble-free week. I find that the vast majority of parents are fine with this expectation, at least in principle and prior to their actually being involved. Where it gets tricky sometimes is in the exploration of the parent's own ideas, emotions, and behavior patterns. I will sometimes get the alarmed "We're not here to talk about me" from a parent. I then know I have to spend some more time describing the importance of the parent in the change process and the necessity of understanding the whole picture, including what is distressing the parent and how she is managing distressing situations. The vast majority of parents come around to this idea, this necessity. But it remains something to be clear about from the beginning: "I will be interested in understanding the whole picture, including what it's like for you in those moments, so that I can recommend new and more helpful ways everyone can respond in those situations."

Along with the necessity of parent involvement, the frame needs to provide realistic expectations for how psychotherapy actually works. Parents often bring their child to therapy with a model based, if not on dry cleaning, at least on visits to the pediatrician. This model, which may be the only one with which they have experience, involves a quick examination, notation of symptoms, and maybe some "tests." A clear and straightforward scientific diagnosis is arrived at quickly, if only provisionally, and a straightforward treatment is recommended—for example, "Take two of these a day for ten days." The illness has been cured. The problem has been fixed. Sadly, psychological diagnosis and treatment doesn't operate this way, and that can be confusing and frustrating for parents. Therefore, it's important to explain within the frame what they can expect on the therapeutic journey.

THE THERAPEUTIC JOURNEY: ONE STEP AT A TIME

As clinicians, we can get caught up in the contagion of the anxious parents: they are confused, we are confused; they become frantic, we become frantic. (I will have more to say about parent *and clinician* resilience in Chapter 9.) At this point in the therapy/assessment process, you will want to model patience while validating the parents', and the child's, desire for a quick fix.

There's a wonderful observation by the novelist E. L. Doctorow who describes the often mysterious process of writing a novel as comparable to driving at night. Doctorow says that the car's headlights illuminate only so much of the road in front of you, but you can make the entire journey that way. I mention this to parents and say that it is a good description of the assessment process and even well into the treatment phase—we can't see all the way to the end, but we can see enough at any given time to have a good idea of what to do next. Step by step, listening, assigning small tasks, gathering more information along the way, we move toward our treatment goals.

A relevant observation comes from the late Gestalt therapist Miriam Polster. I heard her speak at a therapy conference many years ago. She said, "You can change someone's life in fifteen minutes. But sometimes it can take six months to get them to the point where you can change their life in fifteen minutes." The audience laughed, but we all knew it was an accurate description of the therapy process and of the patience that is often required of all parties.

Shaping Ideas About Process

Parents often believe that their kids think about anxiety the way they do: It's an irrational emotion to be overcome. And it's overcome by rational discussion, "reality testing," and letting reason prevail— or by just sucking it up and being brave. But this mature and logical approach (even when it works) is predicated on skills and capacities that the child may not possess even on a good day and while in a good mood. Recall what I said in Chapter 1 about regression under stress to the cognitive state of a typical four-year-old. That aroused child, in the heightened anxious state, is in the throes of that all-or-none, rigid, egocentric, fused, literal thinking. That child does *not* want to "work through" the anxiety or fear. He does *not* want to even think about these feelings and thoughts, let alone reason through them. And he most certainly *does not want to take deep breaths*! He wants this feeling *gone, now,* and he will do whatever it takes to get the parent to make it go away.

In some ways, this problem-solving or "control" approach to anxiety makes sense, as primitive as it sounds and is. After all, if you step on a tack, you don't spend time thinking about it—investigating where the tack came from, trying to understand the meaning of the pain or to work through the pain. What do you do? You pull out the tack. Unfortunately, anxiety cannot be removed like a tack, or hacked up like a hairball. But children, and many adults, don't appreciate this about fear and anxiety. If the child cannot "solve the problem" of anxiety (which is different from solving the problem that *causes* the anxiety), then he will elicit (demand) problem-solving help from the parents. Thus, the dance.

Grace and the Malfunctioning Vending Machine

As stated, parents are problem solvers and children see them as such. Also, very young or regressed children see their parents as these magical, omnipotent beings who can do anything, make it right, or make it all go away. An additional twist to this primitive, preschool-age thinking I've been describing is the lack of awareness or appreciation that other people are actually *people,* in the sense that they have their own feelings, ideas, needs, and so on. The psychodynamic folks refer to this as "subjectivity": Only I am a *subject,* an individual with a world view, thoughts, feelings, and so on. Everyone else is an *object.*

Let's take a look at this phenomenon in the life of Grace and her parents, Holly and Alistair.

CLINICIAN: Describe for me the "popsicle incident" that you mentioned on the phone.

HOLLY: That was awful. I asked Grace to go to the freezer in the garage to get popsicles for herself and her three brothers. It was a hot day last summer.

ALISTAIR: I was staining a chair in the garage and there was something you were doing in the house.

HOLLY: That's right. We were busy and couldn't just drop everything like she demanded.

CLINICIAN: Grace went to the freezer . . .

HOLLY: Yes, and there were only two popsicles. She freaked out—I mean, she started screaming, calling for me. I thought she'd been hurt. When I got there she was standing in front of the freezer just shaking and hyperventilating. She kept saying,

"There's only two. There's only two." She knows the family rule: everyone gets equal amounts of whatever there is. So we were going to have to divide the two popsicles into four.

CLINICIAN: What did you say to her?

ALISTAIR: I jumped in and reminded her of the rule. I remained calm. I said, "You know the rule. Just calm down. Go into the kitchen with your mother and divide those up." But she wouldn't even look at me. Just kept screaming at her mother, all kinds of stuff: "The babies don't care, they don't need popsicles," "Take me to the store to get more right now!" Lots of demands. Holly tried to be calm and reasonable too, but Grace just got more and more upset and said, "I hate you" and other hurtful stuff. It must have gone on for twenty minutes.

HOLLY: I can only imagine what the neighbors were thinking!

CLINICIAN: Is twenty minutes typical for one of these episodes? [*Duration is a key variable in the change process, as we'll see.*]

ALISTAIR: That's on the long side. Typically, it's more like ten minutes. But twenty to thirty minutes can happen."

CLINICIAN: Feels like an eternity, I'm sure. How did it end?

HOLLY: I could see that Alistair was getting frustrated, so I took Grace inside and up to her room where it was cooler and we sat on her bed for a while, just not saying anything. She cried. I cried. We hugged and then it was over.

CLINICIAN: And then . . . ?

HOLLY: Well, we went downstairs and I tried to get her to help me divide up the popsicles, but she wouldn't have anything to do with it. So, nobody got popsicles. We went on with our day. But a little while later, I took her to the store and we got another box of popsicles.

So, what does this episode have to do with anxiety? It would be easy to frame this as the behavior of a selfish child who doesn't want to share with her siblings. And that may be the way one parent or perhaps both see it. But Grace could have easily slipped out a single popsicle for herself, left the garage, and enjoyed her ill-gotten prize alone, begging forgiveness later. But she didn't. How I think this relates to anxiety is through the very young, or in this case *regressed,* brain and the fight-flight-freeze-or-freak-out reaction.

Grace goes the the freezer in the garage with popsicles *in mind.* Because of psychic equivalence, or *fusion* as it's called in acceptance and commitment therapy, her thoughts map directly onto reality and vice versa. There *are* popsicles in the freezer, enough for everyone to have their very own. Grace lacks the meta-cognitive executive skills to consider the possibility that it might be otherwise.

Then, reality bites and her limbic system goes off. She experiences what I call a *pantrum*: a cross between a panic attack and a tantrum. She is in a much heightened state of arousal. She freezes up (sorry!) and cannot use her parents' words to build a bridge to some compromised reality. At that moment, in that regressed, all-or-nothing state, Grace's only salvation lies in the power of her parents to *change reality.* They are, in her regressed mind, these omnipotent beings who *could* make this and many other situations right. But they're not making it right.

This situation is infuriating, as well as anxiety provoking in its own right. It is infuriating because Grace's parents are not using their superpowers to make the world conform to the reality Grac-eshe has in her mind. At that moment, they are to her the equivalent of a malfunctioning vending machine; they are "objects," devoid of their own ideas, feelings, or needs. It's as if she put in the right amount of money, pressed the right buttons, and the bag of chips (or in this case, the popsicle) starts to move but then just dangles there, mocking her.

This further provokes Grace's anxiety because her parents' unwillingness to rescue her, when they surely could, says something awful about her worth and their love, or lack of it, for her. It likely evokes sharp-edged internal working models, perhaps not dominant ones, but the kind we all harbor: "I'm not good enough," "People can't be trusted to help me," and so on.

But one more point about the "popsicle incident." Why, when Grace's father was right there in the garage, did she call (scream) for her mother, who was in the house? It is not uncommon for one parent or the other to be a child's "primary dance partner," as I think of it. This dynamic is a significant part of the overall anxiety picture and process. One can get some traction around change by identifying which parent is most often pulled into the dance, or how each parent (or other adults) brings his or her own characteristic choreography. I will have more to say about exploring the details of the dance in the next chapter. Again, one must be diplomatic about this inquiry; the clinician wants to avoid casting blame and potentially alienating one or both parents while also feeling she can tell the parents what she feels is important and necessary. It's a tricky balancing act and all a part of the ongoing therapeutic journey.

CHILD DEVELOPMENT: JUST BECAUSE IT'S NORMAL DOESN'T MEAN WE SHOULD IGNORE IT

One common topic with parents is the question of what's "normal." Often parents (or one of them) will present with some trepidation around seeing their child, or someone else seeing their child, as somehow abnormal or deviant. This is understandable. Virtually all parents want others to think well of their child. After all, it's a reflection on them as parents. One parent or the other may say, "But all kids do that, don't they?" or "I was like that at his age" with the implied or stated, "And I turned out fine."

In truth, anxiety and fear (as well as a certain amount of sadness and defiance) are part of every childhood. And the range of what's normal, of when a child typically attains various skills and developmental milestones, is quite broad, especially in younger children. This includes when children walk, are toilet trained, learn to read, and many other important tasks, including managing one's behavior in the face of strong emotions.

The Snapshot Versus Trajectory View

My early graduate work was in developmental psychology, so I tend to conceptualize children and the concerns that parents bring to me in terms of development gone awry—impeded or "snagged" somehow. The child is in some way not meeting expectations. Are those expectations reasonable, given who this child is? What's getting in the way of growth? The goal of therapy is less "cure" than it is promoting psychological growth, maturation, and increased competence.

I will often describe to parents a method for considering a particular child's development set against these rather broad expectations for maturity. First is the "snapshot" view. This is a quick and wide take on how this child is doing here and now in terms of behavior, given his age and circumstances. Sometimes the snapshot is one of quite flagrant deviation from the norm—for example, the child who is not speaking by age three or is engaged in serious and repeated self-injurious behaviors. These behaviors would be cause for alarm and immediate intervention. A school-age child might refuse to go to school more days than not and experience panic attacks on a daily basis. This picture, too, would warrant quick assessment and action.

On the other hand, you and I will see children who do fall within the boundaries of these rather broad norms for child behavior and milestones. This is the child who has a mild or even subclinical symptom picture. The distressing episodes may be infrequent and have little impact on the child's overall functioning and growth. Perhaps there are obvious stressors impinging on the child and the family that are temporary or somehow potentially manageable, such as a kitchen remodel or a change in schools. We might reassure the parents that their child is "normal" and make a few simple recommendations (see Appendix E), and send them on their way, grateful and relieved.

However, you should also ask parents to consider what I call the "trajectory" view. The trajectory view takes into consideration the various constitutional and contextual factors involved in describing this child: temperament (as discussed in Chapter 1), cognitive maturity, family issues such as siblings, birth order, marital difficulties, parent skills, attachment, social environment, and other current or potential stressors impinging on the child and family. Then, this complex mix is imagined projected out into the future, perhaps a year or two, to speculate on what we might be dealing with then.

For example, a child may be holding his own in terms of anxiety and stress in a small, supportive elementary school class with a sensitive and flexible teacher. But next year this sensitive and social-dependent child will enter a middle school with 1,200 other students and will contend with six or seven teachers, some of whom will be cranky and insensitive to his needs. What then? This view may suggest a course of treatment to develop coping skills, self-advocacy skills, resilience, and so on. Other trajectories may predict challenges due to the impending birth of a sibling, the anticipated passing of a beloved grandparent, a divorce, or major relocation due to a parent's job change. Your task may then be to help gird the child, and the parents, for the emotions, cognitions, and behaviors that will likely be provoked by these events. Even a seemingly simple and expectable developmental event, such as entering fourth grade, can have a significant and disruptive impact on a child who is temperamentally vulnerable. Or, behaviors that were tolerated by peers or teachers at one age are suddenly deemed "weird" or "inappropriate," as in the case of Brayden.

Brayden and the Unlucky Shirt

Brayden is a ten-year-old, fifth-grade boy, the only child of Salma and Geoff. Salma is an artist and Geoff works as a senior programmer at major software company. Geoff was recently promoted to project manager.

Brayden has a lot of "big picture" anxieties. He'd heard about the Mayan calendar predicting the world's end in 2012 and spent a number of months distressed about that, subjecting his parents to almost nonstop questions about it. More recently, he has developed half a dozen obsessions and compulsions having to do with numbers and "lucky" and "unlucky" objects. These ideas rotate through on an almost weekly basis. He can spend ten minutes going through the shirts in his closet, feeling, taking out, and putting back shirts, trying to ascertain which among all of them is the one and only lucky shirt that he can wear that day—or more accurately, which is the not *unlucky* shirt. This and his other little rituals slow routines down to a crawl, and the rhythm of the household is determined by Brayden's ability to proceed from one task to the next. Picking the shirt determines when breakfast is eaten, which determines when the rest of the morning routine is completed. Other rituals determine when homework gets started or when Brayden starts getting ready for bed.

Brayden is very picky about lots of things. In addition to seeing shirts as lucky or unlucky, he has a narrow range of clothing he will wear based on the feel of the fabric and the amount of constriction the garment creates. He is very sensitive to certain smells. This becomes as issue at school during snack periods and lunchtime, when Brayden will gag and loudly complain about and denigrate a classmate's food choices. His male peers who are on a more typical trajectory are moving toward ball games, which Brayden has begun to loudly and publicly disparage. Brayden is suspicious of his peers generally, preferring one or two companions who still share his interests in Pokémon.

Brayden attends a small, elite private school that caters to the children of tech entrepreneurs, brain surgeons, and MacArthur genius award recipients. The school reports that Brayden is quite capable and can produce work of great depth and imagination. However, this academic year it seems Brayden will only engage in a very narrow range of topics and assignments, and he complains to his teachers that most of his expected work is "boring," "stupid," or "irrelevant." Given the school's mission to create an atmosphere of tolerance and acceptance, much of this behavior was accommodated until Brayden called the daughter of the chair of the auction committee a "Philistine." The girl wasn't exactly sure what it meant, but she was deeply hurt nonetheless. The school thought an evaluation "would be in everyone's best interest." Here's a glimpse of the first session with Brayden's parents:

CLINICIAN: So, tell me about Brayden. Can you give me the snapshot of how he's been doing generally lately, and then we can get into the specifics of what brings you in today.

GEOFF: He's a great kid. Charming. You're going to love talking to him.

SALMA: We have wonderful conversations about an amazing range of topics: politics, art, history. He comes up with the most amazing ideas. Sometimes we call him "The Little Professor."

GEOFF: We have no secrets in our family. We can talk about anything. My new job has been very stressful, lots of travel and long hours, and it's been a strain on everybody. Marital stress is way up. But we all talk it out and Brayden is right in there as a part of every conversation.

CLINICIAN: I'm looking forward to meeting him. I understand some of his ideas have to do with lucky and unlucky objects—shirts and the like.

SALMA: That comes and goes. I think this week it's numbers; he has to do something, anything, four times.

GEOFF: I thought it was three times.

SALMA: That was last month. It changed when you were in China.

CLINICIAN: Can you tell me more about how numbers matter? If I were there, what would I see Brayden do?

SALMA: He would enter a room and then go back out again and come back in a second, a third, and then a fourth time. It only takes a few seconds and he doesn't seem upset by it. When I ask him about it, he says, "I just like to." But the week Geoff was in China, Brayden was saying everything four times and demanding that I do the same. It was exhausting.

GEOFF: I used to do that sort of stuff as a kid.

CLINICIAN: What do you remember doing?

GEOFF: Touching things a certain number of times. Counting things, like in class at school. I was bored in school, too. I tell Brayden it's normal to be bored in school and that my teachers were idiots, too. But you have to follow the rules, even the stupid ones.

CLINICIAN: Does any of this get in the way of Brayden doing things he needs to do?

SALMA: Not really. We try to just get through the repetitions as quickly as possible. When it's trying to avoid something he thinks might be unlucky, like a shirt or a towel, it can take ten or fifteen minutes to get going again, and that can slow things down. It's not a problem at home since we're not real rigid about schedules and things. At school, they have their rules and such, and sometimes Brayden comes home saying that a teacher was impatient with him for making everyone wait.

CLINICIAN: And the worries you mentioned on the phone?

SALMA: They come and go, too. One week it's death. Then it will be rising sea levels or Ebola. He can get pretty worked up, almost frantic. He comes to me—he knows he can do that any time, day or night. We talk it out. Use some common sense, reason. And he calms down in an hour or two.

CLINICIAN: How often might this happen?

SALMA: A few times a week, I think.

GEOFF: Listen, I know the school has a lot of concerns. And there was that girl Brayden was joking with. Truth is, they're all Philistines in my opinion. Way too sensitive and PC. I think they need to relax. All boys do this sort of thing, don't they?

SALMA: But next year Brayden will be going to the upper school, which is much bigger and he'll have six or seven teachers a day instead of two. I've heard that some of the upper-school teachers aren't very tolerant. I'm afraid it will crush his spirit.

The snapshot of how Brayden is doing contains a number of concerns. But Salma and Geoff have a very positive, accepting, and loving stance toward their son, which is an asset. On the other hand, the generational boundaries appear to be rather weak and you would wonder if Brayden is privy to too much adult-level information, which could contribute to his stress and worry.

Diagnostically, Brayden appears to have some worries and compulsions that would make a traditional diagnostician think of generalized anxiety disorder and obsessive-compulsive disorder. Brayden also presents with an odd mix of sensory and social issues that would make me wonder about the very mild end of the autism spectrum. Here in Seattle, as I imagine in any tech hub, we have many children I call NQAs: Not Quite Asperger's. While not meeting full criteria for the syndrome, these boys (invariably boys) present with various mixtures of mild social oddities, narrow but not extremely narrow interests, a very horizontal view of the world wherein children and adults are more or less equals (a worldview that is sometimes supported by the parents), and linear, detailed, egocentric, and rigid thinking that includes a very strong sense of fairness. As such, this mixture can predispose the child for conflicts with the world when things aren't fair (that is, when they don't go the child's way), adults assert their authority role, and the situation requires perspective taking and a cognitive and emotional flexibility that is hard to summon.

Given this presumed temperament or personality style, Brayden is at risk for anxiety and interpersonal conflict as his natural trajectory takes him into more complex and demanding social and academic challenges. As with Grace's parents, the trick will be helping Salma and Geoff see their role in helping the child meet societal expectations for behavioral regulation in the face of his strong, uncomfortable emotions and compelling but unhelpful ideas. Here's one way a clinician might handle it:

CLINICIAN: I think it's wise of you to be thinking about what the current situation might look like if we project it out into life in the upper school, or even beyond. If we did nothing at this time, how confident would we be that Brayden's trajectory would take him through those coming challenges without some real problems showing up? He could be just fine. But some of the things you're describing suggest to me that Brayden is feeling quite a bit of anxiety and is having trouble coping with it. Put another way, his current strategies for coping are themselves causing problems.

CLINICIAN *continues*: I think it would be prudent to invest some time now in increasing our understanding of what Brayden thinks and feels, what he needs in order to cope better, and how to help him meet today's challenges in preparation for the future opportunities he'll have. It's a tricky business. We certainly don't want to do anything to dampen his spirit, *and* we don't want him to drift over time and see his emotions, ideas, or social interactions get in the way of his being successful, however you and he want to define that.

THE ANXIETY DANCE: NO ONE'S FAULT, BUT EVERYONE'S RESPONSIBILITY

If we are going to make real changes in a child's anxiety, then we're going to have to change the system in which the anxiety typically emerges and is acted out. That might include systems or contexts such as the school or other situations, but generally we're working with the family system. And changing the family system means involving the parents.

As I described in Chapter 1, anxiety and fear are normal, built-in mechanisms that we humans have used for millennia to keep ourselves out of trouble. Among these built-in mechanisms is the natural drive to seek protection from caregivers, as demonstrated by the earliest of infant behaviors described in the attachment literature. And because these important parent-child transactions involve infants with poor communication skills and their often sleep-deprived, distracted, overwhelmed, and inexperienced parents, this attachment dance does not always go smoothly. Kinks, gaps, unwarranted assumptions, and bad habits develop on both the child and the parental sides. Both child and parents are daily dance partners in an intricate, intimate, and often barely conscious set of moves and countermoves, which, as I mentioned earlier, I call the *anxiety dance*.

My assumption is that we're all just trying to get our needs met. And in the vast majority of situations these needs—affection, security, esteem, enjoyment, to name a few—are legitimate. The central problem, *the central process,* that confronts us every day in our therapy sessions is that the anxious child's attempts at getting his needs met are making everyone confused, frantic, frustrated, and crazy.

Conveying the Dance Concept

Let me describe, so that you can convey to the parents you work with, the idea that a child's anxious *behavior* (as opposed to anxious thoughts and feelings per se) is at the heart of the struggle. The child's various and characteristic anxious behaviors (crying, clinging, freezing up, defiance, aggression, and so on) can be thought of as a *gambit:* "a maneuver by which one seeks to gain an advantage" (Random House College Dictionary, 1980). For example, in chess a player might move a piece into position with the intention of having the opponent take that piece, thereby enabling the first player to spring a trap.

In much the same way, although without much if any conscious planning and thought, anxious behaviors are a maneuver on the child's part. These anxious behaviors serve two important, even vital, functions: (1) to communicate the child's distress to the parent and (2) to engage the parent in an interaction that will lead to the parent rescuing the child from his distress. Typically, this rescue involves escape from the anxiety-provoking situation in the present and avoidance of that situation in the future. There are times when rescue/avoidance is appropriate. But a pattern of habitually avoiding challenges undermines the development of accurate views about the world and the child's ability to tolerate distress and effectively cope with challenges.

Through careful questions (and even diagrams) assessing the form and function of the child's anxious behavior (see the next chapter), it will become quite clear that parents, one or both, are key players in how anxiety presents itself in the family. This involvement is thoroughly expectable; children necessarily regard their parents as rescuers, as a vital source of relief and of problem solving. That's a good thing, when communication is clear and there's an actual problem to be solved. But it's a problem *when there isn't a problem;* a reasonable parent is not going to "rescue" her child from going to school or somehow rid the world of dogs in order the rid the child of fear and anxiety. The parent's job in those anxiety-provoking situations is instead to orient the child to some effective coping response.

So, and this is important, changing this problematic process (the dance) will involve less changing the child's thoughts and feelings in the moment, less trying to eliminate all sources of fear and anxiety, and instead working on (1) improving how the child communicates his distress, which relates to (2) better ways of motivating the parents to help him, which requires (3) other possibilities for managing these anxious situations besides escape, avoidance, or inappropriate control efforts. This old dance will be replaced with a new dance—one based on effective mutual communication between parent and child and the availability of broad range of positive coping behaviors marked by flexibility and courage.

Common Elements of the Anxiety Dance

In order for the old dance to be replaced with a new dance, however, three issues need to be addressed—automaticity and immediacy of behavior patterns, and awareness. Let's take a closer look at each of these issues.

Automaticity

Jean Dumas (2005) describes how behavior patterns become routinized, automatic, and therefore largely unconscious. He calls this process *automaticity*. We can see the process at work in all the many habits, routines, and behavior patterns we execute every day. These patterns include how we interact with others. Whether it's a quarterback lofting a pass to a receiver, pilot and copilot landing a plane in bad weather, or mother and child getting out of the house in the morning, overpracticed routines are highly effective and efficient, when they work well.

When behavior patterns aren't working well for us (we call these "bad habits"), we can feel very frustrated because behavior patterns that are largely automatic are also largely unconscious and therefore resistant to change. Stepping outside a highly automatized pattern takes a great deal of awareness and effort. For example, as Dumas (2005) points out, compare saying the alphabet forward with saying it backward. One direction has been "practiced" over decades and the other has perhaps never even been attempted. The former takes little to no effort. To execute the latter is a great demonstration of the executive skill of effortful control. The kinds of parent-child patterns of interest to us, these anxious transactions between parent and child, Dumas calls *automatized transactional patterns,* or ATPs. I simply call this "the anxiety dance" because it has a certain predictable choreography, leading and following, moves and countermoves.

Immediacy

Another important aspect of these ATPs or dances, in addition to being largely automatic and unconscious, is what Dumas calls their *immediacy*. By this, he means that these behavior patterns lie close to the surface, as it were, and in situations or contexts of the kind that historically led to the development of the routine (for example, anxiety and stress), these patterns will appear first, which means more practice, which means more automaticity. This can be a good thing if you instantly and automatically go into the overlearned procedure for steering out of a skid on an icy road. But it's bad when Wyatt and Sara or Holly and Grace or Elena and Mycroft find themselves yet again in a maladaptive dance.

I don't mean to pick on the moms here, but it is my experience that moms tend to be the primary dance partners for the anxious children I see. This is because, in our society, the management of the child's emotional life still tends to fall upon the mother. I have seen plenty of two-Dad families and two-Mom families where there is still one of the parents who, by default or tacit agreement or temperament, is the primary dance partner.

Again, these patterns have emerged through no one's fault. Everyone's just trying to get his or her needs met and get through the day. But erring on the side of just getting through the day or just the next ten minutes, of yielding to and accommodating anxiety and fear, leads to a deficit in experiences where anxious emotions and ideas might be challenged by reality and new cognitive structures or internal working models created. Over time, dependency on the parent increases, or at least doesn't decrease with age, and the child falls further behind in developing confidence and self-reliance. At some point, as seen in Wyatt, this dependency evokes resentment and even rage on the part of the child toward the parent he's become dependent upon.

Awareness

Parents will say that they sometimes can observe themselves and hear themselves falling into an unhappy and unhelpful behavior pattern, helpless to avoid it or change it once it starts: "I just listen to myself saying these things, and I think, *Why am I even talking?* But I can't stop." This is actually good, because changing any habitual behavior pattern can only be achieved by first increasing your awareness of what you're doing in the moment. (Keep a food log for a week. You'll be eating better by the third day.) With increasing awareness comes the ability to change behavior patterns away from the old anxiety dance to a newer, psychologically healthier dance.

MESSAGE TO PARENTS: YOU'RE VITAL TO THIS PROCESS OF CHANGE

It is important to convey to parents that they play a vital role in changing these anxious dances or processes. More than the anxious thoughts and feelings themselves, it is the anxiety dance that lies at the heart of the presenting problem. After all, if Wyatt "simply" got up and marched off to school, taking his anxiety with him, it's likely the family would not be bringing him to see you. Let's take a quick look at how this message of parental importance might be presented, generically, to a parent:

CLINICIAN: From what you're telling me, it seems that your child gets stuck in some quite powerful feelings and ideas.

PARENT: Very powerful. Overwhelming.

CLINICIAN: And in those desperate moments, your child looks to you as the rescuer, the one who's going to somehow make it okay. And you would make it okay, if you could.

PARENT: I would, but sometimes, often, I have no idea what he wants. But even if I did, there are just things we need to do.

CLINICIAN: Yes, some things can't be avoided, not without some cost anyway, which you appreciate. You're the adult. But your son often doesn't appreciate the long-term cost of these behaviors. He lacks that perspective, especially in those times of distress. You are, as it were, the Keeper of the Bigger Picture. You know what's at stake—not just in the short-term, but in the long-term as well. So, our job, working as a team, will be to do three things. First, we'll see if we can better understand what's going on during these episodes of distress, and by "we," I include myself, yourselves as the parents, and your child also, at an age-appropriate level. Second, we need to get the communication going better. It's hard to know sometimes, as you said, what your child even thinks and feels and needs in those moments. I imagine sometimes *he* doesn't even know. And he's often unable to benefit from the help you're trying to give him. Third, we need to look at changing the direction of the behavior away from upset and conflict and toward solving problems, if there's one to solve, or coping strategies for when, as you said, "There are just things we need to do." As you can see, you're the lynchpin here; everything is going to pivot around you as you lead the new dance.

CAN'T WE JUST MAKE IT ALL GO AWAY?

It's true that if the anxious thoughts and feelings weren't there at all, any child would likely function much better and cope well with the challenges he faces. But sadly, children are confronted every day with anxiety-provoking situations or stressful events, such as schedule changes, disappointments, frustrations, and so on. They will think and feel this anxious (or angry or sad) stuff, and they will readily fall into unhelpful behavior patterns unless and until we work with them—and their parents—to weaken the automaticity of the old dance and establish a new, more age-appropriate, supple, spacious, and effective dance.

We can certainly help parents find ways for reducing stress and anxiety in their lives. Simple actions can be taken, such as reducing the bombardment of negative news stories from all the media sources, being careful about the adult-level information, or partial information, that our children are privy to, and making home life as predictable and structured as possible. Obviously, parents can't raise their children in bubbles, and even if we could, it would not prepare them for life. Instead, parents must manage all of the components of family life with an eye to creating opportunities for growth, even if it is sometimes anxiety-provoking for both child and parent.

A LOOK AHEAD

In the next chapter, we will explore the importance of awareness. Increasing the parents' and the child's awareness of what each is thinking, feeling, and doing is the key to changing the old dance and developing and establishing a new dance. Even with growing awareness, parents can still slide into their old pattern of interaction with their child. However, as awareness grows, they can halt that slide a little more quickly and a little earlier in the process, until it can be avoided altogether. The expectation is that, with diligent practice, the new, more effective and adaptive dance will become the new routine and habit. A large body of therapeutic work promoting *mindfulness* will be brought to bear on this task.

At the level of technique I will describe the use of the *functional analysis* in eliciting information from the parents regarding the parent-child dances of importance. By creating this visual picture of the common family anxious processes, parents will become more aware of what antecedent or *activator* conditions contribute to their child's anxious behaviors. The child's behaviors will be defined in specific and tractable terms ("standing at the bottom of the stairs, not moving, crying" rather than "acting like a baby"). Explicating the consequences that follow anxious behavior will help our understanding of the "feedback loops" or contingencies, notably *negative reinforcement,* that maintain the status quo.

Finally, I will discuss some ideas for changing the "choreography" of the parent-child dance, step-by-step. In fact, there are three steps in this change process; increase awareness, shift attention, and take goal-directed action.

Summary of Key Ideas

- Understand how this child has come to you.

- The first step in talking to parents about their child's anxiety is to *listen* to them.

- My treatment goal in a nutshell: to be comfortable with being uncomfortable, in the service of a worthy goal.

- The goal is less "cure" than it is promoting growth, maturation, and increased competence.

- A child's anxious *behavior* (as opposed to anxious thoughts and feelings per se) is at the heart of the struggle.

- With increasing awareness comes the ability to change behavior patterns away from the old anxiety dance to a newer, healthier dance.

- The referral path is important because it defines your early work with the parents: allowing their own concerns to be heard apart from the concerns of others, discovering what all this means for them as parents, exploring who "owns the problem."

- Facilitated listening is an interpersonal experience, one that can help soften and shape a child's, or a parent's, internal working models and rules.

- The frame is important because it creates a set of expectations for how assessment and treatment will be conducted, the various roles and responsibilities of the individuals involved, and the "deliverables" that treatment will provide. It makes the treatment process clear, predictable, and stable.

- The central problem, *the central process*, that confronts us every day in our therapy sessions is that the anxious child's attempts at getting his needs met are making everyone confused, frantic, frustrated, and crazy.

- Parents play a vital role in changing these anxious dances or processes.

- Speaking the words is the beginning of many exposure exercises, big and small.

- We can't see all the way to the end, but we can see enough at any given time to have a good idea of what to do next.

CHAPTER 4

Changing the Choreography

Holly is sitting at the kitchen breakfast nook table with her computer, attempting to finish up some work emails. She knows she doesn't have much time. Grace has been alone for the past several minutes in the family room just around the corner and out of sight. But not out of earshot.

"Mom." Holly ignores Grace, but picks up the pace of typing and clicking.

"Mom!"

"I'm busy," calls Holly. "What do you need?"

"Mom!!" calls Grace with intensity. Holly tries to get her last clicks in when a great, wailing, wordless scream comes from the family room. Holly goes running in, imagining her daughter's mortal wound but rationally, and historically, knowing that Grace is unharmed. And it's true. Grace sits in the middle of the family room floor, arms crossed, greeting her mother with an icy stare. "What was that all about?" asks Holly. "I thought you were hurt."

Grace curtly turns her head away, saying nothing. Holly starts to go back into the kitchen.

"Mom!!!"

As I described in Chapter 3, much of our daily lives is built around routines: getting out of the house in the morning, driving familiar routes to work or school, completing routine tasks within our jobs, and so on. These familiar procedures are made smooth and efficient by the fact that they are habits and involve little or no thinking. A good routine makes life predictable, stable, and efficient. A bad routine can be a nightmare.

CHANGING THE ANXIETY DANCE: INCREASE AWARENESS, SHIFT ATTENTION, AND TAKE ACTION

I would assert that the barely conscious routines that make up the anxiety dance between parent and child *are* the presenting problem. This dance includes the child's anxiety-related behaviors, such as Grace's increasingly insistent calling for her mother, and even her punishing "icy stare." The process or dance also must include the parent's behaviors, such as ignoring, attempting reasonable responses like "what do you need?", and appealing for Grace's empathy by pointing out how her behavior is distressing Holly, as in "I thought you were hurt."

All this transpires, in some form, multiple times a day; day in, day out. For some families with anxiety issues in the middle of the night, the dance can almost be performed in one's sleep. These are overlearned behaviors. Although the task is challenging, these behaviors can be un-learned.

To change these routines or dances, to change the choreography as it were, we must start by making important parent-child routines more conscious, more a part of the ongoing awareness of both the parents and the child. Only then will the dance be less automatic and more amenable to change. Making the *process* of child anxiety (the adaptive transactions between temperament and environment) more conscious begins with the first interview, described in the last chapter, when parents are assisted in making their stories clearer, more specific, and more coherent. Facilitated listening, an important and ongoing component of working with parents of anxious children, plays a significant role in the choreography change process because it helps make unconscious actions as behavior patterns are described in detail, perhaps for the first time.

The goal is to replace the old, maladaptive dance that brought the family to see you with a new, more effective dance. As with changing any habit or learning a new routine, the new behavior patterns will feel awkward at first. There may well be some resistance to making these changes. The anxious child, in particular, may be quite alarmed at even small changes to her expected routines, and you must prepare parents for the possibility of an *extinction burst*, the behavioral therapy technical term for "things may get worse before they get better." But with time, practice, and patience, the new dance will also become more automatic, efficient, and—most important—more positive and helpful.

Three basic dance steps will profoundly change the anxiety dance for the better. We might think of these steps as subprocesses within the larger process that will be the new and improved parent-child dance:

1. Increase awareness, generally and in the moment.
2. Shift attention.
3. Take values-driven action.

I call these "steps" in keeping with the analogy of the dance, but in practice they are broad categories of behaviors of both parents and child. These behaviors will help the parents and child more effectively face anxiety, fear, or any distressing emotion or idea. All three steps undermine the automaticity of the old processes and align behavior with better coping and problem-solving goals.

STEP I: INCREASE AWARENESS

Making behavior more conscious allows us some opportunity to make a different decision (that is, to act differently), which habitual routines do not afford. So, the first step in changing the maladaptive parent-child dance is to increase awareness of what happens in these anxiety-provoking situations. As I mentioned earlier, this process of increasing awareness starts with facilitated listening and the sharpening and elaborating of the parents' narrative.

One of the best techniques for increasing parent awareness is *functional analysis.* It also provides a continuation of the assessment of behavior patterns.

Functional Analysis

Classic functional analysis increases awareness and helps you understand the important behavior patterns at work. Functional analysis has a long history in the assessment of behavior problems among children and adults with developmental disabilities in which the function, purpose, or meaning of a behavior may be difficult to ascertain. This technique can be quite extensive, with pages of checklists and observational data. However, the variation I will describe is quite simple but can yield a wealth of information.

Every psychotherapy office should have a good-sized whiteboard so that routines and processes can be diagrammed, made clear and concrete, pondered, and redrawn to reflect new possibilities. I find that dads in particular resonate with a good diagram of the problem situations and routines. They can *see* what word descriptions may fail to fully convey. Take your time with this valuable activity. It can easily take up an entire therapy hour and may have to be repeated in order to capture more than one situation or set of behaviors.

To begin, make three columns on the whiteboard, or a sheet of paper, and label them A, B, and C (see Figure 4.1) for antecedents (or activators), behavior, and consequences. Then ask the parents to describe a common situation in which there is a lot of anxious upset and avoidance or controlling behaviors that are of concern.

Antecedents or Activators

In the A column, write down one- or two-word examples or descriptors of the antecedent conditions or *activators.* These are the elements that make up the context in which the child's anxious behaviors tend to occur. Obviously, there may be more than one context to describe and discuss in order to get the full picture of what's going on in this particular family. That's fine. Be specific. There may be subtle but important differences between anxiety experienced

ACTIVATORS (ANTECEDENTS)	BEHAVIOR	CONSEQUENCES
Situation Common variables Setting Events Proximal Triggers		
Wyatt's bedroom 6:30 a.m. Monday morning A project (unfinished) is due today. Sara comes in and tells Wyatt it's time to get up.		

Figure 4.1

in the morning compared to bedtime compared to the weekend. Some of these contextual factors can be noted as "setting events" (described next). The point is to not try to compress all of a child's anxiety experiences into one analysis.

Elicit from parents a few possible activators. You can also ask about factors you suspect may be important: "How long had Grace been by herself before she started calling for you?" You will have to use your judgment about when you've obtained the necessary and sufficient information so that you can move on to the next portion of the analysis. It may be somewhat arbitrary to say that the anticipation of a spelling test that day is an activator for school refusal worth noting but the child's favorite baseball team losing the night before is not. That will depend on the child. But you don't want to get bogged down in minutiae. Use your best judgment.

Activators should include a description of the situation itself—for example, Wyatt's bedroom, 6:45 A.M., and so on. Also included here are any potentially relevant factors or variables, if known: Monday morning, a spelling test that day. This can sound like the stage directions of a play: "Wyatt's bedroom, dawn, Wyatt is somewhere under a pile of blankets, enter Sara stage right."

Setting events: An important class of activators are the *setting events*—the circumstances or stimuli, past or present—that change the *functional properties* of another stimulus. The functional properties of a red traffic light are to get you to stop before you reach the intersection. For me, the functional properties of a cheeseburger are to induce me to eat it. At least most of the time. If, however, I've eaten many cheeseburgers of late or if I've just watched a documentary about slaughterhouses, I may pass on the next cheeseburger that comes along. The cheeseburger has not changed. What has changed is what *I bring to the situation*—a new or different predisposition toward that same stimulus, based on some event or condition: same stimulus (the cheeseburger) but different functional properties (no longer inviting the same response from me).

So, hunger, fatigue, the presence or absence of another person (think about classroom behavior when there's a substitute teacher), and many, many other events and conditions will change a person's "set point" for frustration, resilience, approach, avoidance, and so on. Setting events are so common and so important that it is worth spending some time exploring these situations and events with the parents you're working with. Setting events influence the behaviors of the child as well as the parents.

Proximal triggers: Oftentimes it's possible to make a clear connection to some single event or trigger (a spider comes into view) and the sudden onset of anxiety or fear behaviors (Grace shrieks). In a functional analysis, the spider would be considered a "proximal trigger"—something that happens temporally close to the behavior in question (shrieking) and is presumed to have caused the behavior. Proximal triggers tend to be rather straightforward and easy to understand. They may or may not be easy to deal with. At other times, the triggers may be less obvious or the behaviors of concern appear far removed in time from the triggering event. This can make understanding the process or dance more challenging. Additionally, there may not be a clear and straightforward cause-and-effect connection between activators and behaviors. As you explore activators with the parents, together you may discover a variety of quite different antecedent conditions generating quite different behaviors or consequences. Under the influence of setting events, what served as a trigger yesterday may not serve the same function today, and so the same situation itself may pass without difficulty.

Through these discussions, the parents—and the older clients whom you also can involve in these discussions—will begin to increase their awareness and understanding of the dance in its many variations. Clarifying the variability inherent in the system—that is, the contexts that change how the dance proceeds—will help parents recognize that they are not dealing with a monolithic, invariant (and intractable) situation. Instead, there are often a number of places along the path where it's possible to make small but important changes to the process and, most important, to start focusing on the times when things in fact go well.

Where to put worry and fear? What about the worry and fear? Are they setting events, triggers, or behaviors? Technically, worries and other negative thoughts, along with anxious and fearful emotions and bodily sensations, are behaviors. They are something the child is *doing,* even if not conscious, volitional, or observable. Worry and fear are what we sometimes call *private events,* in contrast to the outward behaviors or *public events* we can observe others doing. However, for the purposes of the functional analysis, I put relevant thoughts and feelings in the activator column, as either a setting event or a proximal trigger. As I've stated, I'm interested in changing the child's overt anxious *behaviors* as a first step toward reducing anxious thoughts and feelings. When we talk about changing the child's behavior—for example, through an exposure exercise—we can expect the presence of some anxiety or fear, at least in the short run. In fact, as I'll discuss in Chapter 6, it's not good to have the client *completely* free of anxiety during an exposure exercise. I will refer again to the presence of anxious thoughts and feelings as antecedents when we talk about "contrast" later in the chapter.

Behavior

Once the activators are sketched in, you will move to the B or *behavior* column. Here you want to elicit descriptions of the child's outward behavior that is of concern, given this set of activators. As I mentioned above, I consider the child's anxious thoughts and feelings to be among the activators and will have explained that to the parents. Still, as discussed in previous chapters, parents may describe their child's behavior in vague, global terms that include the child's presumed emotional or cognitive state: "He becomes upset," "She's unreasonable," "He goes from scared to angry."

Your job then is to patiently ask for a description of what the child is doing: "Yes, that sounds very frustrating. But tell me, if I were there, what exactly would I *see* Wyatt doing?" Ask for specificity: Does "becomes aggressive" mean a slapping motion that misses by two feet, a punch to the body, or angry or mean words? Given the differences in activator conditions, are there different behaviors that make up variations on the core anxiety dance? Obtain concrete descriptions/definitions of "uncooperative," "out of control," "miserable," or "just can't function." For example, describing the "icy stare" and "curtly" turning her head away at Holly's attempts at engaging Grace would be useful. It would be reasonable to see the function of these specific and colorful behaviors as attempting to "punish" Holly for her laxity in responding. It would certainly be more helpful than simply saying that Grace had been "rude."

Consequences

Now for the C or *consequences* column. Most people equate "consequences" with punishments. For this exercise, I tell parents that *consequences* are any events that follow the behavior we've just described and written down in the B column. Included will be the observable behaviors of others, typically of one parent, but also anyone else who might be involved—for example, a sibling, another parent, or the nanny. Keep it simple to start. You can go back and analyze more detailed and complex situations later. Again, I want good, concrete descriptions: "I reassure him by saying . . ."; "His sister starts telling him he's acting like a baby"; "We just leave." For our purposes, consequences will also include the *parents'* emotions (embarrassment, guilt, sorrow, their own anxiety) and thoughts ("I don't have time for this"; "I'm a failure"; "Why can't she just get in the damn pool?").

Also, it's easy to see that any one consequence can serve as the activator or trigger of yet another behavior, evoking yet another consequence, and so on down the line. As such, and with limited white-board space, each functional analysis will be somewhat—or even greatly—truncated and simplistic in terms of the actual day-to-day processes. When conducting the analysis I will, as illustrated in Figure 4.2, toggle back and forth between behavior and consequences as the sequence unfolds.

ACTIVATORS (ANTECEDENTS)	BEHAVIOR	CONSEQUENCES
Situation Common variables Setting Events Proximal Triggers	Observable Specific	Observable Other's (e.g., a parent's) thoughts and feelings

Wyatt's bedroom
6:30 a.m.
Monday morning
A project (unfinished) is due
  today.
Sara comes in and tells
  Wyatt it's time to get up.
	1. Wyatt does not respond.
	2. Wyatt moans and curls
	  deeper into the blankets.
	3. Wyatt complains
	  about his stomach, head,
	  underwear.
	4. Wyatt becomes loud
	  and provocative.
	5. _____
		1. Sara reminds him of their
		  agreement.
		2. Sara, feeling tense
		  and sad, leaves for ten
		  minutes, then returns.
		3. Sara calmly reassures
		  Wyatt.
		4. Dan enters room and
		  angrily shouts at Wyatt
		  to get up or else.
		5. _____

Figure 4.2

And Then . . . ? It's clear that the behavior-consequences iterations can go on for a while. At some point, the episode appears to end. But I like to pursue the consequences out a ways further by asking, "And then . . . ? What happens next? And after that?" Sometimes down the line, maybe even an hour or two later, there are important transactions that may be providing a feedback loop, a set of contingencies that holds the entire process together, gives it meaning, or simply increases the probability that the problem behavior will happen again in the future. Recall that Grace's mother took her to buy more popsicles after her tantrum. Was doing so a mistake? Did this somehow reward Grace's "bad behavior"? It's hard to say based on one example. But if there is a pattern of delayed contingencies possibly creating a feedback loop of positive or negative reinforcement, I want to know about it.

I will always remember a heartbreaking story related to me by a professor in graduate school. He was working with a very conservative and traditional family that had been having difficulty with their six-year-old son. They described a repeated and upsetting scenario. The boy would dress up in his sister's clothes. His mother, alarmed and angered by this behavior, would scold him and do the "just wait till your father comes home" routine. Father would come home. Mother would tell Father about the boy's transgression. Father would severely spank the boy.

And then . . . ? Reliably, about an hour or so later, the father, perhaps partly out of guilt and partly to give his boy a "manly" activity, would take his son outside and play ball with him. My professor said he asked the father if there was any other time when he played ball with his son, other than an hour or so after a beating, which followed the boy's dressing up in his sister's clothes. Somewhat sheepishly, the father admitted that, due to his busy work schedule, he did not have a lot of time to play with his son. So the answer was no. As I said, heartbreaking. Here was a child who, very likely, had stumbled upon, unconsciously no doubt, a set of contingencies that allowed him time with his father, and the price for that time together was the beating.

The contingencies you uncover may not be that dramatic or obvious, at least to an objective observer. Instead you may discover more subtle but equally important "feedback loops" that help explain and maintain the entrenched behavior patterns at the heart of your work with the family. Again, we're all just trying to get our needs met, children and parents alike. There's no blame here. And sometimes there is a "payoff" for the child (for example, avoiding school), and sometimes it's the parent who feels relief through avoiding another confrontation or having to feel his own distress. This is the power of the negative reinforcement paradigm.

Contrast: Leave some room at the bottom of the behavior and consequences columns, separated from the above information with a solid or dotted line (see Figure 4.3). Typically, and unfortunately, you won't need much room. Recall the question my professor asked the father of the boy who was dressing up in his sister's clothes: "Is there any other time when you play ball with your son?" I want to know if there are exceptions to the patterns the parents and I have just explicated, in terms of either behavior or consequences. I want to know what happens when things go well, even if these are rare occurrences. And I want to know when things go well *under the exact same antecedent conditions.*

ACTIVATORS (ANTECEDENTS)	BEHAVIOR	CONSEQUENCES
Situation Common variables Setting Events Proximal Triggers		
Under these same conditions, what do you want her to do or expect him to do?	• Observable • Specific	However infrequently, what happens next?

Figure 4.3

I point to the activator column and say, "Okay, under these *exact* conditions—Monday morning, he's slept poorly the night before, you're fighting a cold, you have to be at work early, he's starting to express worries about fire drills at school, all of it—what do you want him to do?" Again, we're looking for concrete behaviors, not just "He'll be happy," or "He'll stop being unreasonable," or "He'll appreciate the importance of being on time." After a quizzical look and a pause, you may get an answer such as, "He'd get out of bed without complaining and start getting ready for school." I write this down in the bottom portion of the behavior column.

Ah, and what is the typical consequence for "getting out of bed without complaining and starting to get ready for school"? This usually draws another quizzical look and an answer such as, "Well, he just does that and I go get breakfast ready." The parent might possibly say, "I thank him for getting out of bed and starting right away without fussing." Or worst of all, "I say, 'Wow, who's this child? Have you seen Wyatt?'" Sadly, for many children (and adults), the consequences for doing what's expected of them are often pretty lame or perhaps they are nothing at all. For a child like Wyatt who has a high tolerance for drama and a strong need for engagement, or for the behaviorally inhibited child who needs a lot of encouragement, doing what's expected can leave him or her feeling invisible.

Contrast this with what is often in the upper portion of the consequences column. As negative as the fussing and cajoling and fighting may be on one level, for the child (and even some parents) these episodes are passionate and intimate and "real." No one's invisible here.

So, I will ask the parents, would it be possible to drain some of the energy, passion, and intimacy found in the maladaptive dance and instead put that energy and passion into consequences for expected behavior? While being sensitive to a particular child's tolerances for energy levels and intimacy, can we *consistently* respond to her positive, brave, coping behaviors in ways that clearly and energetically show pleasure and esteem?

Admittedly, this has been a very cursory description of the technique of functional analysis. As I mentioned, you may do several of these analyses over the course of the first few weeks of assessment and treatment. Keep it simple. Keep the discussion moving along. Get some detail, but don't get bogged down in detail. This technique is an artform and gets easier with practice and experience.

STEP 2: SHIFT ATTENTION

So, you've started to increase awareness and established some understanding of how the anxious processes are "held together." What's next? You will turn to Step 2 in changing the dance: shifting or changing the focus of attention.

Three General Strategies for Shifting Attention

As described in Chapter 1, anxiety and stress generally constrict attention as well as direct it toward negative stimuli in the environment and negative thoughts in the mind. Wherever the attention of the child and parents goes, their thoughts, feelings, and behavior will follow. So how do you shift their attention? Three strategies are to (1) "change the channel," (2) expand awareness, or (3) change the "breadth" of attention. Let's take a closer look at each of these options.

"Change the Channel"

Recall my description of the "hairball model" of thoughts and feelings (from the Introduction): the idea that private events are actual physical entities "in" our minds that must be expelled in order for behavior to be "appropriate" and life to be good. Physiology, and even our own experience, does not support this model. No one has yet found the place where feelings reside as physical entities somewhere inside us. Yes, there is increased activation of certain limbic centers during strong emotions. But again, strong emotions activate many centers of the brain. Yes, scratching an itch will cause it to end quickly, but then again, simply ignoring an itch and attending to something else will result in the itch evaporating soon enough.

The basic fact is, thoughts, emotions, and itch sensations are not physical things taking up space. Our experience of these events is the product of electrochemical activity in the brain. While these experiences are very real and the very basis for our feeling alive in the world, their origins and nature are similar to, or analogous to, the words and symbols that appear on my computer screen at this moment: a product of the electrical activity within my laptop. If I want to change the content of the screen, I simply click on a few icons and now I'm looking at a silly cat video on the Web. I did not have to purge this Word document from the computer (that would have been a huge mistake) in order to switch over to the Web. I merely had to change the electrical activity of the computer and thus the content on the screen. In a similar way, I don't have to expel one program from the television set, say *Dancing with the Stars,* in order to then watch *Masterpiece Theatre.* I simply need to change the channel. Anxiety (or anger or joy) represents particular electrochemical activity of the brain, with participation by other body parts, such as the lungs or muscles. Changing the electrochemical activity will change the emotion or thought I experience, by definition.

So, given this electrochemical activity of the brain, instead of the rather pointless and frustrating exercise of trying to forcibly get rid of unwanted thoughts and feelings, I suggest what I call "changing the channel": focusing on something else that is more pleasant or at least neutral (McCurry, 2009). This is the classic "think about something else," redirection, or distraction technique. However, it is important to remember that, as I mentioned in the Introduction, trying to *not* think something doesn't actually work well (Wegner, 2011). True redirection, or changing the channel, means thinking about something else entirely and not *not* thinking about the annoying, inconsiderate, immature, and vulgar sound of your little brother's chewing at the moment.

In reality, every time we change the focus of attention from one topic to another we essentially "change the channel." So, we all have a great deal of experience doing this. But, of course, changing our mental channel is not often simple or easy when it comes to "hot" topics or overlearned behavior patterns. It can be quite tricky. But the take-home message is that it is simply not necessary to *get rid of* or *get out* an emotion or thought we don't want in order to have new and more helpful content. The key to changing the mental channel is in managing our attention, regardless of the content or its emotional valence. It is the executive skill of effortful control (see Chapter 1), practiced and practiced and practiced some more.

Anderson, Smith, and Christophersen (2011) describe several types of "channels" a child might switch to, each corresponding to a different cognitive-behavioral "anxiety management" skill. I will provide examples of these skills in Chapter 6. Let me hasten to point out that the treatment strategies and skills, as I use them, are less about "managing anxiety" and more about managing choices and behavior (parent or child) *when* anxious (parent or child). This is a critical distinction.

Virtually all parents attempt to get their anxious child to do some conscious breathing. Virtually all anxious children struggle with this task. Yet breathing remains one of the better tactics for shifting one's attention. In his article on attention and mindfulness, Carmody (2009) describes the breath as an "affect neutral stimulus" toward which one can direct attention and thereby disengage from the troublesome and compelling stimulus in the present environment. This can be an initial step or "pivot" away from an unhelpful thought or feeling that can direct the process toward a better outcome. I cover breathing and strategies for overcoming resistance to the practice in Chapter 6.

Expand Awareness

The second way of shifting attention relates to changing or expanding awareness. It is a more subtle shift than changing the channel. Here attention remains on the original content, the original thought or feeling, but this move helps the child and parent to see those thoughts and feelings in a new light. Instead of simply thinking about something else, expanding awareness has more to do with seeing the current set of thoughts and feelings from a different angle or within a different, often expanded, context. I will spend more time on this type of shifting attention in the next chapter when I describe the technique of validation. But the general idea of expanding awareness relates to the concept of mindfulness.

Mindfulness: Interest in the skill and art of shifting and expanding one's attention has a long history in psychology as well as in philosophical and spiritual traditions. We often hear this practice described as *mindfulness.* Ever since Jon Kabat-Zinn's (1994) groundbreaking work with mindfulness and stress reduction, clinicians have been finding applications for mindfulness in the areas of eating disorders, depression, chronic pain, and anxiety, to name a few of the psychological and physical conditions this set of practices has helped.

More recently, mindfulness has been applied to parenting (Duncan, Coatsworth, & Greenberg, 2009; Eyberg & Graham-Pole, 2005; Kabat-Zinn & Kabat-Zinn, 1997). Jean Dumas, whom I've already mentioned in relation to the habitual nature of parent-child behavior patterns, has his own mindfulness-based parent training (Dumas, 2005) from which I borrow quite a bit throughout this book. I have more to say about mindfulness and parenting an anxious child in Chapter 7.

Mindfulness is understandably associated with Buddhism and

other Eastern philosophies and spiritual traditions, but there is also a very rich tradition of Christian meditation and mindfulness (Keating, 2006). However, this association with religion and spirituality may be off-putting to some parents. But these techniques can be separated from spiritual traditions and presented for what they are at their most basic level: attention management skills (Carmody, 2009). This is how I present mindfulness to children and their parents, as attention training or "radical monotasking."

Mindfulness is one of those concepts that is hard to pin down. There isn't agreement on how to define mindfulness; is it a state of mind, a skill, a technique? One definition is, simply, "bringing one's complete attention to the present experience on a moment-to-moment basis" (Marlatt & Kristeller, 2009).

One often comes across Kabat-Zinn's (1994) classic definition of mindfulness: "paying attention in a particular way: on purpose, in the present moment, and nonjudgmentally." This is a fine definition, but I struggle with the requirement that one must be "nonjudgmental" in order to be "mindful." I agree with Carmody (2009) that the "nonjudgmental" component of this definition is too limiting, as well as difficult to achieve. If I am being judgmental at the moment, and I am able to step back from that thought just a bit and hold the judgmental thought a little more lightly, then I think that qualifies as being mindful. I think many people feel they fail at mindfulness practice, or don't even attempt it, because they just cannot avoid judgmental thoughts. After all, if I smugly think to myself, "Here I am being nonjudgmental," that's a judgment!

Two other definitions of mindfulness that I especially like are "stepping back from unproductive ways of coping . . . in order to see more clearly how best to respond" (Dumas, 2005) and "an open, probabilistic state of mind . . . finding differences among things thought similar and similarities among things thought different" (Langer, 1990). I call these more "active" definitions of mindfulness. These definitions approach mindfulness as more than just a state of mind, but as a place from which I can see the world in new ways and make new decisions.

Ellen Langer's definition of mindfulness evokes both the "state of mind" aspect of mindfulness and the action of reorganizing the world through disconnecting and reconnecting ideas, feelings, and decisions. Recall the mind of the very young child, or of anyone of us if we're stressed and regressed, as described in Chapter 1. We make these connections between events, cause and effect, based on our earliest and ongoing experiences. These connections form our internal working models or barely conscious rules that we live by: "If I'm angry then I'm going to hit." Langer's mindfulness suggests we can revisit some of these connections and assumptions and perhaps create some new and more effective rules to live by.

Content within context: Recall the technique of the "time stamp" I mentioned in the previous chapter when I touched upon *validation* (covered in detail in Chapter 5). Saying, "Ah, you're having some of those worry thoughts *now*" or "I'm wondering if the test *tomorrow* is causing you some worries *today*" provides a little containment for the anxious experience and/or connects it to a source. It implies that these thoughts and feelings are transient inner events that are expectable under certain circumstances, *And,* rather than dwell on them, let's find a solution to the problem or cope with the condition. By placing the current experience (worried thoughts) within a time frame, the experience becomes *content* within a larger *context,* that of the rest of time.

I was working with an eight-year-old boy who was struggling to get homework done. It was just a dreadful battle every night, full of "I can't do it" and parent cajoling and threatening. Homework had grown into a monster that was devouring every evening during the week. When I met with the young man, we pulled out my whiteboard and started diagramming the homework process, much like a functional analysis. But the exercise took a wonderful turn when this child took over the markers and began to draw a top-down view of a world, not unlike one might see in a video game. The objective of this "game" was to get to the Castle of Screen Time that lay on the edge of the board. To get there, however, he had to pass through the Valley of Frustration, which represented homework. He was coming up with this stuff by himself. I was mostly just trying to stay out of the way.

He acknowledged that sometimes he felt quite stuck in the Valley of Frustration. I wondered aloud if there might be a way of getting some help at those times. Together we came up with the Bridge of Asking for Help, which could take him across the more difficult portions of the Valley of Frustration and get him to the Castle of Screen Time more quickly and efficiently. We live for these therapy sessions.

There's a saying that "It is only fish that do not know it is water in which they swim." When homework, or any distressing situation, expands to encompass *everything*, becomes one's whole world and existence in the moment, then there is no perspective, no goal to move toward other than frantic escape. Homework had become the all-encompassing context of the evening, for both this child and his parents. When homework became *content* (the Valley of Frustration) within a *context* (a larger concept of what the evening could hold for him), this child was able to consider other possibilities for making the process work. The frustration and other distress became just an *aspect* or condition of the bigger picture. It was something to be coped with and gotten through by way of staying on track to reach the goal, nothing more.

Similarly, placing worry or anxious feelings in a larger context can "normalize" the experience and redirect attention toward the bigger picture or goal. For example, "Ah, you're feeling nervous about the party because you don't know if Timmy [the best friend and source of emotional support] will be there already. If he's not, I'm sure he'll be there soon after you get there and it will be great to see him. I can stay until he gets there if you want me to."

Changes in vocabulary: I will talk more about the importance of nuanced vocabulary in the next chapter. I'll simply point out now that changing one word for another can help shift attention. For example, there is a difference between "scared" and "nervous," between "angry," "frustrated," and "indignant." If we have slightly different words that convey slightly different experiences, we might be able to better discriminate among these feeling and thinking states and consider them in ways that are new and perhaps more useful. For example, expanding a parent's awareness might involve facilitated listening techniques used by the clinician, such as reflecting back what the parent says but with a slight change in emphasis or vocabulary:

PARENT: She wouldn't listen to me at all.
CLINICIAN: Yes, she was too distracted by her own worries to even hear what you were saying.

Or

PARENT: I just get so *angry* when she does that.
CLINICIAN: That would *frustrate* any of us.

Change the "Breadth" of Attention

A third means of shifting attention is changing the breadth of one's attention. Think of a camera that can change from a wide-angle view, taking in a lot of information, to a telephoto lens, focusing on more concentrated and detailed information. Each view has its applications.

To the extent that attention can be too broad or narrow for the circumstances, problems can arise. Mycroft focuses on his shoelaces at the expense of focusing on getting off to school. Brayden, as we saw, focuses on finding the "lucky shirt" (or more accurately, trying to avoid the unlucky shirt) instead of focusing on getting around to eating breakfast so that he can get to school. Wyatt, on the other hand, is likely overwhelmed with the too-big picture of "school" instead of just focusing on getting out of bed. Freya, whom we met in Chapter 1, is absorbed in her worries about her older brother who is in the Army and recently deployed overseas. She then misses out on the conversations around her, and her friends are drifting away due to her perceived aloofness.

Breadth of attention and anxiety—"We can go around the leaf": I draw from movies and other aspects of popular and kid culture for analogies and metaphors. One of the best illustrations of the relationship between breadth of attention and anxiety comes from Pixar's *A Bug's Life.* A twist on the old fable of the grasshopper and the ant mixed with *The Magnificent Seven,* the story line is of decent, hardworking ants who are being extorted by a gang of lazy, scary grasshoppers. The grasshoppers demand that the ants pay them tribute in the form of food, which the ants must harvest for them. In the opening scene, a leaf falls from a tree. It floats gently down to the ground and lands smack on top of a column of ants bearing food for the grasshoppers. The ant the leaf lands in front of screams, "I'm lost! Where's the line? What do I do?" The long line of bearer ants halts. Paralysis and panic ensue.

The leaf has become a roadblock. The ants, being ants, are accustomed to following the chemical trail set out by the ants ahead of them without having to think about it; it's the automatized ant dance. With the leaf in the way, they are bewildered and panic-stricken, not knowing what to do. An old ant appears off to one side and tells the others, "Don't panic. We are going around the leaf!" Confused and uncertain at first, the ants hesitate. The old ant continues to tell them, gently but insistently, "We can go around the leaf. This is nothing compared to the twig of '93." After some reluctance, the ants carefully step around the leaf. Once the new lead ant makes it safely to the other side, the rest of the ants in line follow readily and the column marches on around the leaf. This slight detour is now an accepted part of the path.

This scene nicely illustrates what can happen when a real or imagined roadblock shows up for a child and "the picture" instantly becomes too small. The bigger, metacognitive picture that includes perspective, the original goal, important aspects of the context, or the ability to draw on experience becomes constricted. Someone else, typically the parent, must come along and say, "We can go around the leaf."

Later in the movie, due to circumstances I needn't go into here, the ants are forced to give what may be *all* of their food to the grasshoppers. The ants quickly assume that they will not have enough of the harvest left to avoid starvation in the coming winter. Panic again ensues. From one fact ("We must give even more food to the grasshoppers!"), catastrophic conclusions are drawn in their little ant minds ("We will surely starve!"). This time the picture has become *too big* and the ants are again overwhelmed, frightened, and paralyzed, much as Wyatt panics with overwhelming thoughts of school or separation from his mother as he "tries" to get out of bed. Sara, too, experiences the picture getting too big as she thinks about how she "gave" her anxiety to Wyatt or worries about his ability to ever get an education, leave home, get and keep a job, and put away enough for retirement.

The solution in cases of the picture becoming too big *and* too small is the same: to focus less on the picture itself and instead find the one small "next step" you can take. And then the next, and the next, and so on until the wave of distress passes or parents and child have moved sufficiently into the future and away from the activators so that the anxiety is no longer evoked. For the ants, they must take a deep breath and then take the next helpful step: go around the leaf on the one hand and start gathering more food on the other. For Wyatt, he needs to shift his attention to just getting out of bed, not *trying* to get out of bed, and then taking the next step, and then the next. Sara needs to focus on leaving Wyatt's bedroom and starting breakfast while she lets Wyatt, as Yoda said in *Star Wars,* "Either do or do not; there is no try." And they must be able to do these next steps, at least initially, *while* they are worried and anxiously aroused, and not just when it feels good to do so.

Exercise: Dueling Tubes

Here is a concrete way of illustrating what often happens in situations such as Wyatt and his parents, or Mycroft and his mother, find themselves. For this exercise, you will need to invest in a pair of high-quality, professional-grade cardboard tubes, the kind you find at the center a roll of paper towels.

Holding a tube in each hand, I will say to Elena, "It is morning and Mycroft is utterly focused on getting his shoelaces just right." I hold one tube up to my right eye and train it on my shoe. "He has tunnel vision. A one-track mind. At that moment, Mycroft's whole world has shrunk down to this one thing: the length of the laces. It actually helps him push out all other unpleasant thoughts and feelings—thoughts and feelings linked to being overwhelmed with anxiety." I indicate the presence of these other thoughts and feelings by waving my free hand in the air around "Mycroft's" tube.

I continue, "This narrow view helps Mycroft cope in the moment, but it's not adaptive because it's interfering with the bigger picture"—I take the tube away and indicate the rest of the room and point to the door—"which is the clear and necessary task of getting out of the house and to school on time."

Elena acknowledges that this is Mycroft's reality at the moment.

I press on, holding the second tube to my left eye. "And you, as the responsible parent, have your own ideas about what needs to be happening. Your focus is on getting out of the house and getting Mycroft to school on time and yourself to work on time. And as the sand runs through the hour glass, your vision gets narrower and narrower as well." I turn "Elena's" tube toward the door while "Mycroft's" tube remains trained on my shoe. "This is a prescription for miscommunication and frustration, each person digging in a little deeper, attention getting a little narrower, and each moving further away from a solution and toward more upset."

I go back and forth between the two tubes and their respective centers of attention. Elena gets the point. How she effects this shift in perspective and what she does with it will be the subject of the next chapter. In short, she will learn to look with one unflinching eye on the details of the current situation, unpleasant as those details may be, and with one eye on the larger picture of what's possible and good. But let me describe one more application of the tubes that can be done in session with the child and parent.

I often play board games with children, and parents too, while we talk. To give children and their parents a taste of the limitations of the narrow "tube " view, I ask the child and parents to play a game, such as checkers or ConnectFour, *looking only through a tube held to one eye.* Of course, the child will cheat and look with the other eye, but she can get a sense of how very difficult it is to play these games when she can see only a limited segment of the "playing field." The somewhat wider view, taking in the whole board, works much better for decision making. But on the other hand, stepping too far back and taking in the whole room with its furniture, diplomas on the wall, the view out the windows, and so on might not be efficient and effective either. We might become preoccupied with something out the window and forget we're playing this game. Instead, we must find the breadth of attention that is "just right" for the situation.

STEP 3: TAKE VALUES-DRIVEN ACTION

The third dance step, or key component, of changing the old choreography is to take action in the direction of one's valued goals. Among the acceptance- and mindfulness-based therapies, this is known as *values-consistent behavior* or *values-driven behavior* (Michelson, Lee, Orsillo, & Roemer, 2011). In reality *all* behavior is goal directed. The child's crying, pleading, pulling the covers over her head, freezing up, and saying, "I'm stupid" all have a purpose, even if that purpose cannot be fully articulated by the individual in the moment. The key assumption of the dance model is that the child's anxious behaviors are *goal directed* (escape, avoidance, some semblance of control) but not necessarily *values directed*. Now, we wouldn't expect Mycroft to have an articulable set of values he might use to guide his behavior, but Elena likely does. Among her many values is getting to work on time and having her son arrive at school on time. She also values Mycroft's feeling good about himself, and she values a positive relationship with him. In those moments when Mycroft is really stuck, all these values collide and it's a challenge knowing which values to honor in the moment and thereby decide what action to take.

I will have more to say about values and values-based behaviors in the coming chapters. At this time, I simply want to acknowledge that the *crucial* step in changing the dance is to change the direction the dance is headed. And to do that, you need to know where you're supposed to be going.

Fake It 'Til You Make It

In Chapter 1, I described the "fusion" characteristic of young or regressed thinking. Similar to "rules," fusion dictates that certain relations must hold—certain connections are so much a part of the natural order of things they are not even conscious, let alone subject to change. For example, if I'm *scared,* I can't do the thing that I find scary. In order to do that thing (for example, go off the diving board), I must no longer be afraid—or perhaps less afraid. The assumption is that, in order to behave well, effectively, or properly, I must *first* have my thoughts and feelings in tune with those actions.

However, we may wait a long time for the anxiety to go away. We may never quite extinguish thoughts of doubt or worry before taking necessary action. But then, we don't need to. We shouldn't put our clients in the untenable position of having to change in order to change: "I'll be able to do scary things when I'm no longer scared." Similarly, we can't set up the impossible criterion of needing a situation to be different in order to act differently in that very situation: "I'll be able to do scary things when they no longer scare me." Recall the "contrast" portion of the functional analysis: "What do we want your child to be doing *under these exact antecedent conditions?*"—not "when everything is just the way she likes it." Those aren't the situations that have led to the referral. And those situations are not likely to change appreciably in the future.

What must happen, however incrementally, is for the child (and parents) to take action in a better direction, under those very challenging circumstances. There are things we can do to help make the situation a bit less challenging—preparation and "inoculation" strategies, practicing "next step" and coping behaviors, "transition tasks," and so on, which I will talk more about in the next chapter. But at some point one has to either get in the pool or not get in the pool. There is no "try."

There is a long history of thinking that basically says, "Fake it til you make it." Aristotle said, "We acquire [virtues] by first having put them into action . . . we become just by the practicing of just actions, self-controlled by exercising self-control, and courageous by performing acts of courage." William James, considered the father of American psychology, said, "If you want a quality, act as if you already had it" as well as "Begin to be now what you will be hereafter." The psychologist O. H. Mowrer said, "I can act my way into feeling better sooner than I can feel my way into acting better."

We see this in psychotherapy. Behavioral activation is a well-established treatment approach for depression. Get out and do things. Sitting around the house when depressed only tends to make matters worse. Chronic pain is another area wherein patients must not wait around to feel pain-free in order to get out and to do things. For some, sadly, that day will never come. For their mental health, and in many cases to keep the pain from getting worse, chronic pain patients are urged to be as physically active as they safely can be—not just as physically active as is comfortable.

We know that, for anxiety certainly, exposure is a critical component of treatment. (Exposure/response prevention is discussed in Chapter 6.) We must get out into the world and discover that action leads to a more vital and expansive life. We discover through interacting with the world that virtually all these worries were unnecessary and all these emotions were transient, if we allow them to be transient. We discover our competence and confidence as a consequence of our actions, not as qualities that we can obtain as a prerequisite for effective living. A good pep talk or a threat or the promise of a reward can get a child into the pool. But it's the successful "getting into the pool and discovering it's actually okay" that leads to the shifting in thinking ("I guess it's not so bad"), and it's that experience of success the child can draw upon when in that same situation in the future. Again, for the child and for the parent, having a goal, a direction to be heading in, a commitment to honor, allows them to slog through the many valleys of uncomfortable thoughts and feelings and resist the urge to merely retreat. To aid in carrying this out, I will describe the technique of "motivated action plans," or MAPS (Dumas, 2005), in Chapter 6.

Problems and Conditions:
An Important Distinction

As part of this discussion about taking action, I need to take a short but valuable detour to cover the important difference between *problems* and *conditions*. This is something my father, a consultant in the manufacturing field, used to talk about. It is a thought-provoking distinction that can help parents and their children recognize where to put their attention and energies as situations arise. It will help the families you work with better focus on actions that will be helpful and not just more-of-the-same escape, avoidance, or misdirected control.

A *problem,* my father would say, is a situation that gives you trouble. You look around for some solutions to the problem and apply one or more solutions until *the problem is solved.* A *condition,* however, is a situation that gives you trouble *but for which there are no solutions.* By definition, a condition is not a problem, because it can't be solved. The weather is a condition. The weather may itself cause problems—floods, for example—but in and of itself we cannot solve (control) the weather. Homework is a condition. Having a younger sibling is a condition. Little brothers may cause problems, but there is no real legal or ethical *solution* to the fact of having a little brother. Mom and Dad's divorce is a condition.

What conditions call for is coping, adaptation, perhaps some planning ahead. Here in the Pacific Northwest the weather is famously a condition. If you're going to have an outdoor event in Seattle, you had better think about where your guests are going to get shelter should it rain. Given certain circumstances, a given person, due to temperament, other aspects of biology, and experience *will* feel anxiety. The circumstances might be facing an exam at school, being apart from a parent, visiting the dentist, or going off the diving board. Perhaps these circumstances are important to that person's life, are aligned with her values and goals, and are avoided or overly controlled only at a price. Perhaps these circumstances can be avoided without significant cost to one's growth or the vitality of life.

Parents are great problem solvers. We have to be. But as Abraham Maslow said, "It is tempting, if the only tool you have is a hammer, to treat everything as if it were a nail" (Maslow, 1966, p. 15). Parents can get into the habit of regarding every troublesome situation as a problem to be solved. And the child learns this bias from the parents. Unfortunately, Western culture supports the notion of anxiety and other "negative" emotions as problems to be solved (or hacked up like a hairball) as the prerequisite for good functioning. But if circumstantial anxiety is regarded as a problem, then the child's and the parents' attention will be directed exclusively toward "solutions"—usually avoidance, escape, or overcontrol, which may be largely ineffective at best. Frustration grows and coping suffers. We must therefore help parents, and their children, distinguish *problems* from *conditions* and help them to wisely direct their actions: problem solving or coping.

Acceptance: Regarding Life Honestly and Courageously

Another way to think about the idea of "conditions," as opposed to problems, is to think of how we use that word in terms of circumstances that we're not happy about but that are a necessary or inevitable part of a larger and valued situation. For example, random drug tests may be a *condition* of your employment as an airline pilot. You value being a pilot and are *willing* to accede to this condition in order to remain in your job, even if you have a number of negative feelings and ideas associated with that aspect of your job.

Acceptance does not mean passively acquiescing to every challenge or threat that comes along. It is regarding life honestly and courageously. It is the opposite of denial, which is a fine defense if used sparingly and properly—what my dear friend and fellow child psychologist Emma Waddington calls "a responsible dose of denial."

Acceptance, in its various guises, has had a long tradition in psychotherapy. Carl Rogers regarded the central goal of humanistic psychotherapy to be "openness to experience." These words—

"openness" and "acceptance"—are functionally synonyms. Rogers went on to say that acceptance, as he defined it, allowed the client to "take in the evidence in a new situation, as it is, rather than distorting to fit a pattern which he already holds" (Rogers, 1961)—in other words, to resist passively assimilating one's experiences into the old internal models, which are no longer working.

So, I will tell parents that the kind of acceptance we are going for is not of the commonly held "to agree or consent to" or "to regard as true or valid" definitions. Instead, we will be cultivating acceptance of the "to take or receive what is offered" and "to accommodate or reconcile oneself to" variety. Acceptance is not just "gutting it out" or "putting up with" difficult situations or noxious inner events. It is not even merely "going with the flow." Acceptance is seeing things somewhat differently and, as such, is related to mindfulness. It is necessary for change, for action. We can't change what we are in denial about. And we can't often wait for things to get better on their own. As the imperial Roman Stoic philosopher and statesman Seneca observed, "The fates lead him who will, him who won't *they drag.*"

Willingness Versus Wantingness

There are many, many things that we must do every day, usually starting with getting out of bed, that we may not *want* to do. Instead, for a variety of reasons (valued goals), we are *willing* to do these things. Wyatt does not want to get out of bed and go to school. Sara does not want to insist that he do so. Brayden does not want just to pick the shirt that's hanging in front of him while his mind gives him all sorts of unhelpful commentary. Can Brayden thank his mind for its concern and just grab a shirt?

Changing the anxiety dance is an exercise is *willingness*—the act of just doing it. In Chapter 7, I will describe strategies for promoting willingness. But it's important to emphasize, to both parents and child, that it is unlikely that you or I, as skilled as we are as clinicians, will get our clients to actually *want* to do these anxiety-provoking tasks. But if they can be *willing* to do these necessary life tasks, anxiety or not, the promise is that they will feel more successful, more competent, more in synch with life, and less feeling "dragged."

The New Choreography:
From Reacting to Responding

One might sum up the anxiety dance (or the anger dance, or any number of parent-child dances for that matter) as involving these major steps:

1. Child becomes distressed (and regressed).
2. Child, seeking rescue, acts out her distress in dramatic, regressed, or confusing ways.
3. Parent becomes distressed (and regressed).
4. Parent seeks escape from this situation.

The immediate goal *for both parent and child* becomes escape or control in the present and avoidance in the future. Negative reinforcement cements the pattern. Parent and child both enter similar situations in the future with some tension and trepidation, conscious or subconscious. The likelihood of another unfortunate episode is increased. And so it goes.

When coming up with a description for the "old dance," I often characterize these child and parent behaviors as a series of "reactions." The process is typically kicked off by the child's initial reaction—emotionally, cognitively, and behaviorally—to the provocative situation. The "tubes" appear. The parent then reacts to the child, the child back to the parent, and off they go across the dance floor. The core feature of the new dance will be *responsiveness* rather than reactivity.

Responsive Parenting

This distinction between reacting and responding should be fairly clear. But I go over it with parents, just to be thorough. I think of *reacting* as what I have been describing all along as the automatic, habitual dance between parent and anxious child. Now, sometimes parents just have to just react—for example, their child is about to be hit by a car. But for most situations, a parent can take a moment to consider what is actually going on and then act from a more thoughtful, strategic mindset. Reacting is the polar opposite of being thoughtful and strategic. And what you are doing as a clinician, as described in the two previous chapters and throughout this treatment approach, is laying the groundwork for a new way of thinking about a child's anxiety and fear, one that is more mindful and leads to strategies that will guide the tactics, or the "in-the-moment" actions, the parent will use in those difficult situations.

A Responsive Dance

By conducting the functional analysis, we can help parents see that their child's anxious behavior is meant to serve the purpose of obtaining relief and rescue from the parents, however confusing and off-putting that behavior may be on the surface. With this new way of looking at old, distressing situations, we can begin to change the parental portion of the dance to something like this:

1. Aware of history and experience, parent is alert to and ready for possible distress and regression in this situation, when:
   - child becomes distressed and regressed
   - child, seeking rescue, acts out her distress in dramatic, regressed, and/or confusing ways
   - parent becomes distressed (this is still going to happen, at least for the near term), *but then . . .*
2. Parent endeavors to step back mentally and take a more spacious and flexible view of the situation, without losing contact with the original needs/goals of the situation, in order to understand the message behind the child's behavior.
3. Parent acknowledges the child's likely ideas and feelings using specific language.
4. Parent redirects the child's attention to some neutral or more helpful aspect of the situation.

5. Parent and child take action, if incrementally and heavily supported, toward a necessary and valued goal.

No problem, right? Admittedly, this will be a tall order for many of the families you see. For some, it may be impossible at the time you're seeing them, but it's the goal. And we will get them there, most of them, if incrementally and heavily supported.

Duration, Frequency, Intensity: Knowing When Real Change Is Happening

Here is something I have abstracted from twenty-plus years of doing this work. There are three basic ways an "event," such as a temper tantrum or an anxiety attack, can be measured. There is the *duration* of the event: does the tantrum or anxiety episode last five minutes, twenty minutes, up to an hour? Then there is the *frequency*: do these events occur once a week, once a day, multiple times each day? Finally, there is *intensity*: is it a mild reaction or one with great energy, emotions, or even physical dimensions?

In my experience, when real positive change begins to happen, the first noticeable difference in the pattern is a decrease in the *duration* of the event. It may be gradual and uneven, but one begins to see that the forty-minute event is now thirty minutes, then twenty, then maybe five, on average. This can be a very long five minutes, to be sure, but the trend of briefer duration of events begins to emerge. This decrease in duration appears to be largely due to the ability of parents to effectively work "the back end" of the event once the child's anxious behavior is activated (see Figure 4.4). This results from the parents doing the change steps of increasing awareness through validating the child's thoughts and feelings, and then shifting attention by redirecting the child away from the source of distress (if possible and without "paying off" the regressed behavior), and then moving toward some more productive, adaptive behavior or valued goal.

Soon after one sees a decrease in duration, the *frequency* of events will begin to decrease. This will come from proactive efforts

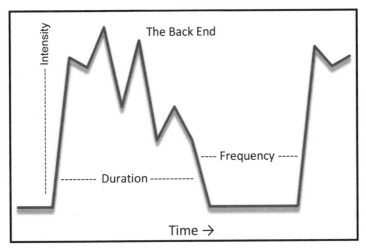

Figure 4.4

by parents to head off the child's anxious reactions through "appropriate" avoidance or working the antecedent conditions. We can also count on the positive benefits of the child's building distress tolerance through adaptive experiences and maturity, especially the development of executive skills such as effortful control. This will lead to less "anxiety sensitivity" and better self-regulation in the face of anxiety and fear.

The last measurable quality of the anxious, reactive event to change in any appreciable way is the *intensity*. It is important for parents to understand that the child's big reactions to fearful and anxiety-provoking situations may continue to be quite intense for a period of time, even as the duration and frequency diminish. This is because the intensity is based on fight-or-flight arousal, which the child and the parent have little to no control over. It is all-or-none. What "all" looks like on any given day will depend on fatigue, blood sugar level, and a dozen other situational variables, so-called because they vary. As such, the child (and parent) will continue to react to provocative situations with a variable level of intensity; highly intense one day, perhaps mildly the next. This inconsistency can be very frustrating and invite the parents to think they (or more likely, *you*) are doing something wrong.

It is important to alert parents to this phenomenon because the intensity of the child's reaction is often what parents want to "fix" first, as it's often the most upsetting feature of these events. You should acknowledge that even a brief and infrequent episode of panic or anxious acting out can be very distressing to both parent and child. When the parents come in and say there was a horrific meltdown over the weekend, in public, with the in-laws in town, the temptation will be great to abandon the strategies that have been successful to date or even to drop out of treatment altogether. Your response will be to validate the parents' distress, frustration, and discouragement. Then gently inquire as to whether the duration and frequency of events remain on the decline. If so, you and the parents are still on the right track.

So, we can inoculate against premature treatment dropout by providing this description of the change process. Again, I use the whiteboard for a variation of the functional analysis (see Figure 4.4). I begin by drawing a base-line moving from left to right saying, "Here you all are, going about your expected routine, when 'Bam,' something happens, some trigger that provokes the anxiety (or any other emotion) and sends it shooting up in intensity." I send the waveform upward to the first peak and continue my description. "This goes on at a high level for a certain duration. Maybe it starts to come down, but a sibling looks at your distraught child the wrong way and it spikes again." More shallow valleys and high peaks are drawn. I say, "Eventually, it does come down and you go on with living until the next one. The distance between events is the flip side of their frequency; four times per week, four times per hour, whatever your experience has been." I put in the "trigger," "intensity," "duration," and "frequency" labels.

At this point, I check in to make sure this description conforms to the family's experience. It rarely does not. I continue. "So, it's this pattern we want to change. You're probably most interested in eliminating these triggers, or getting Wyatt to no longer react with quite so much intensity." Nods all around. "We'll get there," I say. "But, in my experience, when our efforts start to pay off, what you will see happen first is a decrease in the *duration* of these events. In fact, you've already described some examples of this happening over the last several weeks. This is a good and real trend I commonly see. Our work is to continue getting these events to be briefer and briefer by responding effectively at the 'back end' of the process with validation and redirection so that when the emotional reaction *starts to* come down, it actually continue to come down until you're all back at baseline."

I then draw dotted descending lines that show the event coming back to baseline after the third peak, then the second, and eventually after the first for a much briefer, but still intense, event. "Now, that doesn't mean we're going to just let Wyatt do whatever he wants or in some way 'pay off' demanding or aggressive behavior. It means we'll be coming up with ways of redirecting his behavior away from what has been painful and unhelpful to something more helpful or at least neutral.

"We will work on these triggers, the front-end stuff, and his reactions specifically. But in my experience, since Wyatt has, and we all have, so little control over how intense our reactions will be, it's best to focus on what we can control; some activators certainly, but mostly *how you and others will respond to him* when intense reactions show up.

"And because you and Wyatt will start having more success managing these situations, the frequency of these events will decrease. This will be in part due to your better managing the triggers and Wyatt's increased resilience and distress tolerance. But a good percentage of the success will come from the more confident and mindful approach you'll take when approaching situations that have been difficult in the past. This new approach will allow you and Wyatt to navigate life's inevitable frustrations, disappointments, and anxieties so that they are not so triggering to begin with."

Keys to Changing the Dance: Redirection and Validation

The key strategy for reducing the duration of anxious events is acknowledging what is going on for the child (or *validation*, which I will cover extensively in the next chapter) followed by redirection.

As described earlier, we needn't get rid of thoughts and feelings so much as we can learn to "change the channel" and set our attention onto some other topic. This could be in the form of a distracting interlude to dislodge the child's mind from an unhelpful "tube" view (the frustrating shoelaces) or a redirection of attention onto a more important and useful aspect of the situation (heading toward the door and to school). To truly change the old dance, there must be a redirection toward *what's important and necessary in the particular situation*.

The old standby "Let's find something else to think about" might be appropriate and useful on some occasions. But parents must be careful not to enable avoidance or escape. The true and final direction of the new process must be toward what life is calling the child, and the parent, to do in that moment: go upstairs on your own and get your shoes, get your shoes on and head off to school, say a quick good-bye to your mother, head into the classroom, ask if you can join the game at recess, and so on. That is not always an easy or pleasant thing, but it's where life is leading the child and where the real learning about what's okay and what's not okay, what works and what doesn't work, will occur.

A LOOK AHEAD

To change the anxiety dance, parents and child must increase their awareness of behavioral routines, shift their focus, and take action. These "steps" undermine the automaticity of the old processes and align behavior with better coping and problem-solving goals. Functional analysis—which examines activators, behavior, and consequences—both increases parent awareness and provides a continuation of the assessment of behavior patterns. Clarifying that contexts can change how the dance proceeds helps parents recognize that they are not dealing with an intractable situation. It is important to look for patterns of delayed contingencies that may create a feedback loop of positive or negative reinforcement as well as for times when things go well under the exact same antecedent conditions.

When parents have some understanding how the anxious processes are "held together," it's time shift the focus of attention by "changing the channel" (focus on something else that is more pleasant or neutral), expanding awareness (see original thoughts or feelings in a new light), or changing the "breadth" of attention (find one step to take). Next, taking action moves parents and child away from escape, avoidance, and control toward values-directed goals. (Concerning action, it's important to distinguish between *problems* for which there are solutions and *conditions* for which there are no solutions.) Changing the anxiety dance requires willingness (not wantingness) and responsiveness (not reactivity).

The next chapters describe the tactics that flow from this overall strategy of (1) recognizing the intent or function of the child's behavior, (2) the parent's mindfully recognizing his own thoughts and feelings in the moment, (3) resisting the urge to go with the old flow or dance, and (4) changing both parent and child attention and intention from escape, avoidance, and unhelpful control behaviors to values-driven behaviors.

This entire strategy is predicated on good communication, and communication is the subject of our next chapter. Effective communication actually starts by *refraining* from communicating, at least long enough for the parent to think of something helpful to say rather than going with the first words that come to mind in the heat of the moment. In these anxious situations a parent's first and best move will often be to express to the child his understanding of what she, the child, is feeling and thinking and wanting in that moment. This basic strategy is sometimes called validating, reflecting, or mirroring. This understanding, effectively conveyed, will allow the child to hear the rest of what the parent may have to say and will increase, if only marginally, the child's willingness to be redirected toward valued goals.

Summary of Key Ideas

- The *functional analysis* is a powerful tool for gaining information about the particular parent-child dances you are being asked to modify. This exercise helps parents articulate and increase their awareness of the important daily processes. Everyone can then see how the contingencies, or "feedback loops," can hold behavior patterns in place and influence the probability of anxious behavior and reactivity under the same conditions.

- I've found that mutual (child and parent) *negative reinforcement* is the primary factor maintaining these anxious parent-child dances.

- The treatment strategies and skills, as I employ them, are less about "managing anxiety" and more about managing choices and behavior (parent or child) *when* anxious thoughts and feelings are present (parent or child). This is a critical distinction.

- It is simply not necessary to *get rid of* or *get out* an emotion or thought we don't want in order to have new and more helpful content.

- Increase awareness, shift attention, take goal-directed action.

- For the child and for the parent, having a goal, a direction to be heading in, a commitment to honor, allows them to slog through the many valleys of uncomfortable thoughts and feelings and resist the urge to merely retreat.

- Acceptance does not mean passively acquiescing to every challenge or threat that comes along. It is regarding life honestly and courageously. Acceptance is necessary for change.

- The core feature of the new dance will be *responsive* rather than reactive.

- Changing the electrochemical activity of the brain will change the emotion or thought experienced.

- For a child with a high tolerance for drama and a strong need for engagement or for the behaviorally inhibited child who needs a lot of encouragement, doing what's expected can leave her feeling invisible.

- We shouldn't put our clients in the untenable position of having to change in order to change.

- The *crucial* step in changing the dance is to change the direction the dance is headed. And to do that, you need to know where you're supposed to be going.

CHAPTER 5

Helping Parents Develop Effective Communication Skills

The session was coming to an awkward end. Celeste, Jack, and their fifteen-year-old daughter, Freya, sat for several minutes without speaking, each looking down at the floor. I carefully broke the silence.

"This is just an idea that came to me this week as I thought about you all coming in today. I'm not sure if it's important or not, you can think about and tell me what you think next time we meet. Here's my idea. I was anticipating that this would be a difficult discussion, that you'd feel tired and maybe have some discouraging thoughts when we got through it. And my thought is that, from what you've told me, if J. J. were here right now (all three family members stir a little in their chairs), he would be working very hard to lighten the mood, to cheer everyone up, and get things on a hopeful track. He's just that kind of guy, isn't he? (*smiles and nods, but no one looks up*) He serves that role in the family. Like a positive, sunny glue that holds everything and everyone together. And now that he's deployed overseas, it's so much harder to remain positive and brave and hopeful even with the everyday stresses and strains, let alone the big stuff. Finding a way to do that for yourselves has been challenging."

Jack Sr. looked up, eyes brimming. "We just feel lost." Freya added, quietly, "But we never talk about it."

"We never talk about it," Freya says. How often do you hear clients say those words or something similar? What is so difficult about communication, and what happens when anxiety is added to the challenge of communicating? In this chapter, I describe useful concepts and offer tips to increase helpful language use between child and parent, and between the parents themselves. To begin our exploration of building communication skills, let's reflect a bit on children and communication.

LANGUAGE AND COMMUNICATION

What allows children to manage their behavior, control their impulses, and tolerate uncomfortable emotions? What separates the typical three-year-old from the seven-year-old? In my experience, it is the ability to use language to communicate and negotiate with others and to utilize "inner speech" to self-regulate. As I have described earlier, much of what is problematic about childhood anxiety is the child's *behavior* when anxious and the subsequent, largely ineffective reactions by the parent to those anxious behaviors. My hypothesis is that the function of those anxiety-related behaviors is to communicate and to motivate. The child is attempting to communicate his distress and motivate the parent to help in some way, typically by aiding and abetting escape or avoidance.

What makes the anxious or fearful child's behavior ineffective is not so much the *clarity* of what's being communicated. For example, if we go back to the cases of Wyatt and Grace, often it's quite clear what each child wants to gain or accomplish. The problem is that the child's behavior in those moments is "costly" in terms of the disruptions to routines and to getting tasks accomplished, not to mention the wear and tear on the parent-child relationship. The quality of the communication is part of the solution to that problem. In short, replacing ineffective communication with effective communication is key to changing the anxiety dance.

As I described in the last chapter, a key component of changing a reactive dance to a responsive one is increasing the child's and parents' ability to follow these three steps:

1. Increase awareness of what's happening in the moment.
2. Shift attention.
3. Take values-driven action.

In practice, all three steps involve changing one's attention, particularly the "attention spotlight" in terms of where it's pointing and how expansive or restrictive its coverage is. This may be a change in *what* the parent is focusing on—for example, from "Everyone's going to be late for school and work" to "'How can I help my child through this situation and perhaps learn something in the process?" The change might also be in terms of how *wide or narrow* the parent's focus may be—for example, "I'm already worried about how she's going to do at camp next week. I need to just focus on getting through this immediate task and do that well."

SLOWING DOWN THE COMMUNICATION PROCESS

If you've worked with couples in therapy, you know the benefit of pausing to collect your thoughts, of asking for clarity when you're unsure, and of using techniques such as repeating back what someone has said to confirm what you've heard. (This is true both for you in your communication with the couple and for the couple in their communication with each other.) As discussed in Chapter 3, vague, global, or diffuse descriptions of a situation do not lend themselves to understanding or addressing that situation. Just as you encouraged the parents to tell a clear and specific story, you also want them to encourage clarity and specificity in their child's reports of ideas, feelings, wishes, and intentions. To do so, it's crucial to slow down the communication process.

These tactics serve to slow down the process and make it more conscious and mindful. Our thinking may not be serene and nonjudgmental, but it can be clearer and less compulsive. As Dumas and Langer described mindfulness, it can lead to stepping back from unhelpful ways of reacting, and it can create more flexibility and new possibilities for responding.

The habitual and maladaptive dance lunges forward if we surrender to the automatic, unmindful behavior patterns, especially communication behavior that is both verbal and nonverbal. Slowing down allows for opportunities to actually hear and see what is going on and to perhaps make new decisions in the moment. Finally, slowing down sends a message to the child that, in spite of the fact that we're all feeling some uncomfortable emotions and thinking some distressing thoughts, we are at this moment safe and in control, and we can bear these circumstances, feelings, and thoughts and help one another get through them.

THE SOBER WORK OF PARENTING

One of the pioneers of acceptance-based treatments was the late Alan Marlatt at the University of Washington. He was known for his work in substance abuse, mainly the treatment of problem drinking. He developed an acronym that I find very applicable to the work of parenting (Bowen, Chawla, & Marlatt, 2010). It is SOBER: Stop – Observe – Breathe – Expand – Respond. Let's take a brief look at each element.

Stop

When parents confront one of their common anxiety-rich situations and are feeling the pull of the old dance, they need to *stop*. As I mentioned in the last chapter, if the child is about to be hit by a car then the parent should *react*, and react quickly. But barring such life-and-death situations, a parent can stop what he is doing and take the ten seconds or so required to run through the SOBER sequence of actions.

Observe

The parent next takes a clear-eyed look at what is actually going on at the moment, in terms of both the actual events out in the world and what the parent himself is thinking and feeling. The idea is to *describe* to oneself the situation *as one sees it*. In the case of Elena and Mycroft, Elena might see the situation and describe it this way: "He's sitting on the floor working at his shoelaces." At the same time, Elena takes note of the feelings, judgments, and elaborations that habitually show up when she is distressed: "Frustration"; "He's going to make me late for work again"; "I can't do this anymore." Simply observing feelings, judgments, and elaborations and not reacting to them is extremely challenging, especially at the beginning of the change program when the old habits remain strong. It is the mindfulness move. It is a skill that requires practice and patience to develop. In acceptance and commitment therapy, to move away from the judgments and elaborations in our mind, we sometimes say, "Thank your mind for its concern" and then reorient to the present moment out here in the world.

Breathe

Taking a deep breath buys a little time before deciding what to say next. Also, slow and steady breathing is incompatible with maintaining the brain's fight-or-flight reaction, which the parent may experience at that moment. With this deep breathing, the parent models for the child a useful self-regulation tactic. Finally, switching attention to the breath can be an interim step, sometimes called a *pivotal response,* that allows attention to shift or "pivot" in order to break the grip of the parent's automatic private events.

Expand

Recall the "dueling tubes" from the last chapter. *Expanding* is the "anti-tube" move. Elena uses her own effortful control skills to pull back from the narrow tube view and take in the larger context— to discern how Mycroft might be thinking and feeling at the moment, to look at her own thinking and feeling states and hold them lightly, and to consider the possibilities of the situation: How much time do we really have? What's the most important objective at this moment?

For Elena, what may be most important is to somehow use this situation as a teachable moment, as an opportunity to make a sensitive and helpful connection with Mycroft, create some understanding, and help him learn to more effectively deal with this situation. Crafting such an experience may be worth being a few minutes late to work for, at least initially.

In some critical situations, parents such as Sara or Celeste and Jack Sr. may actually need to bring their attention *in* rather than expand it. For them, the picture often gets too big and they feel overwhelmed and ineffective, not knowing which of the many competing ideas and values to honor. To say "Expand or Contract" would mess up the acronym, but it is important to acknowledge that contracting somewhat may be an appropriate response in some circumstances.

Respond

After running through the first four steps, "respond" is the action step. Here the parent makes a values-driven, goal-directed *response,* as opposed to the old, habitual *reaction.* Such a response might look like any number of actions on the part of the parent. An effective response could be a simple acknowledging (validating) of the child's ideas and feelings in the moment. It could be ignoring the child's behavior altogether. A goal-directed response could be leaning in and taking command of the situation—for example, Elena's tying Mycroft's shoes for him and gently but firmly guiding him to the door. A values-drive response could even be an escape or avoidance move (e.g., leaving the overwhelming birthday party) if it is clear to the parent that the child is simply not going to be successful in that situation at that point in time. Discretion is the better part of valor. *And,* in the face of a lot of escape and avoidance, you would want to work with that parent to develop some more appropriate *exposure* situations (see Chapter 6) in order to strategically build that child's capacity to manage birthday parties and the like.

The central idea is that, by utilizing the SOBER procedure, parents can have a flexible and strategic response to their anxious child in the moment. The parent will not be wedded to a "one size fits all" approach to managing anxious situations, and she will be able to expand or narrow her focus according to the needs of that situation and the overall therapist-parent determined program for helping her child.

On occasion the parent may, after taking the SOBER steps, respond in the way she has in the past, at least outwardly (e.g., leaving the birthday party with the child). But in my experience, it will be a different action in that the parent's behavior will be an actual *response* and not a reaction. The parent's actions will be more conscious and less automatic. The exchange between parent and child will have a different quality to it, one marked by increased poise, confidence, consistency balanced with flexibility, and more sensitivity to the child. In the vast majority of situations, the parent's initial response will be one of *validation.*

GRAYBAR'S FIRST LAW OF HUMAN BEHAVIOR, OR THE IMPORTANCE OF VALIDATION

So where and how does validation come in? Parents, as I pointed out earlier, are problem solvers. If we see a problem, we try to solve it—the sooner the better. We have things to do. The kids have things to do. Because anxiety is often regarded as a problem or an inconvenience, parents move quickly to "solve" the anxiety by trying to change the situation (escape or avoidance) or by trying to get the child to not be so anxious. This includes the take-deep-breaths "suggestion" (which is often met with resistance) or attempts at talking the child out of thinking and feeling anxious through logical arguments or reassurance.

The child may be all too eager to avoid or escape the anxiety-provoking situation, such as school. At the same time, because his anxious behavior is an attempt to communicate and motivate, he is unlikely to give up the anxious behavior, and move on to problem-solving or coping behavior, until those twin goals of understanding and rescue have been accomplished. This is where validation comes in.

A friend in graduate school, Steve Graybar, used to say, "All behavior is a message, and a behavior won't begin to change until the person knows the message has been received." I call this Graybar's First Law of Human Behavior. It is very important to remember. Unless and until the child (or any of us) feels heard, really *feels* heard, the problematic behavior (withdrawal, escape, defiance, agitation) is likely to continue, if not escalate.

To help the child really feel heard, the parent uses the technique of validation. *Validation* (or mirroring or reflecting) is the simple act of "playing back" to the child so that she knows the listener has truly received the message behind the behavior. Not that the caregiver agrees with the cause of the upset, condones the behaviors conveying the message, believes the intensity of the behavior is proportional to the situation, or anything of the sort. It is a simple act of conveying "message received." (See Appendix A for a validation handout that I give to parents.)

Therefore, to help the child know that his message has been received, it is incumbent on the caregiver to convey to the child—in some meaningful way—that she gets the message, or is at least attempting to apprehend the message behind the behavior. Doing so won't quickly turn off the problematic anxious behavior like flipping a switch, but it can shift awareness. It can also allow for a change in the direction of the behavior toward something more useful, such as solving the problem (if there is one) or coping with the situation (if it's a condition). The technique of validation is the primary means for delivering this message to the child that the parent got the child's message. For example, Elena may say to Mycroft, "Ah, you have the *idea* that your shoelaces need to be exactly right before we can leave." Or, "It's *so frustrating* when we can't get things just the way we want them to be." One parent can validate the other, as when Sara can say to Dan, "I can see how frustrated and angry this is making you. I really appreciate your letting me handle it."

Validation establishes the supportive and empathic connection between parent and child in the moment. Validation is an important tool for parents to use with each other, as in the example with Sara and Dan. Validation is a critical component of the *acceptance* that makes room for *change*. Validation, like acceptance, does not mean I agree with what you're thinking, share your feelings, or condone your actions. It means I recognize that this is the reality of the moment.

As part of the anxiety dance change process, we want to increase a child's awareness of how he thinks and feels. You would think the child would know full well what his thoughts and feelings are, but with any child, especially a younger child such as Mycroft, there may not be a great deal of awareness of what's going on inside. Young children, and those of us in a regressed state, lack an "observing ego," or metacognitive functioning, that enables them to step back from experience and name it, think about it, and respond appropriately to it. Instead they get the flooded, dysregulated, inchoate experience that can sometimes only be expressed physically through fight or flight.

Sometimes the child's message is quite clear: "I'm too anxious to go to school!" or "Will there be a fire drill at school today?" Sometimes the message is confused or obscure, as when the child cries, clings, or throws a tantrum. As I said earlier, it is incumbent on the parent to convey to the child—in some *meaningful* way—that she gets the message. If she does not, and the child continues to feel unheard, the child is likely to continue the behavioral display or even amplify it until the parent does get it. As I described in the last chapter, Step 2 of changing the anxiety dance is shifting the focus of attention. In my experience, neither the child nor the parent is willing to shift focus until his or her message has been received.

Especially at the beginning of the change process, the old rules or internal working models are in full command of the child's inner workings. There may be deep suspicion of any change in tactics on the part of the parent. As such, the best validating messages may not get through to the child initially. Perseverance and flexibility are required. (I will have more to say about resilience for both parents and clinicians in Chapter 9.)

What Validation Accomplishes

Proper validation accomplishes several things. First and foremost, it provides the message *to the child* that the message *to the par-*

ent has been received. It replaces ineffective *reassurance* in the many situations when the "but-what-ifs" always have the upper hand. Reassurance is like a promise, and it can be helpful when the situation is relatively straightforward and the promise can be kept: "Will you be there the whole time?" "Yes, I will be there the whole time." But reassurance about some future event over which the parent and child have no control is more problematic: "I'm scared." "You'll be fine." "But what if . . ."

Validation provides the child with some vocabulary, some language, that describes his state in the moment with accuracy and perhaps nuance. There is a difference between feeling "scared" and feeling "nervous," or between "angry" and "frustrated," let alone "indignant." In the example above, Elena uses the word "frustrated" over "angry" to label Mycroft's emotion when he's struggling with his shoelaces. Holly might use "impatient" to describe Grace's feelings when Grace herself may state she's "angry." Not that we want parents and children arguing about what everyone is *really* feeling. But a parent might suggest a more nuanced word based on the situation and what she is observing in the child's behavior. If the child rejects the label, the parent should shrug and move on, perhaps saying something like, "Okay, well, that's how it looks to me."

Validation is not just another trick for getting the child to be less anxious, as if saying "Ah, you're feeling *pensive* right now" will by itself change long-standing behavior patterns. We're endeavoring, as both an initial and as an ongoing therapeutic move, to promote *mentalizing:* the awareness of, and curiosity about, one's own thoughts and feelings and those of others, in both child and parent. As I will describe later in the chapter, we're trying to establish a new and different relationship to the historically problematic situations, thoughts, and feelings. This new relationship makes room for some curiosity and flexibility about the inner life of parents and child instead of automatically regarding all thoughts and feelings as real and true and powerful.

Validation can also help connect internal events such as thoughts and feelings with the external events that provoked them: "Ah, you have a test today; I'm guessing that's why you're feeling nervous this morning." Note the time stamp of "this morning." It conveys the idea that this nervous feeling is situation specific and time limited. This kind of validation also normalizes the anxiety; it's expected that one should feel such emotions or have such thoughts under these conditions. It's not wrong or bad or pathological. What we do about it, however, is what matters.

In keeping with Langer's definition of mindfulness, that of seeing differences among things thought to be similar and similarities among things thought to be different (see Chapter 4), validation can help a parent shift attention from the habitual reaction to a potential new response: "Ah, we got here early and none of your old friends have arrived, just these new friends you haven't met yet. I wonder if you're having some nervous feelings and ideas about wanting to leave. Well, let's see if we can think about something else we might do until your old friends get here. What are your ideas?" Or simply, "Feeling shy doesn't mean it's okay to be rude."

Validating Ideas

In Chapter 1, I described a child's (or adult's) regressed and literal thinking, whereby thoughts are not regarded as ideas or possibilities but as absolute and immutable facts. Validation can draw attention to the idea that the child's cognitions are not facts but simply ideas; it can suggest other possibilities. For example, Elena might say, "Ah, Mycroft, I think you have an idea right now. Your idea is that the shoelaces have to be perfect. Let's think about some other ideas we can have. Let's think about Isaac and Peter. They're getting ready for school right now, too. They're tying their shoes. They're going to their cars. They can't wait to see you. Let's get to the car so you can see them."

Note the short sentences, moving the content away from the shoes to some actionable goals. Represented are the three steps to changing the dance: increase awareness of what's pushing our behavior around, shift attention to something more useful or simply neutral, take action in the service of your goals.

For the popsicle incident, Holly or Alistair might have validated

Grace's *expectations*: "Oh, no! You were *expecting* lots of popsicles to be there!" (See also "Validating with the Whole Body" later in this chapter.)

Validating Rules

Recall, too, from Chapter 1 that, from our earliest interactions with our caregivers, we developed internal working models, schema, or "rules" for how the world works and for our relationship with others. Finally, recall that "fusion" can create unhelpful connections among emotions, thoughts, and behaviors—for example, "If I feel nervous, I can't do . . ."

When a child operates in the moment from an unhelpful rule, validation can call out that rule, give it a name, and gently question that rule's usefulness. Here, too, the parent should err on the side of keeping the sentences short and the language simple and direct. As an example, let's return to Sara and Wyatt. Keep in mind that Wyatt, who is chronologically older than Mycroft, may be about the same age *emotionally* and *cognitively* (or even younger) when in that regressed state.

Sara might say, "So, I'm wondering about this rule of yours: 'If I'm having any bad thoughts about school or having any bad feelings on a school morning, I cannot go to school at all.'" Sara provides a slightly exaggerated version of the rule to start, just to encourage a little push back from Wyatt. Maybe Wyatt then feels compelled to defend and clarify: "Not *any* bad thoughts, just scary ones. And it's not a rule." Sara, continuing to breathe and keep an eye on her own anxious agitation, shrugs and says, "Okay, that helps me understand better; any scary thoughts and school is impossible." From there, they might talk about what exactly this rule states and how *useful* the rule is—as opposed to how "true" the rule is or what "costs" following the rule imposes on the Wyatt and the rest of the family. More likely, at least initially, Wyatt will quickly devolve into the old behaviors of repeating that he is too scared to go to school, period. Sara is then faced with the decision to either continue engaging Wyatt or to bail out. This is a delicate situation, and I will have more to say about it in Chapters 7 and 8 when I bring up dealing with resistance and helping parents know when to lean into a situation and when to bail out. It's also important that validation in its many forms be done with sincerity and compassion. It's easy for these messages to come across as sarcastic or dismissive if the tone isn't managed carefully.

Validating the Parent's Ideas and Rules

Recall from Chapter 3 that an important part of facilitated listening is validating the parent's experience and reflecting back specific and nuanced comments in response to the parent's story. This will be an ongoing part of your work with parents of anxious children—validating their experiences as the treatment progresses, giving them accurate and nuanced vocabulary to label and observe their own thinking and emotions, identifying and normalizing the connections between outer events and inner experiences. What are their ideas about anxiety, the connections between external events and internal experiences, their rules about what can and cannot be done? And, what is the price they and their children pay for holding on to these ideas and following these rules? Validation can also help get at fundamental parental values, which can help parents locate and claim common ground. Let's look at how this might work with Dan and Sara in a therapy session.

DAN (*to clinician*): Every kid has to go to school. Everybody has to do things they don't like to do. That's life. Wyatt needs to learn this, but his mother doesn't think all this applies to him, that somehow life's going to give Wyatt a free pass on being responsible. He's going to be living in our basement when he's thirty.

SARA (*to Dan*): I never said he doesn't have to learn to be responsible. But how can he learn if he's too scared to even get out of bed?

CLINICIAN: Sara, I can see that you have some strong feelings about what Dan just said, and I want to hear about them. But I just want to quickly respond to Dan to make sure I'm hearing him correctly.

SARA: Okay, but I don't want Wyatt living in our basement either.

CLINICIAN: Excellent, we're all in agreement about the basement. So, Dan, you're saying it's just a basic expectation that Wyatt must be willing to do things, even if he doesn't want to do them. Sara, is that your expectation as well?

SARA: Yes, I know Wyatt has to learn to do these things. But he can't when he's so anxious. I know what it's like.

DAN: He has to start somewhere.

CLINICIAN (to Sara): You've struggled with anxiety and you know what it's like. (to Dan) I wonder if he hasn't already started. I'm sure there have been times when Wyatt has been courageous, although that's not a word we tend to think of when it's learning to ride a bike or going to school. We could probably come up with many examples of times when Wyatt does show willingness, when he can override his anxieties and do what he needs to do. [recall the overlooked positive behaviors discussed as part of the functional analysis]

SARA: It's an act of courage for Wyatt just to get out of bed.

DAN (snorts): He just needs more discipline.

CLINICIAN: I was thinking about this a few minutes ago, Dan, when you first mentioned the idea of Wyatt needing discipline. I remembered that the root of the word discipline is "to teach." Let's think of some ways the two of you can start systematically teaching Wyatt about willingness and courage.

Validating with the Whole Body

When a child is physically hurt, caring parents immediately and automatically display sympathetic affect and language toward their injured child with a pained face and a concerned tone. But when a child is in psychological distress, parents will often assume an outward affective state that is the *exact opposite* of what the child feels. Typically, it is the hyper-calm parent trying to manage the hysterical child by saying softly, "I understand you're upset" with that lilting tone that implies the "but . . ." is imminent. You know the tone. And parents recognize it when you gently point it out.

How would this parent, or you or I, feel if someone were to be that dismissive and patronizing to us? It would not go over well. Why? Because it's invalidating. It does not convey the message that the child's message has been received. If this parent *really* and *truly* knew how the child was feeling at that moment, the parent, too, would be feeling some of that upset. It's called "feeling felt." The child needs to know he has been felt by the parent (or the clinician) at a gut level. Not that the parent has to become hysterical, too, but *some* display of affect mirroring the child's state would be welcomed by the child.

This need for, and appreciation of, validation or empathy is wired into our brains. Researchers studied the ability of mothers to soothe their eight-month-old infants immediately after the child received a routine vaccination (Fonagy et al. 1995). All the mothers were holding their infant so that she and child were face to face. The vaccination was delivered. Some mothers immediately began their soothing strategies: the rocking, cooing, and gentle talking we think of when we see someone calming a distressed child. Other mothers were observed to scrunch their faces in a grimace of pain for just a moment immediately after the child received the injection. Then these mothers quickly went into their own rocking and other soothing behaviors. It was this second group of mothers who were able to calm their child much more quickly and effectively than the mothers who did not display the pained affect.

What were these very young, preverbal infants getting out of seeing their mothers "feeling their pain"? The pained facial expressions of these mothers were spontaneous. When asked, they could say they were aware of doing them, but making the expressions was not a calculated move on their part. It just came naturally to the mothers—and the message was naturally "used" by the infant to help it self-regulate.

So, whole body validation could simply be a pained look and a tone that conveys concern. It is hard to illustrate here in print, but something like "Ah, Wyatt, I *know* you're having those 'I just want to stay in bed *all day* and not have to deal with *anything*' thoughts." The parent may be thinking that this is the most trivial, ridiculous issue ever, and can still manage a look and tone that says "I get it," because what the parent is validating is the child's distress and "stuckness," regardless of the *reasons* for the distress and being stuck. And we've all been distressed and stuck, so we know what that feels like.

Here are several other points to emphasize when discussing validation.

Forget the "I Understand . . ."

I find it best to leave out the "I understand" as in "I understand you're disappointed." It's unnecessary, and older children will go right to "You *don't* understand!" When that happens, the parent then argues with the child about whether or not she truly understands. Encourage the parent to just make the statement—for example, "You're disappointed"—to the child. The understanding is a given if the parent is anywhere close to getting the message behind the behavior.

Adjust Emotional Vocabulary to Child's Age

As mentioned earlier, the parent should use emotional vocabulary that is as specific as possible, adjusted for the child's age. Instead of "upset," use a more specific or nuanced word, such as "nervous," "jealous," or "frustrated." This is part of stepping back from and being interested in and curious about feelings and "ideas" instead of being pushed around by them. Introduce the child to new emotion words such as "contrary" or "dudgeon" (look it up).

Just Say, "Ah . . ."

I like simple and specific "Ah" statements: "Ah, you're having one of those 'what's-going-to-happen-next?' worries" or "Ah, I can see you're feeling nervous right now." Parents can use "I wonder" statements if they are not sure what exactly is going on with the child or if they simply want a more subtle or less intrusive approach at that moment. For example, "I wonder if you're thinking you won't know anyone at the party and that thought makes you feel nervous."

Offer Refusal Rights

With older children, who cherish their autonomy and privacy, being understood is a mixed blessing; they want it, but they also find it intrusive. *Refusal rights,* or making it clear they needn't respond right away, can give these children or adolescents a face-saving out when validation is just a little too intimate. An example of granting refusal rights might be to say, "I could be wrong, but you look like you're feeling nervous right now." With Freya and her family, as described at the beginning of this chapter, I deliberately hedged a bit on my certainty about what was going on in the family, and I asked that the family give my ideas some thought. This was in part because of the limited time left in the session (which so often happens). It was also because this was a very tender topic and something of an open family secret, which would require some thinking and perhaps discussion among themselves before baring it in session.

Keep It Brief

Finally, parents (and clinicians) should err on the side of keeping validation very, very brief. If it becomes a parental lecture or devolves into the parent's complaining about the child ("Your brother never has this trouble"), it will defeat the purpose of allowing the child to understand himself better; instead, it will become all about the parent.

INOCULATION: PREPARING FOR FUTURE THOUGHTS AND FEELINGS

If we can't control something, like the weather, the next best thing is to be able to predict it. *Inoculation* describes a way we alert others to some feeling or thought they might have in the future. That way, when the thought or feeling shows up, (1) it is not such a surprise and shock, (2) it becomes something more "normal" or at least expectable, and (3) one can plan for it. Inoculation for a child with a history of stomachaches and school refusal might look something like this: "I'm going to guess that, on that first Monday after winter break, your stomach is going to be unhappy about having to get up super early and go to school. So, we need a plan for when it starts complaining [imitates a mopey stomach] so that you can get to school and see your friends."

Inoculation for the parent might look like this: "Even before you lean in and tell Grace that she must finish her art project because it's time for bed, I would expect you to have some trepidation with visions of tantrums, hurtful words thrown at you, and other difficult behavior to deal with. But it's now clear that walking on eggshells and avoiding confrontations hasn't worked. What's our plan going to be to support your being the consistent and in-charge parent Grace needs you to be?"

One form of inoculation I call "first arrow/second arrow." It's actually a term I borrowed from karate where it refers to techniques designed to fake out your opponent with a move that is a feint (the first arrow) so that the real strike can get past the opponent's defenses (the second arrow). We all tend to be on guard against hearing something that will make us feel bad. If a child is thoroughly defended against hearing something, he may simply not hear it. On the other hand, if a child is completely undefended or unprepared for information, the result may be a shock, a spasm of defensiveness, or some other big reaction.

So, the parent's "first arrow" alerts the child that some information is coming, and this is how the child might think or feel. For example, "I have something to tell you that might make you a little nervous." Then there's a brief two-beat pause before delivering the "second arrow," which contains the information: "There's going to be an assembly at school today, so that's where you'll be going with your class during math time."

You could be delivering information that might cause the child to experience an emotion (anxiety, sadness, anger, and so on) or to have a certain idea: "I have something to tell you, and your first thought will probably be 'That's not fair.'" It won't prevent the child from having that emotion or thought, but it might help take the edge off. Also, you want to "low ball" the emotion or thought. Don't say, "I have something to tell you that's going to *enrage* you." Say "frustrate" or "annoy" instead, even if the news does in fact enrage him. It's important to use emotional vocabulary with both precision and care.

DEVELOPMENT OF EMOTIONAL VOCABULARY

As mentioned earlier, an important part of validation practice is to use words that are as specific and nuanced as possible. There is a difference between feeling *scared* and feeling *nervous*. I have a small folder of two-hole-punched 3" by 5" index cards, each with a different emotion word on it made with a label maker. I have maybe thirty or more cards. I keep finding new words to add to the collection. There are the usual suspects: "scared," "angry," "sad." Some are a little more complex or nuanced: "nervous," "indignant," "jealous." Still others are more old-fashioned or obscure: "contrary," "insouciant," "dudgeon." Children can recognize when they're being contrary or insouciant, and it amuses them that there are these odd words corresponding to these various states. It means these emotions must be felt by others, too.

Using words like "contrary," "indignant," or "pensive" can help create the specificity we want in the parent's storyline. These more nuanced or even unusual emotion words help shift the viewpoint of the parent ever so slightly; it's like looking at what's in front of you with your right eye, then your left eye, and back to your right eye. The scene moves perhaps just enough to bring a new perspective or simply more awareness of what is happening in the moment. I will even make up words to convey mixed emotions and shake up the vocabulary a bit. For example, "sangry" is a feeling that is an amalgam of "sad" and "angry." I have heard parents talk about "hangry," which is a well-known combination of "hungry" and "angry." Consider a discussion of emotions and behaviors with Holly, Grace's mother:

CLINICIAN: So, if I'm hearing this correctly, when there is unstructured time and Grace doesn't know what to do with herself, she becomes increasingly irritable and argumentative.

HOLLY: That's right.

CLINICIAN: There's a rather old-fashioned word that describes kids sometimes: "contrary."

HOLLY: That's a good way to describe it. She just gets contrary and I can't say or do anything without it provoking an argument.

CLINICIAN: Another word I like is "boritable"—that's a mix of "bored" and "irritable."

HOLLY: Yes, that's a good word for it. This definitely shows up when she's bored. It's almost as if she's picking a fight with me as a form of entertainment. She never was good at entertaining herself.

CLINICIAN: That's an interesting thought. Maybe that part of the dance, where Grace becomes provocative, serves a purpose—a legitimate one perhaps. She's bored and needs something to do. Okay, I'm wondering if we could think ahead and plan for these situations, if we can, and have some ideas ready for how Grace might organize herself [*action plans redirecting her attention and behavior*]. Of course, since she's in that contrary mood, she'll resist any suggestion you make [*inoculation*], so you'll need to be ready for that and keep breathing yourself and continue gently redirecting.

THE STRONG, CLEAR VOICE: ASKING FOR WHAT YOU NEED

Consider this scenario. It is 1:30 a.m. and Holly is awakened by a noise, quiet at first but growing steadily louder and more fretful with each repetition. It takes her a few moments to identify the sound as Grace crying in her room down the hall. Holly decides to ignore this noise; perhaps Grace is still asleep and it's just a bad dream that will pass. But the sound is louder and clearly coming from the hallway now. They've been here before.

The expectation is that Holly will get out of bed and go to Grace.

This never seems to wake up Alistair! If Grace is still in her room, Holly is expected to ask her what's wrong. She'll be told that Grace had a bad dream and/or woke up and became frightened. Holly will ask for the source of this fear. Grace will draw from a stock set of reasons for fear that have proved in the past to be acceptable to Holly: the bad dream, a shape or shadow in her room, thoughts of burglars or the cat dying. Holly will reluctantly lie down with Grace, or if Grace has made it all the way into her parents' bedroom before Holly wakes, Grace will be reluctantly invited into their bed, where she will sleep peacefully but knee Alistair in the kidneys for the remainder of the night.

I've been told that young girls like the Disney movie *The Little Mermaid* because it's about a girl who loses her voice and then regains it. I have found that it is often possible to change dances like the one Holly and Grace perform in the middle of the night by giving the child her voice. This will work for boys also, and for any situation where children are not asking for what they need in a clear and confident manner but instead resorting to distress and vagueness to get their needs met. The thinking, if you can call it that, behind the child's "strategy" is that "if I'm not direct about asking for what I want, then if I don't get it, it can't be seen as a rejection." It takes a great deal of courage for a child (or an adult) to risk that kind of rejection—to clearly ask for what one needs. Given the "all-or-none" thinking we're all vulnerable to, a denial of some wish can be devastating. Therefore, I'm going to be covert and protect myself. The downside is that I often *don't* get what I need or only at some cost, such as irritating my parents.

Let's return to Holly talking with her clinician. They're discussing the nighttime situation:

CLINICIAN: Sounds very frustrating and tiring. I'd like to make a suggestion, but your first reaction may be skepticism [*inoculation*]."

HOLLY (*laughs*): I'm desperate!

CLINICIAN (*gentle laugh*): Good. Desperation increases willingness. Here's what I'm thinking. You make a deal with Grace. She can have you come into her room when she's frightened and stay with her until she falls asleep. I suggest you sit in a chair near her bed. I would avoid her sleeping in your bed, if that's possible, because that will become a very hard habit to break. But whether she is in her room crying or you find her standing next to your bed, the deal is you will come with her *if* she asks you in a strong, clear voice. No whimpering, or crying or murmuring will do. It must be in a strong, clear voice. And the deal is, if she asks that way, you will comply.

HOLLY: Until she goes off to college?

CLINICIAN: I don't think it will take nearly that long for this to resolve. My thinking is this: what allows children to settle themselves back to sleep after they wake up from a bad dream or for any reason is the certainty that they are safe, that the parents are right there in the next room, and that they can relax in that security and certainty and just get back to sleep.

HOLLY: Grace knows she's safe. We've never let anything bad happen to her.

CLINICIAN: At that hour of the morning, it's hard to know what she knows. Sometimes we have to go back and revisit questions such as "Am I really safe?" that you would think would be long settled and that wouldn't show up by day. But if kids can practice a little courage in those moments, ask for what they need, *acting* with the confidence that those needs will be met, then in my experience the need to test parents—as in "Are you really there if I need you?"—fades away. Those behaviors may pop up now and then in the future when things are stressful. But the child has her evidence that help is reliably available, and all she needs to do is ask for it. Because this is the case, she no longer *needs* to ask for it.

INTIMACY THROUGH ANXIETY TALK

There is something about bedtime that brings out the talk in a child. It is second only to when the child is in the backseat of the car and the parent is driving. Parents get lots of good information then. At bedtime the tendency to engage the parent in conversation may be an attempt to stall the inevitable separation that is coming with "lights out." Perhaps it's the context as well; the child is a bit sleepy, the bed is cozy, the bedtime ritual helps the child feel secure in spite of the twinge of separation anxiety. For whatever reason, this is often when children engage their parents in a lot of intimate talk that can include a recitation of the day's concerns, distressing encounters, and the current crop of worries. For many parent-child dyads, this is the most talking they do on any given day. And for many parent-child dyads, this is also a variation on the anxiety dance; the child learns that talking about anxiety engages the parent and obtains parental attention.

While parents want and need to hear what their children think about, there is a fine and indistinct line between their facilitated listening to the child's concerns and giving these concerns too much attention, especially if worries and other anxious content regularly dominate the conversation. When working with parents, I gently inquire about the nature of these conversations and, if necessary, suggest that the parent be mindful of balance, to make sure there are opportunities to talk about solutions to problems and offer examples of brave and coping behaviors. Parents must also beware of unburdening themselves onto the child in these situations, offering too much personal information about their own worries or problems.

THINKING OUT LOUD: NORMALIZING CHALLENGING THOUGHTS AND FEELINGS

Children often think that parents are these omnipotent beings who have tremendous power and control over their lives. Don't we wish? I find that it's helpful if parents can gently and judiciously disabuse their children of this idea. One manifestation of the black-and-white, all-or-nothing thinking I first talked about in Chapter 1 is the idea that one either does or does not have control over life, including not only external events but also internal ones, such as thoughts and feelings. Children do not appreciate that we spend the vast majority of our time in what the psychologist Laura Kastner calls "the messy middle." Life gets messy. We're confused, anxious, irritated, *and* we need to not get stuck there but to carry on with dignity and grace toward our valued goals. It's easy for children to develop the *idea* that everyone else looks as competent as they do on the *outside* because everyone else is calm and unperturbed on the *inside*. Since this state of inner calm and certainty is very difficult to achieve, and impossible to hold on to for any length of time, children (and even adults) conclude that they are failing at getting their act together and, without having their feelings and thoughts well sorted out, they are *unable* to function.

So, it is important for children to learn the truth: we're all just doing our best and it's often not pretty, but it works well enough. I encourage parents to "think out load" (with appropriate editing) when they confront a challenging situation. Let the child in on how a reasonably competent adult handles some frustration or anxiety. I mentioned this example in Chapter 2: "Oh, this traffic! Here I am getting really frustrated and having those 'This always happens when I'm late' thoughts. Got to take some deep breaths and just be patient. Shall we listen to some music while we sit here?" Increase awareness. Shift attention. Take action. Perhaps the only reasonable action one can take is to listen to the radio as a distraction from the situation that is clearly a condition, not a problem. Doing so normalizes the kinds of pesky thoughts and feelings that *we all* struggle with and suggests that they needn't be struggled with so much as duly noted, and then turn attention toward solving a problem or coping with a condition.

FRAMING: HOW TO BE INCONSISTENT AS A PARENT

While consistency and predictability are important in order for children to feel secure, parenting must also be flexible and nimble in order to respond to the unique demands of the present situation. This means that parents at times have to be inconsistent, at least inconsistent in the eyes of the child: "But you let me have a sleepover last week!" The parent knows that that was last week and the circumstances this week have changed.

It's important for children to understand the circumstances, or the variables, that sway decisions and make certain actions appropriate or not. Obviously, given the age of the child and other factors, a parent will be thoughtful about how much information a child is given. In my experience, parents will often try to explain too much, too often, in an attempt to have the child see the reasonableness of the parent's decision and then not argue about the decision. I prefer to keep things simple and then move on. One of my favorite authors, psychologist Wendy Mogel, says, "Let 'no' be a complete sentence."

If a parent must be flexible (read *inconsistent*), then she might employ the tactic of *framing*. This is the act of creating an awareness of context for the child by putting a verbal frame around a situation. The classic parental frame is "It's a special occasion." This denotes a temporary change in rules or expectations. Today is a special occasion; tomorrow likely won't be. Today the rules and expectations are a little different from the norm; tomorrow the old rules and expectations will be back and in force. Other common frames include "We're all a little tired today," "While your mother's out of town on her business trip . . . ," and "We have company."

Framing can articulate the connections between external events and thoughts and feelings. For example, "There are a lot of kids here you don't know, so I'm guessing that [*wondering if*] you're feeling nervous." Framing can also link the child's intentions with behavior the parent wants to shape up: "I will go in with you, but you have to ask in a strong, clear voice instead of whining."

EFFECTIVE COMMUNICATION AMONG FAMILY MEMBERS

Freya, whom we met first in Chapter 1, is a fifteen-year-old with a long history of anxiety. Her preschool years were marked by extreme shyness and avoidance and later years by social phobia and somatization. Since about the fourth grade, she has experienced great difficulty keeping up with schoolwork in spite of obvious intelligence. Freya may complete her work, but then she fails to turn it in. Lately, she has been almost completely paralyzed around engaging in and completing schoolwork.

Never very comfortable socially, Freya has few friends. She was, however, always very close to her older brother, Jack Jr. or J. J., who is eighteen and now in the military and deployed overseas. As we saw in the brief vignette at the chapter beginning, Freya and her parents, Jack Sr. and Celeste, convey great love and admiration for him. It's clear that J. J. is a solid, stable, and positive force in the family, providing humor and support. They email frequently and Skype when they can. Mostly they worry about his safety and miss him terribly.

For years, Jack Sr. worked long hours at a local paper mill. But the mill closed, and he has been unemployed for almost a year. Too busy during his working years to have hobbies or much of a social life, he now mostly hangs around the house, disrupting the rhythms and routines of Celeste, who is a stay-at-home wife. They bicker more now and Jack Sr. is likely depressed. Lately Celeste has been relying on Freya as a confidante, complaining about Jack Sr. and other issues, such as her own poor health. Celeste talks vaguely of divorce and makes negative statements, such as "Maybe everyone would be better off if I wasn't around."

Freya's anxiety currently manifests as long stretches of nausea and other bodily discomfort. This is distracting and invites worries about cancer or other serious illness. She excuses herself from class at least twice a day to go to the nurse's office. Her teachers report that while in class, she at times appears to be in a trance.

At this time, Freya reports low mood, low energy, and anhedonia, which suggest an emerging depression. She confided to her mother that lately she has been "trying out" scratching her arms with the tip of a paper clip. This hurts, but it also distracts her from her emotions and worries.

Jack Sr. and Celeste have loud disagreements about what to do about Freya. Jack Sr. is impatient with Freya's moods and favors a "sink-or-swim" approach to academics, with the occasional motivational talk about grit and turning your demons into allies. Celeste insists on treating Freya's "issues" as a medical problem and has brought in nutrition experts, vision therapists, naturopaths, and psychiatrists. Neither parent seems comfortable with emotions and thought processes. Now they've come to you at the recommendation of their family physician.

Listening carefully to Freya, Celeste, and Jack Sr. describe the situation and their concerns reveals a good deal of frustration and anxiety spreading out like ripples in a pond. Some containment is called for. Like Brayden and his family, whom we met in Chapter 3, the generational boundaries in Freya's family have become rather porous. A child's exposure to and involvement with adult-level information, issues, and problems (especially when information is vague and uncertain) is a prescription for anxiety. A first order of business would be to help the adults protect the child from unnecessary and burdensome information and to keep the child from being put into a position of carrying the parent's burden as a confidant or decision maker. The clinician can model this behavior by meeting with the parents without the child present or by deflecting topics that may erode the generational boundaries. Let's take a look at how a conversation with Freya's parents (without Freya present) might proceed.

CLINICIAN: I wanted to meet with you both without Freya so that we could speak freely about what you all have been are going through these past months.

CELESTE: I just feel like everywhere I turn there's something new to deal with. I'm done.

JACK SR.: I'm just trying to stay busy.

CELESTE: Well, your idea of staying busy is starting all kinds of projects around the house that never get finished and just make more work for me.

CLINICIAN: I need to interrupt, sorry. This has been a very difficult year for your family, and I think there are probably lots of important concerns like the one you just mentioned. I would really like to set aside some time in here to talk about those concerns, as we are now, without Freya. Until we figure out what's going on with Freya and get her on the way to recovery, I think it will be important to keep her protected from some of the other stressors you all are dealing with. She has enough on her plate as it is, wouldn't you say?

JACK SR.: How do we do that?

CLINICIAN: I'll have some very specific suggestions to make as we talk and I understand better what you all are dealing with. But generally, I would strongly recommend shielding Freya from issues that are rightfully yours and not hers. This would include [*turning to Jack Sr.*] your job situation and [*turning to Celeste*] how you're managing with all you have going on.

CELESTE: But we need to have open communication in the family. We can't just keep things bottled up inside.

CLINICIAN: Communication is very important to you. It's important to me, too. It's so important that we really need to manage it well. Nothing's going to be bottled up, but at the same time we need to make sure that we don't overwhelm Freya with worries that would add to her stress. There are things that only you as a couple can work out. Let's direct our attention to those issues and start to work them out in here and keep home a calm and safe haven for Freya as we work on restoring her psychological health.

THE FAMILY STORYLINE

For any family, it will be necessary to establish an acceptable clinical formulation (our terminology) or storyline (normal people speak). A good storyline enables the parents, the child, and any important others (e.g., teachers or grandparents) to think about the situation in a way that makes sense to them. Additionally, we want the storyline to help unify the somewhat (or perhaps very) different viewpoints among the various players or dancers by emphasizing basic values and goals that everyone can get behind. We all want Wyatt to be a successful student, even as Sara wants him to not be anxious and Dan wants him to not be disrespectful to Sara. Finally, a good storyline will lead to some agreed-upon goals: Wyatt will get to school, even if anxious, even if he's rude on the way to getting him there. At least as a start.

The clinician can help weave a good storyline by listening for the parents' "key words" found in their descriptions of the concerning behavior. For example, in Freya's case, a story emphasizing the physical manifestations of Freya's anxiety and budding depression would (1) validate the symptoms that Freya experiences every day, (2) fit well with Celeste's formulation of the problem, (3) create a place from which you might help her expand her thinking to include psychological elements as well, and (4) give Jack Sr. a compassionate perspective that will take his thinking about "solutions" to Freya's behavior out of the realm of a failure of character and help him see it more as a struggle with forces that are not under her control, at least not yet.

For Grace, the formulation might emphasize the profound influence and durability of temperament and how temperament can be in conflict with the necessities of learning how to manage in a social and academic environment. For Wyatt again, you could describe the importance of autonomy to boys at this age and the necessity of balancing his strong need for control with the expectations of family and society—for example, going to school even when one doesn't want to. Similarly, for Brayden you could help the parents see that there are societal expectations for respectful, cooperative behavior and that the delicate balancing act is to instill these recognitions and skills in our children while preserving their strengths and creative spark.

INTERPARENT COMMUNICATION

As you help parents develop effective communication skills with their child, you will also often work with them on their communication skills with each other, which may be sorely lacking. The late Neil Jacobson pioneered the use of acceptance-based treatments in couples' work (Cordova, Jacobson, & Christensen, 1998; Jacobson, Christiansen, Prince, Cordova, & Eldridge, 2000). His research looked at the communication patterns in highly distressed couples who had been "engaged in their destructive patterns for years" (Cordova, Jacobson, & Christensen, 1998, p. 438). In other words, the couples had their own maladaptive dance, practiced over years, perhaps decades.

Jacobson and his colleagues demonstrated the power of communicating acceptance to reduce conflict and increase marital satisfaction in couples. It is important for the clinician to model acceptance and to communicate support and avoid casting blame. Again, our definition of acceptance is not one of resignation but rather of an honest and embracing regard for life as it is in the moment, warts and all. It is only from this stance of unflinchingly taking life as it is that we can begin to know where and how to make the necessary changes. It is from this accepting, mindful stance that parents can recognize what is a problem and what is a condition, find common goals and strategies, and be responsive to their child and to each other.

So, parents must apply the SOBER procedure to their own parent-parent "dances" in order to reduce the amount of conflict and crosswise agendas that we often see in families with anxious children. Clinicians can encourage parents to slow down their discussions and allow the other parent time to speak. Asking parents to check in with their own thoughts and feelings during discussions can increase that parents' awareness of what goes on for them when attempting to think about and communicate around these topics. Breathing is always helpful.

The *expand* component of SOBER is helpful to recall often and to manage in session. Is the picture getting too narrow (when, exactly, will Wyatt get out of bed?) and are overall objectives (Wyatt will get to school) being missed? Similarly, the discussion can become too detail oriented and the basic values-driven goals the parents share can become lost. For example, Salma and Geoff both agree that Brayden should be successful socially, but they become bogged down in long discourses on the differences between what is witty repartee and what is rudeness when describing the behavior their son uses to cover his feelings of awkwardness and diffidence around peers.

On the other hand, the picture can get too big and you find yourself discussing possible scenarios far into the future ("What will this be like when he's fifteen?") or one parent or the other brings in too many issues (e.g., last year's cranky teacher). Under these circumstances it is often helpful then to *narrow* and sharpen the focus so that the discussion can stay manageable, relevant to the present circumstances, and action oriented.

IN-SESSION COMMUNICATION

Gerald Patterson and colleagues at the Oregon Social Learning Center (OSLC) have been studying families for decades. They have conducted some interesting research on communication between clinician and clients that is relevant to our work with parents and encourages good parent-to-parent communication (Patterson & Forgatch, 1985). The OSLC group found that the probability of in-session client resistance or noncompliant behaviors (including "interrupting," "confronting," "not tracking") increased when the clinician engaged in behaviors coded as "confront" or "teach." Confrontation included clinician behaviors reflecting disagreements, challenges to the client's thinking or decision making, disapproval, confronting, or limit setting. Clinician behaviors coded as "teaching" included any instruction telling clients what they should do, such as implementing a point system or even describing what it typical for a child at a particular age. Now, parents often come to us, if not to be confronted, at least to be given recommendations and perhaps some insight into why their child is behaving this way. We may not experience a great deal of resistance when we communicate these ideas and give these instructions. But the OSLC data give us pause, especially as we think about and guide communication within a client family. We want to tread carefully and encourage family members to do so with each other, certainly during the tender first sessions of the treatment journey.

On the positive side, what the OSLC study also showed was that the in-session probability of client noncompliant behaviors *decreased* significantly following the clinician behaviors defined as "support" and "facilitate." *Support* was defined as clinician behaviors showing warmth, humor, understanding, and/or encouragement. *Facilitating* behaviors were the basic "back channel" responses we all use to indicate we're paying attention to and engaged in what the client is saying: "Uh-uh," "Sure," "I see." These are the communication behaviors we need to be modeling, teaching (gently), and encouraging in the families we're seeing. The ongoing emphasis is on conveying understanding and empathy as the foundation from which change will become possible. From that place of understanding and support, both children and parents will dare to change their behavior, creating new experiences. New experiences bring about new ways of thinking about situations and new emotions associated with those situations.

ROLE-PLAYING COMMUNICATION SKILLS

Finally, communication is a skill, or a set of skills. As such, it must be practiced—a lot. It's far too common to discuss some plan of action in the therapy session only to have it fail in the real world. I think sometimes the plans we come up with in session start to decay in the minds of parents and their children before they get to the parking lot. So, I try to do some role playing of the plan in session just to give everyone a taste of what it will sound like, and how it will feel, and to work out any possible logistical or technical issues before they "try this at home."

The SOBER procedure is good to practice. Identify one or more typical situations and walk the parent through each step while imagining what feelings will be present and what sorts of parental ideas will show up that will be accepted and let go in favor of a mindful stance. This is not unlike sports psychologists leading their clients through guided visualizations of the action on the field and the athlete's skillful response to each demand that comes up.

Similarly, parents can plan and rehearse what they will say to each other in those heated and stressful moments. Having an agreed-upon, and rehearsed, set of communication skills in their parental toolkit can help parents feel united in their efforts and thus strengthen the generational boundaries. With the parents in the therapy room, without the child, you can role-play a new parental response and anticipate that child's likely reactions when a parent says X or does Y. You can then modify your plan or come up with a decision tree (again using the whiteboard). For example, in working with Salma and Geoff, you might suggest this scenario: "You will validate Brayden's likely ideas about the unlucky shirt. You will remind him of casting the die [see Chapter 6]. If he casts the die and follows the new rule, you will praise his flexibility and courage. If Brayden balks, you will walk away muttering [see Chapter 8]."

I also strongly encourage several quick (two- to three-minute) practices each week at home. There are data to show that active recall or rehearsal of material in the days following learning will prevent rapid decay of that information. To obtain a durable and accessible procedural or body memory for the new behaviors that will make up the new dance, this active, physical rehearsal is hugely important. I will address this issue of rehearsal again in the next chapter on treatment within the family context.

A LOOK AHEAD

The function of a child's anxiety-related behaviors is to attempt to communicate distress and to motivate the parent to help. When both child and parents are communicating ineffectively, replacing ineffective communication with effective communication transforms the old anxiety dance to a new, more adaptive dance. The SOBER technique (stop, observe, breathe, expand, respond) helps parents communicate more effectively by slowing down the dance, connecting the parent with what's true and valuable, and orienting him toward a more strategic and less reactive next move.

However, unless and until the child really *feels* heard, the problematic behavior is likely to continue, if not escalate. To help the child really feel heard, the parent uses validation, which tells the child his "message" has been received, provides the child with vocabulary to describe his state in the moment, and helps connect internal events such as thoughts and feelings with the external events that provoked them. Parents need to assume an outward affective state that reflects their child's state. Validating ideas and rules applies to both child and parents.

In the next chapter I describe some traditional, as well as some innovative, cognitive behavioral therapy (CBT) strategies for treating anxiety in children, with an emphasis on the involvement of the parent as "co-therapist." There will also be opportunities for the parent to be a "co-client" as she joins her child in exposure and response prevention adventures and models courageous and effective behavior. Space does not permit an in-depth exploration of all the many relevant and helpful CBT strategies and techniques available to us. Instead, I will describe a few techniques with case examples and provide resources for your further reading.

Summary of Key Ideas

- Unless and until the child (or any of us) feels heard, really *feels* heard, the problematic behavior (withdrawal, escape, defiance, agitation) is likely to continue, if not escalate.

- Validation is a critical component of the *acceptance* that makes room for *change*.

- It is important for children to learn the truth: We're all just doing our best and it's often not pretty, but it works well enough.

- Conveying understanding and empathy is the foundation from which change will become possible.

- Communication is a skill, or a set of skills. As such, it must be practiced—a lot.

- The ability to use language allows children to communicate and negotiate with others and to utilize "inner speech" to self-regulate.

- An acronym that I find very applicable to the work of parenting is SOBER: Stop – Observe – Breathe – Expand – Respond.

- Slowing down allows for opportunities to actually hear and see what is going on and to perhaps make new decisions in the moment.

- *Inoculation* describes a way we alert others to some feeling or thought they might have in the future. That way, when the thought or feeling shows up, (1) it is not such a surprise and shock, (2) it becomes something more "normal" or at least expectable, and (3) one can plan for it.

- An important part of validation practice is to use words that are as specific and nuanced as possible.

- While parents want and need to hear what their children think about, there is a fine and indistinct line between their facilitated listening to the child's concerns and giving these concerns too much attention, especially if worries and other anxious content regularly dominate the conversation.

CHAPTER 6

Treating Anxiety in a Family Context I: Cognitive Behavioral Therapy

As described in the Introduction, clinical psychology is moving toward *transdiagnostic* models of case formulation and treatment. For the interested reader, a recent edited volume by Ehrenreich-May and Chu (2014) offers chapters that cover a range of topics, all concerned with transdiagnostic assessment and treatments for children and adolescents. Two broad categories of transdiagnostic treatments have been identified: the general cognitive behavioral therapy (CBT) model and the acceptance-based or mindfulness-based models (Norton & Barrera, 2012). In this chapter and the next, I describe the use of cognitive behavioral and mindfulness- and acceptance-based therapies in the treatment of anxious children, with an emphasis on parent involvement.

This chapter covers some of the basic treatments components of cognitive behavioral therapy. Certainly, all treatment plans must be individualized, and space here does not permit developing in-depth treatment plans for Mycroft, Grace, Wyatt, and the other anxious children I have been describing. As in the Introduction, where I explicitly did not go into detail regarding clinical diagnosis, my intention in this chapter is not to describe CBT for child anxiety in detail but instead to focus on how parents can be folded into some of the effective treatments that are out there, and that you no doubt already have some experience conducting.

For the reader who wishes to delve more deeply into cognitive behavioral therapy models relevant to our work, the following references will prove helpful: Cartwright-Hatton (2010), Chorpita (2007), Hirshfeld-Becker et al., (2008), Kendall (1994), and Wood & McLeod (2008).

PARENTS AS CO-CLINICIANS

As I've mentioned before, parental involvement plays a vital part in the therapeutic process. Although I touched on that important point earlier in the book, I want to revisit it now, specifically in relation to these treatment approaches. A number of studies show that involving parents improves treatment success for childhood anxiety subtypes, including separation anxiety, generalized anxiety disorder, and specific phobias (see Barrett & Farrell, 2007, for a review). However, the data are rather "noisy," and other research has not supported any significant improvement in treatment outcome with parent involvement (Barmish & Kendall, 2003; Silverman, Kurtines, Jaccard, & Pina, 2009). But a study by Knox, Albano, and Barlow (1996) strongly suggests that parent involvement, at least in exposure therapy, may be quite important to treatment success.

Parents can be instrumental in the success of CBT with their anxious children in a number of ways. First, parents can be involved in treatment generalization by cuing and encouraging skillful problem solving and courageous behaviors (exposure/response prevention) outside the therapy hour and in a variety of settings.

Second, parental facilitation of treatment-related activities *in the world* (parent as "co-clinician") helps the "transfer" of expertise from the clinician to the parent and eventually to the child herself (Barmish & Kendall, 2005). We want the child to feel age-appropriately empowered to meet her challenges and in doing so, with the parent's active support, degrade any pattern of parental overcontrol, intrusiveness, and low-autonomy granting in the family.

Third, as the parent models good coping behaviors and provides cues and positive consequences for courageous child behaviors, it will undermine the family's "avoidant lifestyle" and instead encourage an "exposure lifestyle" (Chorpita, 2007), in which challenges are seen as opportunities to develop one's knowledge base, skills, and resilience.

PARENTS AS CO-CLIENTS

I want to talk about three often overlapping treatment process goals that pervade the various specific treatment strategies and tactics I'll be laying out in this chapter and the next. My first goal is to enlist the parents in helping with various aspects of individual child treatment—for example, by encouraging skill building and courageous behaviors through everyday exposure exercises. Second, I work with parents to improve the day-to-day processes, or parent-child dances, that so often define the problem of childhood anxiety. I described some strategies for changing the dance in the last two chapters. Both of these goals involve the parents as "co-clinicians" in the child's treatment. Third, and this gets one is tricky, I look for opportunities to work with parents directly on the issues they struggle with—issues that affect their child's courageous behavior and self-efficacy. This is parent as *co-client*. I want to do this "organically"— not forcing it, but always on the alert for any hints that the parents are struggling with their own thoughts or feelings. I can then carefully pursue this issue and see where I can create some new thinking and behavior patterns in the parents' lives. This work was already begun in the first assessment session when I listened for parent distress, anxiety, unhelpful rules, dilemmas, conflicts, and the like.

I often say to the graduate students I supervise, "Do unto the parent as you would have the parent do unto the child"—listen, validate, provide clear expectations, build skills, encourage courage, grant autonomy, but also articulate rules and set limits as needed. These clinician activities help establish and maintain what I have described as the "therapeutic frame," which is so important for the success of treatment.

Similarly, there is a "parental frame" or "family frame" that, explicit or implicit, defines the expectations and boundaries within the day-to-day life of the family and makes this everyday functioning predictable and successful, or not. The work of helping Dan and Sara find common ground regarding their values and goals for Wyatt, and then articulating the steps to achieve those goals, is one instance of the clinician's helping the parents establish and maintain a supple (strong but flexible) and conscious family frame. This work necessarily gets us into the territory of the parent's own internal working models, ideas, and emotions. Putting the exploration of the parent's inner life in the context of helping the child and the entire family can support acceptance of this work on the part of the parent and make it feel less intrusive or seen a search for blame.

THE DIFFERENCE BETWEEN STRATEGIES AND TACTICS

After completing the functional analysis, as described in Chapter 4, I'll know more about what's happening in the situations of concern. Together with the parents and the child herself (if old enough), I start to develop ideas about which positive, adaptive behaviors to increase at the "expense" of the maladaptive behaviors. That leads us into a discussion of specific strategies and tactics (tools) for changing the current behavior patterns.

In talking about treatment, I tell parents that I am interested in helping them develop *both* strategies and tactics. A *strategy* is a "plan, method, or series of maneuvers . . . for obtaining a specific goal or result" (Random House College Dictionary, 1980). It is the overarching set of ideas and concepts that will guide our moment-to-moment decisions and help us select our tactics. *Tactics* are the "maneuvers themselves." When parents come to you saying they want "tools" for their child or for themselves, they are often referring to tactics—useful maneuvers for obtaining a result.

But without a clear strategy, tactics or tools cannot be used consistently and effectively. Without a sense of what one is trying to build, pounding nails, done however artfully, will not result in a useful product. It's good to have a diagram, a blueprint, or at least a mental image of what this pile of wood will apparently look like when you're done pounding nails. Having a good understanding of *why* parents, or children, have these particular tools, and knowing *when* and *how* to use them, is vital for success.

CONTENT AND PROCESS

Parents come to us describing specific behaviors (clinging, defiance) and inner experiences (worries, anger) that make up the situations of concern. These specific behaviors, thoughts and feelings are the *content* or "stuff" of the presenting problem. Mycroft is having tantrums during important transitions. Brayden is demanding that his mother repeat his phrases. Content collects into syndromes.

Content can be important, but it can change with the situation, from day to day, and with development over time. We may find through a functional analysis that different behaviors can serve the same function. For example, sulking, whining, and kicking can all serve to gain attention. *Process,* however, describes what is *happening:* this child is trying to get my attention through these behaviors. Content changes. Process can be quite durable and may be the more important thing to focus on. When we talk about "taking responsibility," "cooperating," "trying your best," "being flexible," and a host of other general goals and expectations for children, we are talking about process.

Process is at the heart of the transdiagnostic approach. In my experience, parents are thrown off by changes in content—a different set of activators, a new anxious behavior, defiance—and become paralyzed or reflexively apply an old tactic only to be frustrated when it doesn't help. Strategies help us recognize and focus on process: "Ah, she's trying to *control* things," "I wonder what she's trying to *avoid* right now," "Oh, this is where I usually start yelling, then she cries, then I give in."

The shift to a focus on process quite naturally involves a stepping back from the details and the apparent uniqueness of this situation and instead attempting to apprehend the process in play. This stepping back was in the very definitions of *mindfulness* presented in Chapter 4. It provides a little psychological space in which parents can see the common and familiar features within any particular situation as well as its unique and important aspects; "Ah, this is one of *those*, only with a twist." With this more spacious view, parents can draw on their budding successes, consider a broader range of response options, and get creative, even playful, with their tactics.

FUNDAMENTAL PARENT SKILLS: ICE

Jill Ehrenreich and colleagues have developed the Unified Protocol for the Treatment of Emotional Disorders in Adolescents (Ehrenreich et al., 2008) and the Unified Protocol for Children: Emotional Detectives (UP-C:ED; Ehrenreich-May & Bilek, 2009; Ehrenreich-May and Chu, 2014). Among its many useful features, the UP-C:ED includes a set of skills for parents to learn and practice. These are called the "ICE skills": independence, consistency, and empathy. I'll look at these in reverse order because I often find the empathy, or validating, move to be the best "first response" the parent can make. Consistency of parental responding is an ongoing goal. Independence, for the child, is the ultimate goal.

Expressing *Empathy* for the Child

Empathy is embedded in the validation techniques I have described so far. Again, if the child's anxious behavior is meant to convey important information about how she thinks and feels in the moment, then an empathic, validating response by the parent helps her have the confidence that her message will be received. It's only from that place of "Yes, I get your message" that the parent can effectively work on giving the child new and better ways of communicating and open up the possibility of the child no longer needing to resort to those aversive behaviors to get her message across and her needs met. Empathy is usually not a problem for parents. However, if the child's behavior *is* particularly aversive or the apparent message is confusing or potentially misinterpreted (for example, fight-or-flight presenting as defiance), then a parent may have a deficit of empathy in the moment. Note the clinician's validation and empathy in this exchange with Geoff about his son, Brayden:

CLINICIAN: We've been talking about validating, which is closely tied to empathy. I'm wondering if there are times when it's hard to empathize with what's going on with your son.

GEOFF: Sometimes Brayden gets worked up about incredibly trivial things; he creates these elaborate scenes with the action figures and LEGO creations and then lashes out if something is disturbed, even minutely. I just don't get it. So, yes, it's hard to empathize.

CLINICIAN: *It is hard.* Especially when there are things to be done, like cleaning the living room or maybe just needing to put your down coffee cup somewhere without disturbing the battle for Hoth. *You then feel frustrated and impatient, I'm sure.* So, there are two ways you might look at this in the moment and perhaps reach down and find some way to be empathic, as a means of letting Brayden know you're in tune with him and as a start to moving his behavior in a better direction.

First, regardless of the source of Brayden's emotional pain— the disturbance of his creation for example—at that moment, he *is* in pain. It may look like frustration or anger or indignation. It may come out as rudeness or sullenness. But at the center, it's pain. Pain is pain, regardless of the cause. *And you've known pain.* You can empathize with that basic experience, even when the cause of the pain seems trivial to you. (*Geoff nods*)

Second, getting away from the content and thinking about process, you've been in these situations and continue to experience them. Maybe no one is messing with your LEGO creations, but your work or your plans get interrupted or thwarted from time to time, I would imagine.

GEOFF: You don't want to get me started.

CLINICIAN: I won't take us there unnecessarily. But my point is that you find yourself in comparable situations, perhaps every day. You feel and think many of the same things Brayden is experiencing in his moments, but you manage all that well because you have all these layers of maturity and experience with self-control that Brayden has not acquired *yet*.

GEOFF: Sometimes it's pretty tenuous. How do we help Brayden develop those skills?

CLINICIAN: Everything we're doing is part of that campaign. Right now I want to identify some plans for what you're going to say and do when Brayden goes to that frustrated place, starting with validating his likely emotions and thoughts, and then directing him to some possible solution or coping strategy.

I might have the same conversation with Dan, Wyatt's father, about the difficulty of empathizing with your child when he's pushing your buttons. With Wyatt's mother, Sara, I would congratulate her on her great empathy skills and then wonder aloud whether that empathy at times becomes so central (the "tube") that the other goals and necessities of the situation, such as getting to school, are lost. With any parents, I would then spend time, going back to the functional analysis, coming up with new and specific parenting behaviors that would follow the child's anxious behavior. These new parent responses would be the new consequences in the new dance and, over time, they will guide the child's behavior in a more adaptive direction. I will spend more time on this later when I talk about motivated action plans, or MAPs (Dumas, 2005).

Responding with *Consistency,* to the Extent Humanly Possible

One of the problems in implementing any new change program, and one that can readily undermine the parents' efforts, is lack of consistency in the *consequences* column of the functional analysis. Many parents are well aware of the problem of being inconsistent, and they will readily admit that they are inconsistent in responding to the child. Sometimes there is "intra-parent" inconsistency, or the variable responses of one parent to the same child behavior. This type of variability is often driven by the factors within or impinging on the parent: fatigue, impatience, time constraints, and other "setting events." I'll have more to say about this kind of impingement later in this chapter.

Then there is "interparent" inconsistency. This occurs when each parent responds differently to the same child behavior. This, too, can be the result of any number of proximal or distal factors impinging on the parents, and can go all the way back to family of origin issues and experiences.

It is important to not cast blame on what is essentially an inevitable phenomenon and thereby induce more parental guilt or resentment than necessary. Instead, validate the difficulty, even impossibility, of being completely consistent. Too many variables interfere with or simply influence decision making in the moment. Parents need to have a certain resilience in the face of their child's accusations of unfairness and other variations of inconsistency. I will cover parent resilience in Chapter 9.

Recall my description of "framing" from the previous chapter. By placing one's own behavior in context ("It's a special occasion") a certain amount of flexibility (inconsistency) can be justified. Another strategy for minimizing inconsistency is remembering the concept of "process over content" mentioned above. By focusing on the underlying process ("He's having some of those scary thoughts and he wants me to go upstairs with him") instead of the content ("We're late and my child is not going upstairs to get his shoes like I told him to"), a parent can focus on the salient aspects of the situation and better access the new, agreed-upon responses that are part of the overall treatment plan ("I'm going to take a breath, validate his feelings and ideas, and then tell him I'll go upstairs with him but he needs to ask me in a respectful voice"). Similarly, focusing on process over content helps the anxious child shift attention to actionable and valued goals: "This isn't about whether or not you can stay home on the day your group is going to present your project to the class, it's about keeping your promise to support your team."

Promoting the Child's *Independence*

Ultimately, we want to teach parents to encourage age-appropriate activities that promote autonomy and confidence. For many parents, this is the opposite of overprotective behaviors. As I'll describe later in the context of exposure and response prevention, increasing independence (decreasing avoidance) will be accompanied by a certain amount of anxiety, for *both* the child and the parent. Almost by definition, increasing the child's independence will be incompatible with avoidance, either the child's or the parent's.

Again, excessive avoidance is detrimental because it prevents "corrective learning": assimilating new information and adjusting one's rules or internal working models accordingly. Excessive control efforts do prevent contact with the real and natural consequences of situations and preclude effective learning. Think of superstitious behavior. How do you know that the good luck charm *didn't* help you do well on the test? It was more likely the studying you did or even the good sleep you got the night before was more influential. But you'll never really know unless you start manipulating the variables; study and no charm, charm and no study. In order for the anxiety dance to change into something flexible and effective, *both* the child and the parent must experience some corrective learning. Variables need to be played with in a systematic way. That's where cognitive behavioral therapy comes in.

COGNITIVE BEHAVIORAL TREATMENT APPROACHES TO CHILD ANXIETY

Empathy, consistency, and promoting independence. Increasing awareness through validation maps onto *empathy*. Shifting attention to ongoing expectations and common processes promotes *consistency*. Orienting to valued goals meshes well with defining and encouraging *independence*. With these objectives in mind, we can now look at some more specific treatment strategies and tactics within the general class of cognitive behavioral therapies. The efficacy of cognitive behavioral treatments for childhood anxiety has been well established (Anderson, Smith, & Christophersen, 2011). Taking a transdiagnostic approach, Barlow, Allen & Choate (2004) have reduced the effective components of CBT to three:

1. Cognitive reappraisal
2. Preventing emotional avoidance
3. Promoting courageous behaviors

I would suggest that numbers 2 and 3 are mirror images; if someone is not avoiding, she is likely leaning into life, which is to say acting with courage. As I mentioned in Chapter 4, the two major classes of anxious child behavior are avoidance/escape and maladaptive control efforts. It's time to say a little more about avoidance. Again, I'm presenting someone else's components out of their original order because it makes sense to me to start with the behavioral problem, which commonly is avoidance, and then talk about the treatment goal, courageous behaviors, which will presumably lead to new ways of thinking or cognitive reappraisal.

Emotional Avoidance: A Common Process

Let's return to some of the children we've already met. What is each child avoiding in the situations we've discussed? It seems reasonably clear that Wyatt is trying to avoid school, or more accurately, the anxiety that thoughts of school provoke. You discover through your assessment that Wyatt also exhibits a great deal of controlling behavior toward Sara, commanding her to do things for him (such as driving him places, as opposed to his father driving him) and generally insisting that she be readily available should he need her. A further bit of information is that anxiety per se over separation from his mother is rather variable, and we find that Wyatt is quite content to stay at home while Sara goes to work. We may hypothesize that Wyatt is trying to avoid feeling scared or perhaps the embarrassment and feelings of incompetence that he "thinks" await him at school. I placed "thinks" in quotation marks because in those getting-out-of-bed situations, Wyatt's inner narrative is probably not very specific or coherent. That is a large part of the problem itself; Wyatt doesn't know what rules he's operating under or what he even wants.

Similarly, Brayden attempts to avoid vague feelings of unease by adhering to his rituals. Freya, in attempting to not think about her brother and the worries attached to him, tries to not think about *anything.* Grace and Mycroft try to control the world around them in order to avoid or contain certain unpleasant emotions. Neither Grace nor Mycroft can articulate what exactly they're trying to not think or feel.

This *emotional avoidance,* also referred to as "experiential avoidance," is defined as a person being "unwilling to remain in contact with certain experiences and [taking] steps to alter the form or frequency of these experiences even when this avoidance causes behavioral harm" (Cheron, Ehrenreich, & Pincus, 2009, p. 384). These "steps" (think *dance steps*) are the escape or avoidance behaviors as well as control strategies that make up the presenting problem. After all, if a child feels anxious or has worries and she just goes about her business, then she has probably not been referred to you. She may simply be suffering in silence, while acting courageously—a sad situation, perhaps, but one that may not alert adults to consider psychotherapy.

Courageous Behaviors: The Heart of the New Dance

What is the "positive opposite" of avoidance and control? As I described in Chapter 4 in my discussion of *wanting* versus *willing,* the opposite of avoidance and control is simply doing what the situation calls for. Sometimes this is not a big deal. And sometimes this is a genuine act of courage.

What maintains the maladaptive parent-child anxiety dance is the mutual negative reinforcement paradigm whereby the child and the parent support each other's emotional avoidance. The "response prevention" component of "exposure/response prevention" specifically undermines emotional avoidance; if the client is not allowed to escape or avoid the anxiety-provoking situation, and if she is prevented from engaging in distracting or mollifying "safety behaviors," then the client will necessarily experience anxious distress and live to tell the tale. Because this is a *mutual* negative reinforcement or emotional avoidance paradigm (*both* parent and child are seeking quick relief), effective treatment for child anxiety will include an exposure / response prevention component for the parent as well. And, we should not think about this process as simply preventing old and unhelpful responses (reactions). What are the child and the parent to do instead? This is where you, the parents, and the child come up with some likely alternatives to escape, avoidance, or control in the form of concrete treatment goals. The emphasis is on acting with courage as opposed to "Wyatt won't be anxious about going to school."

As a combination of "co-therapist" and "co-client," the parents should actively engage in the child's exposure exercises outside of the therapy sessions where they (the parents) will no doubt have some challenging emotions evoked by the exercise. Seeing one's child struggling with anxiety and fear is quite anxiety provoking for a parent. It can also evoke frustration, confusion, despair, and a host of other emotions and thoughts that the parent must accept, and not react to, in order to navigate the situation. These exercises will become the parents' opportunity to engage in response prevention in order to change their own habitual reactions. I will give examples later. Perhaps the process should be called "*reaction* prevention/ response promotion."

The Ongoing Process of Cognitive Reappraisal

"Cognitive reappraisal" is listed as number 1 because that's how Barlow et al. (2004) list these components. After all, it's called *cognitive* behavioral therapy and not behavioral cognitive therapy because of the assumption that changes in thinking will lead to changes in behavior. It is the idea that if I have a new thought about a situation—for example, "That's not actually so scary"—I am more likely to engage whatever "that" is. But, as I tell parents and children, this thinking can slides easily into the worries and the "what ifs" and the "but this time it might not work out." So, we often must engage "that" *even though* we have some anxious emotions or mental commentary about it. After all, that is the very definition of being brave: to be afraid and to do what must be done anyway.

I would suggest, instead, that real and durable cognitive reappraisal—the shift from old, unhelpful rules to new, helpful rules—can occur only as the *result* of new experiences. Some shifting or expanding of attention, as I've described, may need to happen in order for the child, or parent, to take the initial steps toward that new experience, if only for a moment in order to disrupt the old pattern. But an actual change in one's rules *about* the world must come from feedback *from* the world. It is the goal-directed behavior, and the achieving of those goals, that allows for cognitive reappraisal and a consolidation of the new feeling-thinking-behaving patterns.

As such, cognitive reappraisal is an ongoing and iterative process: It involves some shifting of ideas or attention that allows for engagement. The engagement in turn generates an experience of success (or at least survival). That experience then becomes incorporated into new cognitions or schema about that situation, which encourages more engagement, and so on. To the extent that parents and children can understand and accept this process, the more likely they are to be willing to engage in the difficult work of acting with courage and not wait to be relieved of their anxiety as a prerequisite to living a spacious and vital life.

EXPOSURE/RESPONSE PREVENTION WITH CHILDREN AND PARENTS

Recall the three effective components of CBT. Two were preventing emotional avoidance and promoting courageous behaviors. I observed that these are mirror images of each other. Preventing maladaptive reactions that make up the old dance is more than just not doing those old behaviors. What will the child and parent do *instead*? The goal is for them to act courageously. The best way to learn to do this is to do this.

Exposure lies at the heart of cognitive behavioral treatment and of mindfulness-based treatments as well. I will not spend time going into detail regarding particular exposure exercises. There are book-length descriptions of how to conduct exposure therapy with children and adolescents. An excellent and practical resource is Chorpita (2007). My intention here is to describe how these techniques can be integrated into work with parents, both as co-therapists and as co-clients.

Generally, parents and most children will acknowledge that to overcome a fearful and avoidant behavior pattern they must confront and push past the fears. Yet there is often considerable resistance to this approach. This is, in part, because anxiety and fear are regarded as problems to be solved or truthful warnings of actual impending danger. It's always a good idea to spend time, perhaps a considerable amount of time, preparing the parent and child for exposure therapy. When it is discussed with care and an eye toward informed consent, clients will accept exposure therapy and recognize its potential usefulness. Continued discussion and tweaking will be necessary to manage any problems or concerns that come up and to keep everyone on track and moving steadily forward, however slow the pace may be.

Part of the preparation is doing some psychoeducation prior to starting exposure. Clinicians often begin by explaining the purpose of exposure, which is to challenge the old ideas and rules about anxiety-provoking situations and to allow the overlearned anxious reactions to extinguish through habituation. The analogy is one of a "false alarm" or "overly sensitive smoke detector" that can be calmed, more or less, by the experience of success and safety that engaging the world can bring about. Exposure asks us to boldly enter into important situations and experiences while the anxious thoughts and feelings clamor and claim to be alerting us to real and present danger. But we learn to regard and evaluate those situations mindfully and choose to push on, because it works (gets us to our goals) for us to push on.

Presumed *fear structures* (Foa & Kozak, 1986), or internal working models or psychological programming, connect certain situations with certain thoughts and feelings and then certain high-probability reactions. For example, for Grace the presence of spiders, in actuality, in her imagination, or simply the verbal stimulus of the word *spider*, initiates a chain of inner experiences leading to outward behaviors. Her fear structures contain the visual and verbal representations of "spider," connect these representations to evaluations ("bad," "dangerous"), elicit physiological arousal (fight-or-flight reaction), and then initiate a habitual set of behaviors: shrieking, freezing up, demanding that the stimulus be removed and the environment be thoroughly checked for other spiders, perhaps refusing to enter that situation for a period of time. Of course, fear structures can be highly adaptive and keep us safe. They become a problem when harmless aspects of the environment become incorporated into the set of "dangerous" stimuli or when these stimuli provoke behaviors that interfere with adaptation, learning, and growth. We want to modify these fear structures so that they are more flexible and more in sync with reality.

Effective exposure and subsequent corrective learning require that the fear structures be activated or "confronted" so that the habitual process of *stimulus leading to inner events leading to outward behavior* can be interrupted and eventually reconstructed into a more adaptive response to the same situations. In Grace's case, this will be spiders. For Wyatt, it might be the tasks related to *getting to* school. (Historically, Wyatt is fine once he gets to school.) So, an exposure exercise must generate some of the expected thoughts and feelings. The trick is to make the exercise sufficiently evocative that the internal anxiety complex is activated but not so clearly fearful that the child, or parent, won't even attempt it.

Revisiting the Functional Analysis

As part of the preparation for exposure, clinicians often spend some time identifying signs or cues that anxiety and fear are approaching or have arrived. These "early warning signs" might include bodily sensations (for example, nausea), certain thoughts

("This is going to be bad"), or verbal rules ("I can't do this if I'm scared"). These signs will then be repurposed to act as prompts for the child, or parent, to begin using effective coping strategies rather than engage in avoidance or unhelpful coping strategies.

It is useful to include a discussion of the parents' own warning signs of emerging anxious thoughts and feelings, and their own inclinations to react one way or another in that situation. For example, Sara experiences rising anxious physiological arousal in anticipation of waking Wyatt on a school morning. Her response to these feelings is to put off waking Wyatt until the last possible moment, which means there's less time to deal with any resistance he might put up to getting out of bed. For Salma, there is a sudden tiredness, with sagging shoulders and a deep sigh, when Brayden starts to pull her into his compulsions. She's then likely to just acquiesce to his demands but with a heaviness that wears on her and is disturbing to Brayden, making him even more anxious and prone to compulsive behavior. These parents might practice being tuned into their early warning signs so that a conscious decision can be made to resist the habitual behaviors and instead try something new in response to what the child is doing.

Once situations and early warning signs are identified, plans are then developed for what the child, and parent, will do when these feelings and thoughts arise during the exposure exercise. The child's typical avoidance and control strategies, along with the parent's, are identified so that they, too, can be watched for and also become cues for taking a different path—a path of engagement.

This discussion will likely evoke some mildly anxious responses as you simply *talk* about anxious feelings and thoughts. In itself, this talk becomes a gentle inoculation and a bit of exposure. You will also offer reassurances: There will be no surprises, no sudden changes to the rules, and no leaps to much higher situations on the "hierarchy" (described later under "Setting Up the Hierarchy"). The child sets the pace, the child chooses to do the exercise or not, and there will be no negative consequences for choosing not to engage; there is no failure.

Setting Goals for Exposure and Dealing with Setbacks

Classic exposure therapy has extinction or habituation of the anxiety response as its primary goal: repeated exposure without dire consequences reduces the fear reaction and decreases anxious cognitions. Often during the exposure exercise, anxiety is monitored and measured, perhaps rated on a 0 to 10 scale as in a "fear thermometer." With each exposure exercise, and in between when the fearful situations are naturally encountered, the child is asked to notice the anxiety and rate its intensity on this scale. The data are tracked in some visual way, such as a chart on the refrigerator containing a week's worth of daily thermometers. The expectation is that fear ratings will go down steadily over time. Seeing this change will be reinforcing for the child and the parent, and will encourage more engagement. The goal, ultimately, is a good long stretch of low anxiety in these situations.

One problem that may arise is the "setback." We may see a positive trend of decreasing anxiety over time with carefully supported exposure, only to have a day in which anxiety shoots up dramatically. Or, regardless of the reported emotions, there may be an episode of intense anxious reaction after a period of decreased frequency and duration of these behaviors. Or, perhaps the child and parent merely encounter a plateau, a stubborn stretch of moderate anxiety that is not extinguishing further despite continued exposure exercises. When this happens, the understandable reaction on the part of the parent and child is one of frustration, discouragement, and thoughts of "going back to square one": "This [therapy] isn't working" or "I/she can't do this." The family is at risk for abandoning treatment.

To mitigate the impact of the inevitable setback or mere stalling of improvement, it is important to be proactive and anticipate these events before they happen. This is another form of inoculation, as I described earlier. I tell parents and children that there certainly will be days when nothing seems to be working as planned, when—for a hundred reasons—the child's reactions, inner and outer, will fluctuate wildly. I ask the family to recall the conversation we had about frequency, duration, and intensity and that we have so little control over how our emotions are provoked or how intense they might be on any given day or even hour.

Classic CBT, like most classic exposure strategies, calls for challenging the likelihood of feared events and applying reasoning to the rules as a way of getting the client to see that her anxious thoughts are unwarranted. For example, one might ask Wyatt to consider how likely it is that he will be humiliated at school today, given his past experiences. It may be quite clear to the rational observer that humiliating events at school are highly improbable for Wyatt on any given day. But Wyatt and Sara, like many anxious individuals, live in a "parts-per-billion world" where even the most remote and logically improbable odds are still too great to risk. When I talk with children and parents about anxiety, I acknowledge what they already know— that these anxious thoughts can be tough and wily. As I tell parents and child, "The 'what ifs' always seem to win these arguments." I will have more to say about getting around the "what ifs" when I discuss acceptance-based treatments in Chapter 7.

The point of these exposure exercises, however, is not to provide the child with new ways to endure her thoughts and feelings; nor is it even, really, the reduction or elimination of anxious thoughts and feelings. Chorpita (2007) states that "the object of exposure is to present the feared object or situation to the child in a way that fosters new learning" (p. 53). To achieve this "new learning," or cognitive reappraisal, the child and parent must repeatedly practice focusing on goals—healthy goals, not avoidance and control—and aligning their behavior with those goals rather than focusing on transient emotions and unhelpful thoughts and trying to manipulate those inner processes.

If we make strengthening goal-directed behavior patterns the objective of exposure exercises, then as long as the child and parent work toward that new pattern or dance, however fitful the progress may be, they are moving in the right direction. As a by-product of focusing on values-driven goals and successfully engaging the world, anxiety should recede and be less a central and influential aspect of those situations. But for some parents and children, and for some situations, there may always be a twinge of nervousness or murmurs of doubt that must be acknowledged but not allowed to divert them.

So, in my work the more important treatment goal is to change the overall process of behavior such that parent and child can orient away from *whatever* inner events may be activated at the moment and instead orient toward actionable goals. As such, it is critically important to not simply track fluctuating emotions in a provocative situation, but also to track and celebrate goal-oriented or courageous behavior. If life's goals are being met, then thoughts and feelings can fluctuate as they will without that becoming a problem.

Engaging Parents in Exposure/Response Prevention

Again, our goal for exposure exercises is twofold. First, in the classic sense, we set up opportunities for the child to confront anxiety-provoking situations and learn new behavioral responses leading to new ways of thinking about those situations. Second, we set up opportunities for the *parent's exposure* to the child's anxiety, an aversive event for the parent. The goal here is for the parent to explore and develop new behavioral responses along with new parental cognitive structures (narratives) about these particular situations.

When explaining the process of exposure to parents, it's vital to emphasize that the child must be at least somewhat anxiously aroused when you do the exposure. *If the situation does not elicit some anxiety, it's not proper and effective exposure.*

The old fear structure (for both parent and child) must be activated in order for it to be examined, better understood, questioned, and decisively reprogrammed through new behavior. That's the only way the child, and parent, can learn that anxiety is something that can be felt *with* taking effective action.

The old fear structures and their accompanying behavior patterns really never go anywhere; they are forever a part of one's brain architecture. What we work toward is (1) weakening these old, maladaptive patterns through disuse, and (2) promoting new structures (thinking, feeling, and behaving) that will "compete" with the old habitual programming in those provocative situations. If the new behaviors are practiced diligently and mindfully, they will gain traction and become the new normal. The old idea or rule of "I can act in adaptive ways so long as I'm not anxious" can be replaced with "I'm anxious, *and* I can manage in this situation."

When setting up this program, there will be an explicit expectation that exposure will occur outside the therapy session in the child's actual, everyday environment. As such, it's important to give parents their instructions for guiding the child's exposure exercises out in the world. Chief among these instructions is to emphasize that the parents, too, will be experiencing certain habitual thoughts and feelings, mostly unpleasant, while their child deals with the exposure. The goal for the parents is to be able to manage their own anxious behavior in order to remain present in the situation, so as to experience habituation and extinction and increase goal-directed behavior. Parents must allow their child to struggle with the exercise rather than stepping in and rescuing. The parent is expected to do some minimal validating—excessive talking or asking questions can be a way for parents to "bind" their own anxiety during these exercises—and provide some encouragement for the child to remain focused on the valued behavioral goals tied to that particular situation.

Setting Up the Hierarchy

Exposure therapy invariably begins with identifying situations that occasion fearful or anxious thoughts and feelings *and* in which the client engages in maladaptive avoidance or control strategies. This work will have begun with the functional analysis I described in Chapter 4. Working together, the parent, child, and clinician create a list of eight or ten situations or behaviors (for example, thinking about, approaching, contacting) that range in anxiety-provoking power from rather mild to quite arousing. It's important to generate good detail and specificity around the descriptions of these situations, just as was done for the functional analysis. Setting events and other potentially important factors should be considered: for example, "Being dropped off at school by Dad" compared to "Being dropped off at school by Mom." Six to ten situations is best. Too few and the leaps from one situation to the next one "higher up" on the hierarchy can be too great and progress may be stalled. Too many situations and progress may be too slow.

Each situation is then rated as to its anxiety-provoking potential with the Subjective Units of Distress Scale (SUDS). This scale can be from 0 to 10, 0 to 100, or whatever units you decide. A "fear thermometer" or "fear ladder" can be drawn to arrange the situations in a hierarchy from least anxiety provoking to most. This is a living document and can be modified with experience.

Typically, then, one would start with some exposure to the experience that is lowest on the fear ladder. For Grace, this might be simply having someone say the word *spider* or having her sit at the kitchen table in the evening and allow a piece of paper to not be parallel with the bottom edge of the table. The paper would likely have to be blank or otherwise devoid of any significance for schoolwork.

After a series of such exposures, we would expect to see the reported SUDS units drop and remain relatively low. After such a period of habituation—for example, to the word *spider*—Grace would agree to exposure with a stimulus "next up" on the hierarchy, perhaps a picture of a spider or some actual homework that's not parallel with the edge of table. SUDS units would continue to be assessed, expected to drop over time and with repeated exposure, and another situation would be teed up, and so on.

An Alternative to the Hierarchy: The Territory and the Quest

One way to make this idea of a hierarchy more interesting for some children is to tie it to something they already know. For example, video games often involve "levels" within which tasks must be accomplished or opponents defeated before the player can move to the next level. Often these levels and their adventures occur in some fantastical world or landscape. In Chapter 4 I described working in this way with an 8-year-old boy who came up with The Valley of (homework) Frustration. The clinician, parent, and child can make a "map" representing the various challenges found in the hierarchy, with divisions, territories, or "lands" representing the anxiety-provoking situations (Osborne, 2012).

The story or narrative then becomes one of the child confronting and successfully managing these provocative situations as she moves through the territory that is her everyday life. The emphasis in these situations is on reaching the objectives, the valued goals, and not so much on focusing on what the anxious thoughts and feelings are up to. These are the distraction—the siren song that tries, unsuccessfully, to lure our hero away from her quest. Here's how a clinician might present this to Wyatt and his parents, Sara and Dan:

CLINICIAN: Okay, Wyatt. I have this paper on which we're going to create a map that will represent this game, this serious game, of getting to school. Right now I want to just focus on the three steps of Level 1: getting out of bed, getting dressed, and getting downstairs. I want you to think of this the way you would a video game. These actions may seem very ordinary, but they are in fact vital pieces of a larger and very important covert operation. The fate of the world lies in their careful and consistent execution.

WYATT: So, this is a dystopia?

CLINICIAN: That's the idea! Yes, very much so. Tell me more. What's your avatar's name going to be?

WYATT: Wyatt the Wily.

CLINICIAN: Excellent. And your mother's name and character? What role is she going to have in this game?

SARA: Can I pick my own name?

WYATT: You'll be Sara the Servant. You'll set out my body armor and weapons and prepare my rations for the journey.

CLINICIAN (*makes eye contact with Sara and gives her a discreet nod*)

SARA (*hesitates, then says*): I can do that. In fact, I'm already doing that, I think.

CLINICIAN (*turning toward Dan*): Now, I'm wondering about a role for your dad . . .

Imaginal Exposure

There are situations that do not allow for direct exposure to the actual feared situation—for example, extreme events such as tornados and earthquakes that are rare or difficult to just go out and confront. *Imaginal exposure* is the creation of mental imagery that will evoke anxious or fearful emotions, bodily sensations, or thoughts. These images might be generated by the child or parents themselves through their own imagination, or the clinician can elicit images by describing in detail situations known to provoke anxiety. This type of exposure might also be suitable for getting started, as an exercise at the very mild end of the hierarchy. For Grace, this might be imagining a spider or imagining that her homework paper is not exactly parallel to the edge of the kitchen table. For Wyatt, it might be asking him to conjure in his mind a provocative situation: "Imagine it's Monday morning and your mother tells you it's time to get out of bed and get ready for school."

The power of language and imagination, and the well-worn paths connecting events, thoughts, and feelings, will reliably generate some of the expected anxious thoughts and feelings. If the child, or parent, can "sit" with those feelings and imagine new behavioral responses, new paths can be created in the brain.

For the parents, you might have them imagine the same or a similar situation, one in which their child is likely experiencing some anxiety or fear. They can then experience their own fizz of anxiety and reactive thinking. If the parents, too, can focus their imaginal attention on new and more adaptive responses, this "covert rehearsal" will strengthen the likelihood that they will be more responsive and less reactive when those situations actually occur.

In Vivo Exposure

When we think of exposure, *in vivo* exposure is what most of us think of: actually going out into the world and evoking some anxiety or bringing an anxiety-provoking stimulus into the therapy room. This is obviously going to be quite edgy and provocative of all sorts of habitual feelings, thoughts, and action potentials. But you will have gone over all of this with the child and her parents as preparation, inoculation, and obtaining of informed consent. You will carefully but insistently (within the framework of client choice to engage or avoid) lead the child and parents up the hierarchy, acknowledging, validating, and articulating the various anxious thoughts and feelings that arise for both parents and child. You will encourage courageous, goal-directed behaviors, and you will discourage avoidance and maladaptive control. This last component—discouraging avoidance and maladaptive control—is *response prevention.*

Response Prevention

If the child and parents react to the exposure exercise with the same old anxiety dance of avoidance and control, there will be no new experience, no new learning. Response prevention is the blocking or denying of the habitual "safety behaviors" (avoidance, escape, and control) that have to date maintained the current behavior pattern through negative reinforcement. Response prevention might take the form of a complete stoppage of the habitual safety behaviors, or it could entail a gradual fading of these behaviors as the child and the parents gain confidence.

Rather than simply proscribing the *old* behaviors, it's best to come up with, ahead of time, some strategies for what exactly the child, and parents, are going to do *instead.* This is where you discuss goal-directed, values-driven behaviors that would be expected in these particular situations. For example, should Grace encounter a spider, she has certain options for effectively dealing with that situation: for example, she can leave the situation if she can or seek help from an adult using respectful words. If the family decides to target Grace's challenging homework process for exposure, then a set of likely thoughts and feelings would be identified along with some possible goal-directed behaviors. Here's an example:

- Grace will sit down to do homework within two minutes of being told it's time to start homework, *even though* she's having the idea she's not ready.
- She will begin her homework within one minute of sitting down, *even though* she's having ideas about her paper not being lined up exactly parallel to the edge of the kitchen table.
- If Grace is unclear about how to start, she can ask a parent for help.

At the same time, Grace's father, Alistair, will no doubt feel mounting anxiety as he anticipates a struggle over getting the homework started. His goal-directed behavior might be to breathe mindfully (see Chapter 7), set the timer as planned, and say nothing. Sometimes following the admonition "Don't just do something, stand there" (DJDSST) is a useful parent tactic. I will have more to say about this in Chapter 8, "Learning When to Push and When to Yield."

Motivated Action Plans

The talk and planning that go into the exposure preparation can themselves be exposure in a mild, imaginal form. Discussing the processes, the habitual patterns, is an exercise in *mentalizing*—stepping back and regarding a situation with more objectivity and even curiosity. This shift in thinking about situations and about oneself marks the beginning of cognitive reappraisal.

But mostly, preparation for exposure is spelling out, to the extent possible, what will happen during the exposure exercise and what everyone's job will be. This planning and scripting can give both parents and child the confidence they need in order to take that leap of faith and do the exposure exercise.

So, for both parent and child, exposure therapy is not complete without getting to the new, more adaptive behaviors and making them the new normal. That's where having specific behavior plans for these situations comes in. Going back to the functional analysis once more, think of these plans as both the child's new behaviors in the B column as well as the parents' new responses in the C column.

To aid in describing and implementing these new behaviors, I again refer to Dumas (2005) and motivated action plans, or MAPs. Motivated action plans are the blueprint for the specific, goal-directed behaviors that will replace the old, maladaptive parent-child reactions and eventually form the new dance in response to anxiety-provoking situations. MAPs describe the when, where, who, and how of the new dance between parents and child.

Three key elements make an effective MAP. First, Dumas points out that behavioral goals should be specific rather than vague. This goes back to the idea, presented in Chapter 3, that we want the parents' descriptions of the child's behavior to have some specificity as opposed to the more global, diffuse descriptions characteristic of stressed-out parents. In behavioral research, this would be referred to as an "operational definition" of the target behavior. It's easier to work toward the specific goal of "He gets his shoes on" than the less clear objective of "He is aware of the time," especially if the child is a five-year-old such as Mycroft. One can always string small, specific objectives into longer chains that would get Mycroft or Wyatt up, fed, dressed, and out the door.

Second, and also related to specificity, MAPs should address near-time or *proximal* behavioral objectives over more distal outcomes. Rather than state "Wyatt will get to school," "Grace will be a good student," or "Brayden will learn to relax," the MAP would instead call for Wyatt to "get out of bed," Grace to "start her homework right away," or Brayden to "take three mindful breaths." Again, one proximal goal is linked to another to form a chain that leads off into the future.

Finally, MAPs should focus on promoting positive behaviors rather than attempting to prevent negative behaviors. Children are far more likely to comply with "do commands" than "don't commands," and most parents, by the time they come in to see you, are tired of hearing themselves nag and admonish. So, again, Wyatt would "get out of bed in a timely manner" (with "timely" being explicitly defined), instead of "He'd stop defying me." Grace would start her work right away, instead of "She'd stop procrastinating," and Brayden would take those breaths rather than "avoid becoming hysterical."

The clinician develops these MAPs with the parents and with the child, if she is mature enough to be a helpful contributor. The plan can be drawn out on the whiteboard, on paper, or on a computer screen. A copy goes home with the family. A very simplified example of going over a MAP might look like this:

CLINICIAN: Okay, the goal is to get homework started right away and to keep it moving so that Grace can get it done and have time for fun things. We know that all kinds of ideas and feelings will show up when she sits down to do her homework. Some of these ideas will be to make her paper even with the edge of the table, to arrange her pencils in patterns, and other things to make her feel more comfortable. So, the plan is that Grace will bring only one pencil to the table. She'll let the paper be a little crooked if that's the way it is sometimes. Mom will be nearby doing her needlepoint in case Grace needs her, but Mom won't be sitting with Grace. Grace will ask Mom for help is she doesn't know how to do something. Have I missed anything?

Practice, Practice, Practice

It will be important not to just talk about the plan but also to practice it in session. The child can participate if she is present, or you can role-play with the parents, with one of them taking the part of the child. This can be a minor exposure exercise in itself, as it will elicit some of the important problematic thoughts and feelings but under more controlled conditions and without some of the contextual factors or setting events (the annoying little brother, fatigue, medications wearing off) that might complicate the actual situation. Of, course, these factors and setting events would be discussed and anticipated.

Additionally, when parents and their children practice these MAPs and other new behavior patterns in your office, it can accomplish three important things. First, it can help everyone work out the details of the plan through brainstorming—throwing out ideas and "trying on" the behaviors each one will be expected to perform. Second, you and the family can anticipate potential difficulties that might show up when trying to implement the MAP out in the world. Similarly, you can consider variations or exceptions to the basic plan given various nuanced conditions the family will encounter. Finally, with rehearsal, the new behaviors will come to feel more comfortable, natural, and automatic.

In addition to actual in vivo exposure episodes out in the world between therapy sessions, families can and should rehearse the MAP behaviors at neutral times, when there isn't the burden of anxious and fearful thoughts and feelings. This would be something in between imaginal and in vivo exposure, as it would bring up the anxious topic and some of the associated private events but outside of the common contextual cues and activators—e.g., it's not 7:00 on a school morning, the annoying little brother is not present, you're not all actually getting on the airplane. A few quick booster practices during the week, for just a few minutes, will help consolidate the learning that took place in session and will allow the family to continue adjusting the MAPs as necessary.

Brayden: Randomizing the Compulsions

A twist on your basic exposure exercise is to randomize the anxious behavior. This can work well with compulsive and other "rule-governed" behaviors. Your approach is "Let's try something you might find a little odd." The stance is one of a playful experiment in which neither the child nor the parents can fail. Here's what this might look like for Salma and her son, Brayden:

CLINICIAN: Here's what I'm thinking. We need to really shake up this routine, but in a way that might even be a little fun. (*hands Salma a pair of dice*) You and Brayden each get a die [as in one half of a pair of dice]. Keep your die with you at all times. The deal is this: When Brayden feels the urge to say something more than once, he will roll his die and whatever number comes up, one through six, he will say what he's going to say that number of times—no more, no less. When he has the idea that you must repeat what he's saying or repeat yourself and "requests" this of you, you will roll your die and that is the number of times you will say whatever it is Brayden wants you to say—no more, no less, regardless of how many times Brayden repeats himself. Similarly, when Brayden has the idea that he needs to pick a certain shirt and not any other, then he rolls the die. If three dots come up, he picks the third shirt, counting left to right. If the five comes up, he picks shirt number five.

SALMA: So we could repeat something six times! Okay, repeat it five times. That's more than we're doing it now.

CLINICIAN: Sometimes, yes, you'll be doing something one or two times more than is typical now. But there will also be times when you'll only repeat something once or twice. The point is, you're already devoting time to this ritual. Rather than forbid it altogether, which Brayden won't go for and wouldn't really teach him anything, we can start to undermine these iron-clad connections between Brayden's ideas and his actions. We call these *compulsions*. We also call this process "thought-action *fusion*": if I think *this*, I must do *that*. When thoughts, feelings, and actions are fused, there's no flexibility, no adaptability, no choice. *Defusion* is the process of breaking up the old unhelpful connections so that new and more adaptive connections can be made. This is hard because these are old mental habits, so we try things that are maybe a little playful or that take away the overthinking that often goes along with anxiety.

SALMA: I think he'd find this interesting, but I can also imagine him refusing to do it at times.

CLINICIAN: Well, if he refuses, you shrug and say, "Well, that's your choice." But the message is clear that it's now *his choice* to repeat himself and not something he has no control over. Just don't make a big deal out of it. Keep it relaxed. Don't get into a power struggle over it. And it's important that you keep your end of the deal by rolling your die, regardless of what he chooses to do.

ENCOURAGING COURAGE WITH REWARD PROGRAMS

I don't often recommend star charts and other formal reward programs—not because they don't work (they do), but because they all seem to have a life expectancy of about ten days. But a reward program can be a helpful component of exposure therapy, or it can be a stand-alone entity to support behavior change. We hope that the "natural and logical" consequences of living a vital and engaged life will provide sufficient feedback and reinforcement to maintain the courageous behaviors therapy promotes. However, in the real world, we might not be able to count on naturally occurring rewards to be frequent enough, consistent enough, or powerful enough to overcome what may be years of habit and a compelling and entrenched set of anxious thoughts and feelings.

So, the basic idea is to create some short-term rewards in situations where natural reinforcers may be weak or lacking. However, parents must be prepared to put in the necessary work to sustain the program and keep it fresh and responsive. Of course, now that every six-year-old seems to have a smartphone, parents can enlist the help of one of dozens of apps that create and track point programs and chore schedules. Reviews of these apps and their programs can be found on sites such as www.appcrawlr.com, among others.

Parents may resist reward programs for a variety of reasons. A common objection is voiced here by Wyatt's father, Dan:

CLINICIAN: I'm wondering if we're going to need to sweeten the deal for Wyatt by providing some incentives for his cooperation with the plan.

DAN: You mean *bribing* him? I don't think kids should be given a reward for doing what they're supposed to do in the first place. It's not how I was raised.

CLINICIAN: It sounds like, from everything you've told me, you were much more self-motivated as a child than Wyatt appears to be at this time. My concern is that he's in such a negative and stuck place right now that without some external motivators—some positive, short-term, external motivators—he's just going to remain stuck.

Reward programs can be exceedingly simple and naturalistic. In fact, parents do these simple and elegant "programs" every day when the use "when-then" or "if-then" statements. For example, Elena will tell Mycroft, "*When* you get dressed, including socks and shoes, *then* you can watch a twenty-minute video." If Mycroft doesn't get dressed within the time frame allowed by the whole of the morning routine, then he must leave for school without the video. Similarly, *if* Grace can get through the bedtime routine in a timely manner, *then* there will be time for a story. These are very natural and logical consequences. The idea is to focus the child's attention on a valued goal and on the process that will attain that goal. This shift in attention will happen at the "expense" of the child's focusing on anxious thoughts and feelings and subsequent urges for avoidance or control.

If the parent is going to go beyond simple *when-then* contingencies and do a more formal reward program, a considerable amount of discussion and planning is required to set it up for success. A number of ideas for creating and troubleshooting reward programs for anxious children can be found in Chorpita (2007). I have, over the years, identified several important components of creating and maintaining reward programs:

- Identify the positive, courageous behaviors that will earn the rewards. Think back to the functional analysis: Under the exact same provocative activator conditions, what do we want and expect the child to do? Those one or two key behaviors are the ones to call out and reinforce.
- Remember to make the expected behavior specific, proximal, and doable for the child *at the time the program is launched.* The child must be able to obtain some stickers or points *right away,* or she will not be motivated to continue. That means starting with *any* behaviors that could be helpful positive opposites, including the child's simply *not doing* the problem behavior.

Also, start with very short time frames: For some children, even a few seconds of cooperation, calmness, eye contact, or whatever should be jumped on quickly, acknowledged, and rewarded. This is a lot of work. This is why these programs are so hard to pull off.

- For some young children, simply earning stickers or stars on a chart is reinforcing. Older children will need something a little more tangible or valuable to them. Develop a list or "menu" of possible rewards that can be earned through the accumulation of points or stickers on a chart or marbles in a jar, and so on. In behavior therapy terms, these ultimate rewards are called *terminal reinforcers*. These need not be, nor should they be, grand (such as a new game console or a pony). Instead, make the rewards simple, inexpensive, and easily and quickly deliverable. In the long run, it's not the size of the reward that matters. What matters is the certainty and immediacy of the reward, along with parental praise and recognition of a job well done.

- Build in some choice. If there is only one reward, such as picking the video you'll watch on Friday evening, there is a danger that this one reward will lose its reinforcing power after a while. Having a menu of small rewards to choose from will keep the program "fresh," even if the child always picks the same reward.

- Create a "dense" reinforcement schedule at the beginning of the program. There should be ample opportunity for the child to attain stickers and points and larger rewards as soon as possible to avoid frustration and discouragement. One can always *slowly* increase the criteria for attaining the reward. It is easy to move too quickly here, especially since the child's behavior will likely be inconsistent from day to day. A common mistake is to celebrate a day of great behavior and then have that become the new bar the child has to clear *every* day. I remind parents that few of us are always at our best.

- The younger the child, the shorter the time frame between behavior and reward.

- The child needn't have perfect behavior in order to obtain the reward. Most effective reward programs set the criteria for obtaining the reward at about 70 to 80 percent of the maximum attainable "points" (stickers, rewards, and so on) during the time period specified—typically a week for school-age children. That way, if Wyatt has a tough Tuesday, all is not lost; he still has the chance to pull it together and finish the rest of the week strong.

- I like to avoid programs that cause a child to lose points. I would rather instead have the child simply not earn points.

- If there are siblings, there will be accusations of unfairness, even if the parent scrupulously maintains an even and consistent hand in doling out stickers and rewards. You and the parents will want to be proactive about this. The parents, perhaps with your assistance, may want to explain the program to the siblings in terms of helping or encouraging their brother or sister while he or she is learning some new skills.

- If there are siblings old enough to care about it, it may be best to create a program that covers all the children in the family in some way. By identifying process goals such as "cooperation" or "doing what you promised," parents can avoid child-specific content and not single out any particular family member's issues.

- One reason that reward programs wither and die is that the parents become forgetful and complacent: Target behaviors aren't being noticed, stars and points aren't being awarded, terminal reinforcers aren't being delivered. So, make it as simple a program as will do the job. It's better to identify one or two behaviors to focus on and develop a simple tracking system than it is to create an elaborate system that collapses under its own weight.

- Another way to keep reward programs going is to institute a subprogram I call "Reward the Rewarder." In families where there is more than one parent, I will ask each parent to be alert for the other parent's "reward program maintenance behavior." So, if the child's positive behavior is being called out and celebrated—points or stars are registered, rewards are dispensed, and so on—the parent who observes all this gives points or stickers to the parent who is doing the work of the program. The parents can have their own menu of terminal reinforcers; foot rubs seem to be a popular item.

For Mycroft, a simple reward program might be stickers placed on a sheet of paper for each step in his morning routine. Again, a "when-then" contingency can also be used to keep him moving along. Grace may respond well to marbles in a jar that can be turned in at the end of the week for arts and crafts supplies, which she enjoys. For Wyatt, there might be a list of daily "expectations," such as "getting out of bed within ten minutes of the alarm going off," with each expected behavior leading inexorably to heading out the door to school. With each successful step in the overall morning process, points are accrued. These points can be traded for privileges such as screen time.

Please note: These have been the briefest, most cursory descriptions of reward programs. The devil, as they say, is in the details. Again, these programs die an early death if they are not given a lot of attention before they're even launched and given continued attention and maintenance on an ongoing basis.

A LOOK AHEAD

In this chapter I've described some classic, as well as innovative, cognitive behavioral therapy strategies for anxious children and how parents might be engaged in the process as co-therapists. These strategies, such as exposure/response prevention, have enjoyed great success over the past fifty years. And yet, as I will describe in the next chapter, there are limitations to what traditional CBT can do for the anxious child, in both the short term and the long term.

In recognition of these limitations, and in response to the need for new and effective treatment modalities a new family of transdiagnostic therapies that emphasize mindfulness and acceptance has emerged in the last thirty years. In the next chapter I describe some applications of these mindfulness and acceptance strategies to parenting an anxious child.

Mindfulness, as I described in Chapter 4, allows for a more expansive, flexible, responsive set of parenting behaviors when emotions and ideas are running rampant. I will describe the use of metaphor and "playing with language" to create some cognitive reappraisal and new perspectives on old situations. We will revisit parent-child attunement in the context of mindful attention.

It will be important to emphasize to the parents you work with that *acceptance* is not passivity or resignation. In fact, acceptance of what is in the moment is a necessary condition for effectively dealing with that situation. We will also talk about the balance of *surrender* and *action*.

Summary of Key Ideas

- Do unto the parent as you would have the parent do unto the child—listen, validate, provide clear expectations, build skills, encourage courage, grant autonomy, but also articulate rules and set limits as needed.

- Validation is the first step in a new dance.

- Help parents learn to express empathy, respond with consistency, and promote the child's independence.

- Real and durable cognitive reappraisal—the shift from old, unhelpful rules to new, helpful rules—can occur only as the *result* of new experiences.

- For both parent and child, exposure therapy is not complete without getting to the new, more adaptive behaviors and making them the new normal.

- Parent involvement is vital to treatment success.

- The effective components of CBT are cognitive reappraisal, preventing emotional avoidance, and promoting courageous behavior.

- Effective exposure and subsequent corrective learning require that the fear structures be activated or "confronted" so that the habitual process of "stimulus leading to inner events leading to outward behavior" can be interrupted and eventually reconstructed into a more adaptive response to the same situations.

CHAPTER 7

Treating Anxiety in a Family Context 2: Mindfulness- and Acceptance-Based Treatments

The "gold standard" of clinical research is the randomized clinical trial, or RCT. In numerous RCTs, cognitive behavioral therapy has been shown to be efficacious. *Efficacy* means that the treatment group, compared to the control group, saw a statistically significant reduction in symptoms. Treatment *effectiveness* is a somewhat different story. *Effectiveness* is when the treatment works out in the world, with complex clients, against a range of success criteria, and not just measurable changes in anxiety symptoms. Treatment efficacy does not always translate into treatment effectiveness. At follow-up, many "treatment responders" from RCTs continue to report rather high levels of continuing anxiety and impaired functioning (Bradley, Greene, Russ, Dutra, & Weston, 2005).

For fifty-plus years, cognitive behavioral therapy has operated, with success, from a position that anxiety symptoms stem from erroneous belief systems, biased attention toward threat stimuli in the environment, underestimates of personal competence, and other thought-based processes. It is not surprising, then, that the main focus of traditional CBT is to alter these thought processes as a necessary prerequisite for feeling and acting better. This work is generally known as *cognitive restructuring*. For example, one tactic might be to challenge the likelihood of a worrisome thought (for example, "What are the chances, based on your experience, that the other kids will laugh at you when you give your book report?"). Or the person may be encouraged to "talk back" to the anxious thought ("It's going to be okay. I can do this!") in order to reduce its power and influence long enough to get up and give the book report. The expectation is that the book report presentation will go fine, the child's classmates won't laugh (unless it's meant to be funny), and he will engage in some cognitive reappraisal, as I described in the last chapter ("Book report presentations aren't so bad after all"). The next time the child must do a presentation, he will presumably have fewer anxious thoughts and feelings and less hesitation.

LIMITATIONS OF THE TRADITIONAL CBT/PARENT TRAINING MODEL

However, clinicians utilizing basic CBT have found that some conditions—the pernicious worries found in generalized anxiety disorder, for example—do not readily yield to thought-changing strategies (Roemer & Orsillo, 2005). In fact, techniques such as thought suppression ("Just don't think about *it*") can actually cause an increase in the frequency of the unwanted cognitions, specifically in the very situations in which they are unwanted and unhelpful (Wegner, 2011).

More important for our purposes, research suggests that, when it comes to problematic parent-child situations and the effectiveness of traditional parent training, treatment gains are not well maintained on follow-up (see Wahler & Dumas, 1989). With many families, this is how traditional CBT-based treatment often unfolds: There's an increased awareness of the processes at work, cognitive assumptions and rules are challenged and restructured, antecedents and consequences are changed so that behavior changes, and this new behavior pattern is recognized and reinforced with sufficient consistency to keep it rolling along. For a while.

It seems that, for change to occur within the family system, parents need to acquire new awareness and skills ("tools"). But awareness and tools by themselves appear to be necessary but not sufficient for sustained positive change. Something else is at work that erodes improved behavior over time. Wahler and Dumas (1989) suggest that this "something" is inconsistent attention to the child's actual behavior in the moment because of stressors impinging on the parent.

Traditional parent training is predicated on the assumption that it is the child's behavior that determines the parent's next move; child does X, parent responds with Y. But a parent's behavior in any given moment is influenced by a host of factors such as setting events that may be quite distant in time and space from the child's behavior in that moment. Unfortunately, factors such as marital stress, job stress, issues with a client's sibling, and financial stress, to name just a few, can act as setting events that exert considerable influence on the parent's responses (reactions) in that moment. As described in Chapter 2, stress can cause a narrowing of attention, along with a negative coloring of the situation that can lead to maladaptive responding. When the parent is stressed and slips into a narrow and negative view of the child or the situation itself ("I hate Monday mornings!"), we get those overly global and negative descriptions of the child: "He's out of control"; "She doesn't care if she's inconveniencing everyone"; "I can't reach him"; "This is impossible." The result is a description of, or story about, the child or the situation that is high on negativity but low in detail. Further, subsequent parenting behaviors will tend to be inconsistent, out-of sync with, or out of proportion to the child's behavior.

Wahler and Dumas (1989) describe this maladaptive parenting pattern as stemming from an essential "attention deficit" on the part of the parent. Rather than an actual "deficit," the phenomenon may be more accurately described as an attention *allocation* problem. To address this issue, recent therapies have begun using mindfulness strategies and emphasizing acceptance of the moment as the starting point for change. Mindful attention to what is happening in the moment, along with facilitated listening and validation, can help a parent create a new, more accepting, adaptive and flexible description of her child in the moment. From this new stance the parent is more likely to *respond* as opposed to *react* to what the child is presenting. Additionally, a mindful and accepting stance will buffer the parent from the inevitable setbacks, twists, and turns that family life will present as you move forward with the treatment plan. This will help everyone maintain reasonably consistent efforts over time and lessen the probability of discouragement and premature termination.

THE MOVEMENT TOWARD MINDFULNESS- AND ACCEPTANCE-BASED THERAPIES

The newer treatment models that emphasize mindfulness and accep- tance fit squarely within the transdiagnositc paradigm. They are very process-oriented and put less weight on symptom reduction per se, at least as the primary objective. The emphasis in treatment is on developing strategies and skills that will allow the individual to move toward valued goals, regardless of the content of his thoughts or the particular emotions, memories, and bodily sensations he is experi- encing at the moment. As a whole, compared with traditional CBT, these approaches are less concerned with changing the *content* of the thinking or with getting rid of pesky emotions as a prerequi- site to good functioning. If there is a manipulation of one's mental activity, it is more along the lines of learning to shift one's attention *away* from the negative cognitions and emotions and *toward* more helpful or at least neutral feelings, thoughts, and bodily sensations (Cowart & Ollendick, 2010). This is the shifting of attention within the anxiety dance that I described in Chapter 4. This process is one of *effortful control,* one of the so-called executive skills I described in Chapter 1. It is a conscious reallocation of attention in the service of responding to the anxious situation effectively.

This new family of psychotherapies is variously referred to as *mindfulness-based* or *acceptance-based* therapies. Here, too, there are number of good resources for clinicians working with children and parents. The edited volume by Greco and Hayes (2008) presents various so-called "third wave" treatment models (psychoanalysis being the "first" treatment wave and old-school CBT being the sec- ond), which include dialectical behavior therapy (DBT), acceptance and commitment therapy (ACT), mindfulness-based cognitive ther- apy (MBCT), and mindfulness-based stress reduction for children

(MBSR-C), an extension of Jon Kabat-Zinn's work. Other excellent resources include articles by Burke (2009) and by Duncan, Coatsworth, and Greenberg (2009). Coyne, McHugh, and Martinez (2011) as well as Murrell and Scherbarth (2011) review the extant literature on ACT with children. For a book-length, in-depth exploration of ACT generally, there is Hayes, Strosahl, and Wilson (2012). For MBCT with anxious children, there is Semple and Lee (2011). Acceptance and mindfulness books for parents can be found in Appendix E, Resources for Parents. These include Coyne and Murrell (2009), Harvey & Penzo (2009), Kastner (2013), and McCurry (2009).

Mindfulness- and acceptance-based treatment models provide theoretical perspectives as well as intervention strategies and techniques derived from theory. In practice, acceptance and mindfulness techniques are typically combined with other, more traditional child treatment interventions such as contingency management (manipulating activators and consequences—e.g., a reward program) and skill building (e.g., social skills). Let's look at what makes mindfulness-based approaches different from traditional cognitive behavioral therapy.

THE BASICS OF MINDFULNESS-BASED TREATMENTS

Mindfulness-based therapies encompass a growing set of treatment approaches that all share an interest in increasing mindful attention to one's moment-to-moment experience. I gave you several somewhat different definitions of mindfulness in Chapter 4. Duncan and colleagues (2009) describe three core qualities of mindfulness that are relevant to our work with parents of anxious children: Mindfulness embodies (1) a present-centered attention and awareness, (2) an intentional or purposeful component to one's attention and subsequent behavior, and (3) an attitude marked by interest, curiosity, and compassion. These qualities line up nicely, in a slightly different order, with the steps I described in Chapter 4 for changing the anxiety dance: expanding awareness, shift attention, and take goal-directed action. In the context of the dance-changing step of "expanding awareness," I mentioned the practice of *mindfulness*. It's time to go a little deeper into this practice as it pertains to parents of anxious children.

MINDFUL PARENTING

Mindful parenting is a framework or template for attending to, thinking about, and responding to one's child and other aspects of the day-to-day events in the life of a parent. It can be thought of as "place" of intentional awareness of and acceptance of the child's needs, moment to moment, in those challenging situations that make up the dance. Mindfulness-based parent interventions have been shown to improve family functioning and parental satisfaction (Blackledge, & Hayes, 2006; Singh et al., 2007). See also Duncan, Coatsworth, and Greenberg (2009) and Smith and Dishion (2014) for reviews.

Describing and Teaching the Components of Mindful Parenting

As I've discussed, there are several definitions of mindfulness out there and therefore any number of descriptions of what mindfulness ought to look like and how one might find or develop it. A detailed excursion into developing mindfulness practice is beyond the scope of this chapter. I would point the interested reader in the direction of Duncan and colleagues (2009) and Smith and Dishion (2014) for more in-depth discussions of mindfulness as it relates to the parent-child relationship. These authors describe a set of skills or qualities that can be taught to parents and cultivated through practice and everyday parent-child interactions. These skills, or qualities, include listening with full attention, being aware of self and child in the moment, building healthy family relationships, compassion, and acceptance.

Listening with Full Attention

Listening with full attention is the parent's practice of *facilitated listening* that I described in Chapter 3. This kind of active listening is hard work, and it is often frustrating and discouraging for both parent and child when one or the other is only partially listening, as so often happens in our busy lives. Later in the chapter I will describe the technique of child-directed play, which is a vehicle for increasing a parent's mindful attention to the child.

As I suggested earlier, teaching parents to listen well starts with *our listening to them* and encouraging clear, specific, and accurate narratives. We want to emphasize to parents that good listening is not just a matter of accurately hearing the specific and detailed content of what the child is talking about. It should include an awareness of the child's tone, body language, and other "nonverbals" that contain important information about what it going on with the child at any given time. This attention to the *whole child* is the lead-in to full awareness of the child in the moment. Parents may need some prompting to expand their awareness to include important pieces of the situation:

CLINICIAN: When Grace was telling you about presenting her artwork in front of the class and how angry she was at the other students for talking, what could you tell from her facial expressions or her body language?

HOLLY: I remember thinking how angry her face looked but also how sad she seemed at the same time. Something about her eyes looked so sad.

CLINICIAN: And I can hear the sadness in your voice as you describe it. How did seeing that sadness in Grace affect what you did next?

HOLLY: Well, I tried to be evenhanded about it. I was still angry about getting yet another email from her teacher. I told her I was disappointed that she threw her art project at her classmates and that we needed to come up with some better ways of handling nervousness and frustration. I also told her that I could tell that she was feeling sad about it, too. But afterward, I thought about how I could have acknowledged that sadness more; maybe I could have just held her for a few minutes before going into lecture mode. She just looked so small and sad.

Being Aware of Self and Child in the Moment

As the example of Grace and Holly illustrates, listening to the whole child, and not just the child's words, can provide a more expansive awareness of what is going on in terms of the child's thoughts, emotions, needs, and desires in that moment. This can be important when the *outward* message, contained in the child's behavior, is confusing or off-putting—for example, defiance that is covering up fear.

Being mindfully aware of *the other* helps us to be mindfully aware of *ourselves*. To the extent that the parent can be attentive to her own strong emotions and compelling ideas in the moment, she can hold these inner events "lightly" and not allow them to easily trigger old and unhelpful reaction patterns. The thoughts ("I don't need this right now") and the feelings (frustration and discouragement) are still present, still experienced, but their power to influence the parent's decisions can be reduced.

I sometimes describe the process of mindful parenting and the responses that flow from it as "parental aikido": smoothly, not always calmly, meeting the child's behavior and emotional state with a supple stance and redirecting that behavior toward a better outcome. The core component of mindful parenting is managing situations with awareness or attention to the full range of important elements in the situation and not just the narrowed attention (the "tube") that can happen when we become overwhelmed and desperate to find a solution *now*.

Building Healthy Family Relationships

What distinguishes mindful parenting from more common definitions and applications of mindfulness is that here the parent is mindful of the ongoing processes that make up the parent-child *relationship:* what is going on not just for the parent in moment, or just for the child, but for the parent and child as a dynamic system. This is an appreciation that the whole is greater than the sum of its parts and that the situation succeeds or fails in terms of how *both* parent and child fare. So, this is a metacognitive or *mentalizing* task for the parent. This can be a challenge when a parent feels stressed, is under attack, or carries deficits related to less-than-ideal attunement with her own parents. A parent can find herself in "survival mode," just trying to get through the moment—get out the door and to school and work, get the homework done, get in the damn pool for the swimming lesson.

Recall that it's the negative reinforcement paradigm that is behind the establishment and maintenance of these problematic parent-child dances marked by avoidance and control. Mindful parenting is the antidote to this coercive cycle by allowing the parent's attention, and eventually the child's, to consider other goals besides escape— for example, actual problem solving, if this is possible, or coping and adapting if the situation is not a solvable problem. In short, mindful parenting supports *responding* over reacting.

Mindful parenting expands the agenda to include the possibilities of a teachable moment, an "opportunity" in the midst of chaos and anguish for some increased self-awareness, improved communication, coping, or problem solving; whatever the situation calls for. As a parent it's easy to think, "I'll deal with all that when things have calmed down." But when, exactly, is that going to be in the life of a family? Parenting is like the arcade game Whack-a-Mole: a constant, relentless whacking at issues, problems, and conditions that pop up and demand our attention and action, one then another. The time for relationship building through communication and mutual understanding/support is always *now:*

CLINICIAN: So I'm imagining the situation. You're coming home with all the kids after school. Everyone comes crashing through the door. The kids immediately begin demanding your attention for snacks, permission to go over to a friend's house, and so on. You check your phone and there's the email from the teacher telling you in ominous tones about Grace's latest transgression. Grace is standing there watching you. What happens next?

HOLLY (*laughs*): Ideally or in reality?

CLINICIAN: If it were your choice.

HOLLY: If it were my choice? Well, I suppose in reality it is my choice. It just doesn't often feel that way. Okay, I would go to Grace, give her a hug, and say something like "I guess it was a tough day at school today. Let's get a snack and then you can tell about it." I would try and strike that balance between letting her know I love and support her and, as you always say, letting her know that there are rules we expect her to follow, regardless how upset she might be at the time.

ACCEPTANCE-BASED TREATMENTS

Acceptance-based therapies, as the name implies, would suggest that by "making room" for even our most challenging thoughts, judgments, feelings, and urges, we can step back and create more flexibility, more choice about what action to take in the presence of those thoughts and feelings. The distinction between acceptance-based and mindfulness-based therapies is almost nonexistent. Acceptance-based therapies simply articulate the importance of *acceptance* in their theory, strategies, and tactics. Prominent among these therapies are dialectical behavior therapy (DBT) and acceptance and commitment therapy (ACT, pronounced as the word *act*, not the letters *A-C-T*). Both DBT and ACT have small but growing cadres of clinicians who apply these therapies to children and parents. Like all transdiagnostic treatment modalities, acceptance-based treatments are less concerned with reducing or eliminating symptoms than they are with encouraging new and more useful and flexible behavior patterns.

Acceptance: What It Is, and What It Isn't

In Hindu mythology, there is a bird called Hamsa. She is sometimes depicted as a swan, sometimes as a goose. Like all birds, Hamsa has two wings. In the stories of Hamsa, one wing is described as, or embodies, "surrender" and the other wing as "action." The idea is that you need both in order to fly; effective action is predicated on a certain "surrender to" or "acceptance of" one's reality in the moment. The opposite of acceptance is unhealthy denial or self-delusion.

Surrender without action is passivity. Acceptance, as it is defined in these therapies and as I touched upon in Chapter 4, is neither passivity nor resignation. It is not "putting up with" or allowing an unhealthy situation to continue or injustices to be tolerated. One would not accept an abusive relationship in the sense of "agreeing or consenting to" it, a common definition of "acceptance." On the other hand, one would have to accept the *fact* that one was in an abusive relationship as a necessary first step in effectively dealing with that situation. A more mundane example is my needing to accept the fact that it's raining—however disappointed I may be in that fact—in order to dress properly before I leave the house.

Acceptance, as defined in these therapies, is not liking or approving of or wanting a particular situation. It is a clear-eyed "voluntary adoption of an intentionally open, receptive, flexible, and nonjudgmental posture with respect to moment-to-moment experience" (Hayes, Strosahl, & Wilson, 2012, p. 272). As in the definitions of mindfulness I presented in Chapter 4, I struggle with these "nonjudgmental" components. If I am being judgmental, *and* I'm clear about that and can step back a bit from those judging thoughts, I'm okay and can likely make a decent decision in the next few seconds. These states of mindfulness and acceptance need to be obtainable by us mortals.

Recall my distinction between *problems* and *conditions*. The rain I discover upon waking is a *condition*. I should probably accept this obvious fact and cope effectively, such as driving carefully. To do otherwise would be unhelpful or not in line with one or more valued goals, such as avoiding a traffic accident. By the same token, I must accept the unavoidable fact that my tooth hurts whenever I drink something cold in order to make an appointment to see my dentist and get this *problem* fixed, lest it become a more painful and expensive problem.

It is a great challenge for parents of anxious children to get their head around this idea of "accepting" their child's (and their own) distressing emotions and thoughts. After all, they are coming to you with the clear expectation that you will help rid them of these very experiences. Parents hope and expect that you will help *change* things, not maintain the status quo. But acceptance and mindfulness are in fact *not* the status quo if the old patterns are marked by unawareness and struggle with what is in the moment. Mindfulness and acceptance are necessary components of changing the barely conscious, habitual process, because they make real choice possible. You can only get there from here. And given the choice, most parents would choose communication, cooperation, coping, and mutual support in their most important relationships.

So, some work must go into describing these sometimes subtle distinctions between acceptance that leads to action and mere resignation. Here's one possible scenario:

> SARA: So, you're saying I should just accept the fact that my child is anxious all the time and can't go to school and I should just allow him to suffer.
>
> CLINICIAN: If that's what you're hearing me say, then I clearly haven't explained my ideas adequately. Let me take another run at this. You've said three important things. First, yes, Wyatt is *often* anxious, *in certain situations,* such as getting ready to go to school. Realistically, these situations may continue to provoke anxiety in Wyatt for some time to come. Avoiding going to school is the problem. That avoidance is what's interfering with his living a vital life now and what will hurt his future. By *accepting,* I mean we *acknowledge* that anxiety; it is a reality here and now that can't and shouldn't be ignored. You've described your own frustration when others didn't acknowledge your anxiety in the past and when others *seem* to minimize Wyatt's distress in the understandable interest of moving toward action [*a clear reference to Dan*]. *This kind* of acceptance just means we agree that something we don't like is a reality and it's a starting place. We certainly don't like it and we're not going cave to it. Can we agree on that?

SARA (*without conviction*): Okay.

CLINICIAN: Now, I'm *curious* about this second piece—the *idea* that Wyatt can't go to school when he's feeling anxious. Clearly, he doesn't *want* to go and anxiety is part of, an overwhelming part of, his thinking about school. I'd like to spend some time sorting this out and seeing if there aren't other ideas about school that may be part of his *choosing* to avoid school as a way of protecting himself. Right now anxiety is just this giant blob of strongly felt but barely conscious *stuff* that has taken away everyone's power. I'd like to see if we can sort things out, clarify and name some experiences, see what's influencing what, *and see where the choices really lie.*

SARA: What was the third thing?

CLINICIAN: The idea that *we're* just going to allow Wyatt to suffer. He's suffering now, and you along with him, every day. I can't imagine this is fun for Dan either. No, we're all about relieving suffering, when and where we can. It's just that sometimes, if we're going to reach an important goal, there may be some pain along the way. The pain is avoided only at the cost of not getting to our goals. And pain is different from suffering. Suffering is what happens when we get stuck in our pain, struggle with it, think all kinds of thoughts about how unfair it is, and so on. We compound our misery, *and* we don't get to our goals. That's the real tragedy. I'm not saying we go around looking for pain. I'm saying we need to focus on valuable goals and accept that getting there won't always be pain free.

SARA: I just want him to be happy. I want to be happy. Why can't we just be happy?

CLINICIAN: You all deserve as much happiness as possible. And the current setup is clearly not getting you there.

SARA: Some days Wyatt and I really connect and he's sweet and loving and cooperative. I think, "Why can't it be like this all the time?" Then the next day nothing seems to work. It's like I can't do anything right. I just watch myself do everything wrong and I don't know why. Some days we just seem so out of sync.

CHILD-DIRECTED PLAY: TUNING UP ATTUNEMENT

Again, we need strategies for helping parents increase their mindful attention to the child in the moment, over and above the (at times) unhelpful influence of more distal factors or setting events. One of the most effective techniques for increasing parental mindful attention is child-directed play (CDP). The goal here is to strengthen and transform the parent-child relationship through CDP's provision of the parent's mindful attention, unconditional positive regard, and increased parent-child attunement. Attunement means that the relationship is bidirectionally sensitive and responsive.

Clinicians over the years have developed a number of variations of this basic intervention strategy. Child-directed play has been called *floor time* when working with children on the autism spectrum (Greenspan & Wieder, 2006) or *child's game* from the work of Rex Forehand with parents of noncompliant children (McMahon & Forehand, 2003). Many clinicians are familiar with parent-child interaction therapy (PCIT; McNeil & Hembree-Kigin, 2010). When done as an in-session parent-training tool, PCIT typically involves the clinician positioned behind the one-way mirror giving the parent moment-to-moment input through a microphone and "bug in the ear" setup. A recent book-length treatment of mindfulness-based parent-child play therapy can be found in Higgins-Klein (2013).

The goal of PCIT and similar play therapies is to train parental attention to the child in the moment, which is expected to increase the parent's sensitivity to the child's moods and behaviors. The play session itself is supposed to be an explicitly *non-goal-directed* space in which there are no real expectations for what the child is *supposed* to do. It is an exercise for the parent in simply being in the moment with her child without much in the way of an agenda or anything to avoid or control.

These variations of parent-child play therapies have a long and fruitful history in the treatment of childhood externalizing disorders such as oppositional defiant disorder (McNeil & Hembree-Kigin, 2010). Recently, this class of therapies has been applied to child anxiety (Puliafico, Comer, & Pincus, 2012). Parent-child play therapies are well suited for work with rather young children such as Mycroft or with somewhat older children (Grace, for example) who may lack some of the insight, verbal skills, attention capacities, time concepts, or perspective-taking skills necessary for utilizing the more cognitive aspects of CBT. And, to the extent that *control* is prominent in both Mycroft's and Grace's anxiety process, it could be useful to give them an appropriate outlet for this need for control.

Wyatt, too, seems to have a strong need for control in his life, but, at age ten, he might be "too old" for child-directed play. Because of its imaginative and free-form aspects, CDP seems naturally well-suited for younger children, up to about age seven or eight. Beyond this age, most children start moving from "play" to "games," where their activities become more structured, more competitive, and more goal oriented. However, given the opportunity, many older children will engage in "younger" play, as long as their friends or siblings aren't watching. This "allowable" regression can be an opportunity for an older child to revisit some old, favorite play activities and experience the warmth and intimacy that have perhaps been missing and missed in recent years.

But CDP can be modified for older children. For example, it's still possible to engage in the key elements of CDP (mindful attention, conveying unconditional positive regard, attunement) while engaged in a light turn-taking game, drawing/coloring, or some other activity that the parent and child can do together and that encourages interaction and opportunities to be in sync. Watching the child play a video game or playing a highly competitive game of H-O-R-S-E should probably be avoided. But even a walk through the neighborhood can be an oasis of connection and attunement through shared experiences of simple sights and sounds, without a lot of discussion, demands, or expectations.

Child-Directed Play in Clinical Practice

Few clinicians outside of university and hospital settings have access to observation rooms connected to treatment rooms by one-way mirrors and equipped with bug-in-the-ear technology. The child-directed play program I use is described in Appendix C in the form of a handout for parents. It is meant to be done at home, although I will often model the basic elements by playing with the child in the therapy room with the parent present.

The basic idea, as I describe it to parents, is that the attunement process between infants and their parents is invariably flawed, regardless of how present and engaged the parent might have been during that critical early developmental period. Attachment is simply too complex and too much an essentially human process to unfold without some residual kinks, rough spots, and lacunae. CDP is an opportunity to fill in some of those gaps, smooth out the rough patches, and reacquaint both parent and child with how subtle and mutually satisfying their relationship can be.

Child-directed play accomplishes at least four things. First, it sends the message to the child that the parent is so exquisitely attuned and sensitive to the child that the child's "message," delivered through ongoing behavior, will surely and reliably be received by the parent. When the child has the confidence that his message will be received, he can start off with a subtle message. A subtle message means less physicality and more use of effective and nuanced language. It means having the patience to wait for the parent's less-than-instantaneous response and to be flexible when it is not the exact response he was expecting. If, however, a child is in doubt that his message is going to be received by the parent, he will likely come out with guns blazing, just to be sure.

A second goal of CDP is to allow the child to be "in control" of the parent for some fifteen or twenty minutes, reliably two or three times a week. Some programs prescribe daily CDP, for up to an hour. I find this logistically impossible for most families. It is also probably unnecessary. In my experience, two to three CDP sessions per week is a doable and effective regimen. Having it occur as regularly as possible, for example Tuesday and Thursday evenings from 7:00 to 7:15, increases the effectiveness of a limited quantity of CDP, because it becomes a predictable and expected part of the child's life. He is then never more than two or three days from another "dose" of CDP.

Obviously, the child is not *entirely* in control; Mycroft won't get to choose to play with power tools. There will be a few basic rules about safety, treating each other and the toys gently and with respect, time limits, and so forth. But this regular opportunity to control or direct the parent makes *seizing* control of the parent and various life situations less urgent and necessary between play episodes. It should be pointed out that children rarely misbehave during CDP.

A third goal or by-product of child-directed play is the pumping up of the child's self-esteem and sense of self-worth from basking in the parent's mindful attention. The child is regularly given the clear and multilayered message that, at least for those fifteen minutes, "You are the center of the universe, powerful and good, *just because you exist.*" These were things the very young child (each of us) used to take for granted before reality stepped in—in the form of a younger sibling, preschool or kindergarten challenges, and the terrible all-or-none "failures" that invite us to believe that *we* are a failure and therefore unlovable, now and forever.

Finally, it is not just sending the message that the parent is well in tune with the child; the parent *will* become more in tune, more sensitive and able to see the child as he is, and not just his surface behavior in the moment filtered through the parent's transient moods and ideas. This increased attunement and sensitivity will permeate the parent-child interactions beyond the confines of these periods of CDP. As an antidote to the influence of setting events, as described by Wahler and Dumas (1989), CDP will bring parent behavior more in sync with, or "under the control" of, the child's behavior in the moment and less under the control of the parent's moods, stressors, and old, unhelpful rules.

Child-Directed Play with Multiple Caregivers

I'm not aware of any research that has looked at how child-directed play differs between parents when there is more than one parent. My own feeling is that each caregiver deserves good attunement with the child. So, when there is more than one parent or major caregiver, I suggest that each get the chance to engage in CDP on a regular basis. This doesn't mean rigid turn taking, but rather that the parents/caregivers create the opportunity to spread the attunement around. Nor does it mean that six or seven adults will be doing CDP with the child on a regular basis. That would likely dilute the positive effect for any one of the caregivers. So, for Grace, both Holly and Alistair would be invited to participate in CDP—still one-on-one, of course. For Mycroft, I would suggest that his nanny also participate in some CDP.

Child-directed play may be thought of as a proactive or prophylactic strategy that provides a foundation of attunement and sensitivity that will support the parent and child when the relationship becomes strained. Other mindfulness strategies can target specific thoughts and feelings that habitually show up and threaten to be disruptive. One class of techniques encourages the child, and parent, to step back from his or her thoughts and feelings and regard them in a new light or context. One example of such technique follows; it asks the child to consider the tenuous connection between word sounds and word meanings.

MINDFULLY UNDERMINING THE LITERALITY OF WORDS

Recall that very young children, or any of us when stressed and regressed, can forget that thoughts are merely ideas and instead believe them to be actual facts. This phenomenon is sometimes called "literality": the idea that thoughts are invariant and accurate representations of reality. When Grace hears, for example, someone say "spider," or if she thinks this word, her old programming ignites the fight-or-flight response, and it is as if there were an actual spider present—and not just present, but threatening her.

Mindfulness therapies often play with language in order to diminish the literal quality or to change the functional properties of thoughts. There is the nearly 100-year-old exercise of saying a word such as "milk" over and over until it becomes a repetitive, meaningless string of sounds: milk, milk, milk, milk, milk . . . (Tichener, 1916).

Similarly a mild form of exposure, or an initial step in the exposure hierarchy, is to simply speak the fearful word aloud: "spider."

An extension of this technique is to further explore the "mere sound" aspect of words by going to dictionary.com or some other online translation program and seeing (hearing) how that fearful word or idea sounds in another language. With my clients, I demonstrate this on the computer in my office and give the parent and child a "homework" assignment: Together, they are to further explore these translations at home and come in next session with the strangest sounding words and phrases they can find. In some languages, such as Hindi or Arabic with completely different writing, it's difficult for a Westerner to even discern that something is a word, let alone pronounce it.

So, for Grace's "spider" and Wyatt's thought "I can't go to school" we have:

English	Spider	I can't go to school.
Portuguese	Aranha	Não posso ir à escola
French	Araignée	Je ne peux pas aller à l'école.
Swahili	Buibui	Siwezi kwenda shule.
Icelandic	Kongulo	Ég get ekki farið í skóla.

The exercise of looking up the translations necessarily involves contact with (exposure to) the dreaded word ("spider") or an ("I can't go to school"). This helps desensitize the child to the anxiety-provoking properties of the stimulus. Further, this exercise provides an opportunity for the parent and child to talk about these words and the ideas they contain in the abstract, to be curious about them, wonder about them, and even laugh a little. This becomes a mindful new take on an old experience. It is what both Dumas and Langer talk about when they define mindfulness as "stepping back from unproductive ways of coping" and "finding differences among things thought similar and similarities among things thought different," respectively. After looking up some of these words and phrases, the clinician would have a discussion with the child and parent about how to use this new information. For example:

CLINICIAN: So, if someone came up to you and said, "Buibui," would you become afraid?

GRACE: No, it sounds funny.

CLINICIAN: Yes, for you and me, it's just funny sounds. But for someone who speaks Swahili, maybe in Africa, those sounds might cause them to be afraid for a little bit. And our word "spider" [*Grace shudders*] would just be funny sounds to them. Their brains wouldn't have the same reaction your brain has *at first*.

HOLLY: Your little cousin is coming over this weekend. Maybe we can teach her "the itsy bitsy buibui went up the water spout" song.

GRACE (*laughing*): Down came the rain and washed the buibui out.

Now, will *buibui* become the new aversive stimulus through association with "spider"? Possibly, but this will depend on the context in which the new word or phrase is experienced. Is the context one of heightened fear and arousal, of imagined negative consequences? Is it one of curiosity, playfulness, and encouragement of the child's *and parent's* ability to "hold" or "sit with" some mild negative thoughts and feelings and not allow these transient inner events to dictate what happens next? In other words, who will have the power—the words or the parent and child?

NAMING AND CATALOGING THOUGHTS AND FEELINGS

A mindfulness technique found in meditation traditions is one of simply naming or "cataloging" one's thoughts and feelings as they arise. For example, Holly struggles with Grace's rigid and controlling behavior—say, around doing homework. Holly is awash in all kinds of thoughts and feelings that typically accompany these struggles. But upon inspection (mindful attention), Holly might notice that these many feelings and thoughts can be named and sorted or cataloged into a relatively few categories: "irritation," "impatience," "worry." This is very different from becoming caught up in and attached to the "reality" of *content:* "She always does this"; "Why can't she just get this started without all the fussing?"; "What's this going to be like when she's in high school?" Irritation. Impatience. Worry.

It is likely that Grace's thoughts and feelings fall into similar categories under the same conditions; it's homework time- irritation, impatience, worry. The difference is in Grace's inability to "step back" from her rigid ideas and intense feelings in the moment. With some effort, Holly can verbalize what is going on for the both of them in the moment and try for a measure of acceptance followed by redirection. "Ah, yes. Getting homework started. Lots of impatience *in the room right now.* Let's take some breaths and get everything out where we can see what's what and figure out where to begin."

Tomorrow, with a different situation, the content of Holly's, and Grace's, thoughts may be different. But recalling Ellen Langer's definition of mindfulness, seeing "similarities among things thought different" puts all these seemingly different, unique, and uniquely important events into just a few rather predictable and familiar categories. Rather than leading to despair, as one might think ("I'm so impatient. This needs to stop *now!*"), this exercise actually helps us recognize that we have so many of the same basic feelings and ideas, regardless of the shifting details, and somehow we endure and even thrive. Rather than getting caught up in the content of the moment, the parent learns to respond to provocative situations with an "Ah, more 'impatience'" and to even notice, "Wow, I'm having a lot of *impatient* feelings today. I need to just slow down."

Cataloging allows the thought or feeling to be a labeled "event," one that is predictable given a particular situation. Events are just something we experience and then they're gone. With cataloging we take a curious stepping back from our inner events (thoughts and feelings) that allows some spaciousness (think of "expand" from SOBER), flexibility, and choice.

Cataloging doesn't mean the parent won't address the situation. On the contrary, the parent will be more capable of responding effectively when she can think, "Ah, I'm having another one of those 'worrying about her future' ideas. I need to focus on what's going on now and deal with the present."

Here is an example of how a "cataloging" discussion might go with Wyatt's parents:

CLINICIAN: So, we've talked about a lot of different thoughts and feelings that routinely show up for you both and for Wyatt. I'm wondering if we could come up with some basic categories for these events, some common themes, even when the exact wording of the idea in your head or the emotions you're feeling are somewhat different each time. I'll just write down a few as we talk to help me remember. [*pulls out the whiteboard*]

DAN: Anger.

CLINICIAN (*writes it on the board*): "Okay. Anger shows up. [*and, anticipating Sara's comment, hastens to add*] Right now we're just coming up with some general categories. We'll talk more about each of these a little later.

SARA: Dan's anger is the problem.

CLINICIAN (*quickly writes "emotions are a problem" on the board*): Good, that's a common category of *ideas*. We're going to want to spend some more time on that category, but right now I'm wondering about what you described, Sara, as that sick feeling you start to get right before you go into Wyatt's room to wake him up. What label would you give that?

SARA: I don't know—probably "dread." I just dread going in there.

CLINICIAN (*writes "dread" on the board*): Dread, yes. And you can give yourself that self-validation: "Ah, the dread is here, right on time," as you approach his room. And you know that Wyatt will soon to have one of his "I can't do it" ideas. Then there are some decisions to be made. For Wyatt, it starts with "Do I get out of bed or not?" You and Sara then decide whether you're going to lean in or hang back. Hopefully, what drives everyone's decisions will have more to do with *what needs to happen* that morning and less to do with these habitual ideas and emotions that show up. It's not that emotions and thoughts aren't important; it's just that sometimes, maybe often, these inner events deflect us from taking the long view. They're too often tied to the agenda of avoiding pain in the moment, regardless of the

cost of reaching important life goals, including learning how
to manage when uncomfortable thoughts and feelings show up.

What we would want Dan and Sara to do is notice these thoughts
and feelings that habitually arise in various challenging situations
(increased awareness) and step back from them through naming and
cataloging (shift attention), so that they can perhaps make some different choices when it comes to how they will respond (goal-directed
behavior). Discussions like this one, or any of the vignettes in this
book for that matter, are obviously very brief and somewhat stylized
compared to the real thing. Both you and I know they don't always go
the way we planned.

But after a more involved discussion, I would continue to encourage Dan and Sara to look at what a new dance would look like. This
discussion would be founded on the bedrock values and goals I have
been able to establish with the parents—for example, to see their
child resilient, competent, and able to move toward his own valued
goals in spite of the challenges of the moment. This is a shift from
Sara's "I want him to be happy," but it's close enough to "I want him
to have 'tools'" to get the parents' buy-in. The conversation becomes
one of keeping our eye on the goal at the "expense" of focusing on
the discomfort. It may be useful to help the conversation along by
employing some figurative or symbolic language to bypass the verbal
rules that keep the old dance moves in place.

THE USE OF METAPHOR

Because we humans tend to believe everything we think, it is difficult to wrest attention away from our thoughts and feelings and
direct it instead toward what's *actually* going on at the moment
and what we *actually* should be doing in the service of our goals.
In other words, it is difficult to act mindfully in sync with real-time
events outside the skin rather than reacting to compelling internal
states. Additionally, logical and rational arguments often fall on the
deaf ears of highly anxious children and adults. Chief among these

commonsense strategies is *reassurance* ("It will be fine"), which is remarkably ineffective in these high-anxiety moments. Many mindfulness and acceptance treatment techniques rely less on persuasion, direct instruction, and rationality and more on generating an experience of flexibility and possibility that is more *felt* than arrived at logically.

Because of this tendency for humans, especially distressed humans, to regard their thoughts as literal and accurate representations of reality, a clinician at times needs to undermine or bypass logic and even language itself. One example is the dictionary.com exercise described earlier. Another means of getting around habitual and rigid "languaging" is through metaphor. A classic book on therapeutic metaphor for working with children is Mills and Crowley (1986). A recent book by Stoddard and Afari (2014) describes metaphor strategies from within the acceptance and commitment therapy model.

Of course, metaphors, analogies, allegories, parables, and the like have been around for millennia and have a rich tradition in storytelling both for amusement and for conveying important life information in the form of lessons or "rules to live by." But *these* rules, conveyed through action and symbolism, tend to be held not so tightly or inflexibly as some of the logical, language-based rules we develop ourselves, consciously or unconsciously, or have thrust upon us by the social world. Metaphorical "rules," because they tend to evoke very general ideas and themes, are not so tightly fused with particular situations and behavioral responses (reactions). As such, they promote flexible responding in familiar situations and suggest a course of action in new situations; a "good metaphor takes what you already know, feel, or do and maps it onto a domain where adaptive behavioral functions are missing" (Hayes et al., 2012, p. 191).

Some of the best metaphors and analogies come directly from the child's or parent's life. If a child describes the willingness to persevere and tolerate frustration in the service of his baseball team, I can make the connection to what is sometimes asked of him as a member of a family. Parents often come in with a long history of managing challenging situations at work, within their larger family networks, in their communities, and so on. Asking about times when a parent has been successful in life through willingness and distress tolerance, communication and coping, can connect that parent to her strengths and remind her that, while the content may be different, the underlying processes remain the same.

Wyatt and the Mountain Lake

With parents present, I might present the following metaphor to Wyatt as a guided-imagery exercise:

> Imagine you're in the mountains, at the shore of a lake, on a hot summer day. A short way out from the shore is a small island. It has trees and rocky places and looks interesting, like a place where pirates might bury their treasure. Maybe some other guys you know are already there. They're calling you to join them. You're curious and decide to swim out to the island and do some exploring.
>
> You step into the water. It's warm there in the shallows. You feel the soft mud under your feet. You venture further, deeper, until you're waist deep, then chest deep, and then you're swimming. The water's cold now—no longer the sun-warmed feeling from the shallows near the shore. But you want to get to that curious island, to be with your friends, so you keep swimming ahead through the chilly water, keeping the island in sight.
>
> At some point, you suddenly hit a pocket of warm water. This feels so good compared to the chilly water you've been swimming in. You pause there, treading water. You think, *Maybe I can get to the island following this warm water.* Going ahead toward the island brings you into cold water again. It now feels very cold after the warm water. So, you move to the right, but soon encounter cold water again. You retreat to the warm. So you go left, finding warm water for a few yards until, there, cold water again! So you continue to tread water, moving a bit to the right, and to the left, and maybe even going backward, trying to remain in the warmth and avoid the chilly water.

Now, this might be a fine way to spend your afternoon at the mountain lake, swimming back and forth, trying to only feel the warmth and none of the cold. But in doing this, you've abandoned your original goal, which was to get to that interesting island, to be with your friends, and perhaps have an adventure. It becomes clear at some point that a decision must be made. You think, *If I'm going to get to that island, if I'm going to meet up with my friends and see what adventures wait for me there, I'm going to have to swim through more cold water.* If you've made the choice to go to the island, then the decision is to keep swimming.

Now, Wyatt may be unimpressed with this metaphor or argue that he wasn't aware of the cold water before he headed out to swim toward the island and that this new information (the cold water) became a deal-breaker. You might reply, "That's fine. You can change your mind about some things without much of a cost. You just have to recognize when being comfortable isn't always the goal, isn't the best choice."

But the real target audience for these metaphors and ideas may be as much the parents as the child. The clinician would want to impress upon Sara and Dan that, to reach *their* goal of Wyatt getting to school, there will likely be some uncomfortable thoughts and feelings *they* will need to swim through. What allows us to push on through discomfort, what dignifies the hard work and pain, is having a valued goal to keep in front of you. In the context of that goal it is easier to know what to do on a moment-to-moment basis.

CHOICES AND DECISIONS

As a way of thinking about moving toward our goals, such as getting to the island, I find it useful to make yet another distinction between two words that are often interchangeable: *choices* and *decisions*. This is something I learned from my therapy mentor, Steve Hayes, the developer of acceptance and commitment therapy. Steve used to define a "choice" as the big idea or goal, the commitment we make that reflects our values. I choose to be married, to be "a good dad," to live a heart-healthy lifestyle, and so many other goals. With choices, in many instances, one never "arrives" at some goal; these are ongoing commitments. They are journeys rather than destinations.

On the other hand, "decisions" involve the many proximal or near-term actions that support the choice, the bigger commitment. For example, my choice to live a heart-healthy lifestyle means I make numerous daily decisions based on that choice: continuing to be a nonsmoker, getting to the gym even when I don't feel like it, leaving the bacon off the cheeseburger, and other sacrifices. The adult who is committed to her *choice* to be a good parent makes the *decision* to go and watch that soccer game on Saturday morning, in the rain, and cheer heartily. Parenting, marriage, being a good student, work, and friendships are just a few of the commitments or choices people take on that then determine many subsequent decisions.

Increasing awareness of this distinction is important, because it increases our awareness of the choices and decisions we're making. It puts us in touch with the fact that these *are* choices and decisions in the sense that they are taken on more or less freely. Yes, there are potentially dire consequences for not living a heart-healthy lifestyle, but ultimately it remains my choice. And when we make a conscious and clearly stated choice, we become more aware of these many decisions that either keep is on the path toward our goals or allow us to veer off the path.

For Wyatt, the choice could be "to get to school." The decisions flowing from that choice would include each step along the path to that goal: to get out of bed, to eat breakfast, to get dressed, to head out the door, and so on. There is no requirement "to be happy about it." Similarly, Sara and Dan would have their choices—hopefully very similar goals such as "to support Wyatt in getting to school." Their myriad decisions might involve doing things to support Wyatt's efforts: "to fix breakfast," "to give him ten-minute warnings," and so on. Their decisions may also include what *not* to do: "to refrain from nagging," "to not engage in negotiations or arguments that take everyone away from their goals," and so on.

For Brayden and his parents, one choice may be "to live without giving into compulsive ideas" or "to practice patience with others." The decisions would involve all the ways they would resist various urges to do or say unhelpful things, including acquiescing to Brayden's demands, by redirecting attention elsewhere until the urge passes, or by "playing with" the urge as in the dice "game."

I would not expect Mycroft to come up with any goals, but Elena may choose to work on the goal of taking the time to understand and validate Mycroft when he is distressed. From that goal decisions would naturally follow having to do with slowing down, really listening, and perhaps even making room for being late to work on occasion.

For some families a discussion of choices and decisions is important for clarifying and coordinating values-driven treatment goals and the expectations for how the goals are going to be met. For Freya and her family coming up with goals, choices, and decisions is their pathway out of being mired in their oppressive feelings and worries.

Freya and Family

Arditte and Joormann (2014) describe the literature on cognitive bias in child psychopathology. While the data are mixed, there are suggestions that anxiety and depression are associated with a tendency to orient to threat stimuli in the environment. Other research suggests the problem is more that, once threat is detected, it is harder to *disengage* from the negative content over time, at least in depressed adults. This would contribute to the individual becoming *stuck* in a negative mood or cognitive set.

Recall Freya, the fifteen-year-old girl with a history of anxiety and emerging depression. At the level of behavior, Freya avoids friends, schoolwork, and sometimes school altogether. She has many somatic complaints, including headaches and stomachaches that contribute to missing school. The family context includes the felt absence of her older brother who is in the army and deployed overseas. Additionally, Freya's father is recently unemployed and her mother has been self-medicating her own anxiety and depression with alcohol. Celeste, Freya's mother, is inconsistent in her transactions with her daughter. Celeste can be intrusive, using Freya as a confidante and conveying all her own concerns about her son J. J., the marriage, past regrets, and current disappointments. Celeste is also somewhat overprotective and controlling of Freya, in the past not allowing Freya to attend sleepovers at other girls' houses and conveying to her that the world is a dangerous and unpredictable place.

At other times, Celeste is distant, irritable, and dismissive of Freya's difficulties. Jack Sr. tries to maintain a positive demeanor, but the boredom and embarrassment concerning his unemployment are showing up in his own withdrawal and sad affect. Freya and father spend long hours in the evening wordlessly playing chess. This provokes some petulance in Celeste:

CELESTE: I just want to be . . . I just want Freya to be happy again. If she was happier, she would be going to school and seeing friends and we'd . . . she'd be happier. We'd all be happier. She's just not trying hard enough.

FREYA: It's not like I'm trying to be depressed. I want to be happy, too. But I get to school and everybody's *staring* at me—in the hallways, in class, at lunch. They think I'm a freak. I can't stop thinking about them staring at me and what they're thinking. Then I get sick and there's no way I can concentrate in class when my head hurts or I'm going to throw up. I can't do the work when I feel that way. You don't understand what it's like. Everything was fine. Then Margo [*Freya's best friend since grade school*] had to move to Chicago and then J. J. went away with the army. Nothing's been okay since then. Nothing's ever going to be okay. Why bother?

CLINICIAN (*before Celeste can respond*): It sounds awful, carrying around all those thoughts about what everyone else is thinking. Missing your friend and your brother so much it hurts. I'm not surprised that all that stress gets to you physically. What I'm hoping to understand is what we're going to be working toward.

Your mother mentioned being happy as a goal. I'd like to get a little more specific about the goals and come up with some ideas about how to get there from here. Celeste, you mentioned getting schoolwork done and seeing friends. Are those your goals, too, Freya?

FREYA: Sure. But mostly I want to just stop thinking.

CLINICIAN: You just want to turn off the word machine in your head in those situations. Wouldn't that be a relief? I'm guessing that it's a real challenge keeping an eye on goals like schoolwork and friends when you're feeling bad and all those thoughts are coming at you. You probably just want to curl up in a safe place and wait for the feeling and thinking to just go away.

FREYA: That's all I can do.

CLINICIAN: That's all that feels good at the time. Or at least it feels less bad. But I'm concerned that it's not getting you where you need to go. So, maybe we should spend some time thinking about what's important to you right now and what you want to be doing, even if that doesn't seem possible right now.

As I've described, a critical step in changing the anxiety dance is redirecting both child and parent behavior away from avoidance and control tactics and toward useful, goal-directed behaviors. One helpful tool for doing so with late-elementary-school-aged children and adolescents is the Valued Living Questionnaire.

Valued Living Questionnaire

The Valued Living Questionnaire (VLQ) was developed by Kelly Wilson (Wilson, 2009; Wilson, Sandoz, Kitchens, & Roberts 2010). A version of this instrument is reproduced with permission in Appendix D. It is a simple and useful means of identifying what one values in day-to-day life within various domains such as family, friendships, work/education, and so on. There are various forms of this questionnaire and clinicians have used it in a number of ways. I use a variation that ties the client's valued life domain to behavioral objectives or goals for the coming week. Another way to use the

VLQ is to ask clients what they've done in the past week or two, since the last therapy session, to manifest the valued domain. For an adolescent, this can be a good tool for organizing a discussion of values and making some commitments to manifest those values through concrete goals. Like exposure, the idea is to get the client engaged in life tasks and events so that experience provides accurate feedback about what works (engagement) and what doesn't work (avoidance).

For adults struggling with depression, clinical research supports *behavioral activation* as an important change agent (Kanter, Manos, Bowe, Baruch, Busch, & Rusch, 2010). Evidence of behavioral activation as an effective treatment arm for adolescent depression is more scant and mixed (see McCauley, Schloredt, Gudmundsen, Martell, & Dimidjian, 2011; Wallis, Roeger, Milan, Walmsley, & Allison 2012). The VLQ allows for a concrete discussion and plan for getting the client out and doing things that feel important. As with motivated action plans (MAPs), it is good to make these goals specific, proximal, and positive. Here is an example, abbreviated for the sake of space, of how the VLQ might be introduced. One could easily take an entire therapy hour discussing and completing this questionnaire.

CLINICIAN: Here's something that will help us think about what's important to you in your life. There are no right, correct, or expected answers. Everything could be a 10 or everything could be a 1. What's important to you could change from week to week, also. That's okay. And not every domain has to have a goal for the week. Let's talk about what's important to you right now and then choose a few simple goals for the coming week that would help make what's important come alive.

Freya's VLQ might look something like Figure 7.1.

CLINICIAN: Those are fine goals for the week. I'm wondering how your parents might be able to support you in getting a lamp or in getting those walks in this coming week.

CELESTE: I should be doing some of that myself. The exercise in particular. Jack, too. [*turning to Freya*] Would you mind

VALUED LIVING QUESTIONNAIRE

Importance
1–10

1. Family   _6_   Goals _Farmers' market with Mom_

                                                 Email / Skype with J. J.

2. Friends/
   Social Life   _8_   Goals _Eat lunch with Beth_

                                                 Post pictures of cat on Facebook

3. Work   _n/a_   Goals _____

                                                 _____

4. School   _4_   Goals _Desk lamp_

                                                 Get file boxes / organize school stuff

5. Recreation/Fun   _4_   Goals _Not sure_

                                                 _____

6. Spirituality   _4_   Goals _Not sure_

                                                 _____

7. Citizenship/
   Community   _4_   Goals _Not sure_

                                                 _____

8. Physical Self-care
   (diet, exercise, sleep)   _6_   Goals _Walk for 45 minutes 3 times_

                                                 _____

Figure 7.1: *Fiona's Valued Living Questionnaire*

some company on those walks, or would you rather just be by yourself?

FREYA: Could we wait and see? Sometimes I might want you or Dad to walk with me, but sometimes I might want to just be by myself. One thing we keep talking about is getting me that desk lamp for my room and maybe some file boxes to keep my school stuff in. Could we do that this week?

CELESTE: That would be fine. You know, we've been talking about eating better and the farmers' market just started up again. What if we went to the market on Thursdays after school and got some good stuff to make some dinners together?

FREYA: If you promise we won't talk about anything but food and cooking. I don't want that to be an interrogation about my life.

CELESTE (*bristles, but remains composed*): Okay, I can do that.

CLINICIAN: Good. It's a deal. Now, we've talked about how these old patterns are such strong habits and how hard they are to change. So, I'm wondering what sorts of feelings and ideas will show up when you all make steps toward these activities?

At this point, the discussion might turn to how the "old dance" might interfere with work toward achieving these goals in the coming week. For Sara and Dan, this would involve monitoring their respective habitual thoughts and feelings and doing their best to focus on responding rather than reacting. For Sara, as an example, this would be the tendency to step in and rescue Wyatt from his distress rather than encourage him to focus on his goals and push through the unpleasantness. For Dan, there would be a compassionate in-session discussion and identification of his habitual patterns: impatience and frustration leading to hopelessness leading to anger and then reacting with angry and rigid behaviors.

For Brayden and his parents, there might be a discussion of the vague compulsive urges that the repetitive behaviors hoped to alleviate. Cynical thoughts about school, teachers, and peers could be identified as unhelpful, if not untrue. The purpose in talking about goals is to recall the shifting of attention described earlier. What are we focused on—the contents of our minds or the objectives before us at this moment? Of course, if our mind is accurately telling us some-thing important, such as *The room is on fire!*, then we would heed that thought and take appropriate action. However, on examination, much of what our clients (or we ourselves, for that matter) are think-ing is disconnected from present reality and largely repetitive and unhelpful.

For Freya and her family, this would likely include sadness and worry regarding Freya's moods, J. J.'s deployment, Jack Sr.'s unem-ployment, and Celeste's inability to fix it all. Freya could identify spe-cific thoughts, such as "why bother" (*Miks vaeva näha* in Estonian) that frequently interfere with moving toward her valued goals. Some self-validation might help her see these thoughts as the habitual mental reactions they are: "Ah, the 'why bothers' are here." Similarly, physical sensations, feelings, or memories can be cataloged and set aside long enough to focus on the next steps toward goals or shifting attention toward whatever might be useful or simply neutral in the moment. Overall, Freya's family was dealing with great feelings of loss and anxiety and uncertainty about how to move forward. After this discussion, Freya's father made an interesting observation, a spontaneous metaphor of his own:

JACK SR.: You know, all this reminds me of something I used to tell Freya about playing chess. When you play a game, you're bound to lose pieces along the way. That's just the nature of the game. [*laughs*] She'd get so mad when I'd take one of her pieces. But then I'd always say . . . "

FREYA: "You have to keep playing." That would only make me madder.

JACK SR.: But you'd keep on playing. When you play chess, you often lose an important piece at some point in the game, maybe even your queen. But you don't give up. You keep playing. You adjust your strategies, play a more careful game. "Careful" isn't the right word, you don't want to be too careful. Maybe "thought-ful" is a better word. Sharper. You know you need all your wits about you, all your attention focused on the moves ahead. You can't keep dwelling on the loss. You have to stay focused on playing your best game with the pieces you have. It's funny, I haven't thought about that in a long time.

A LOOK AHEAD

In this chapter and the last, I have described some treatment strategies for child anxiety that involve the efforts of the parents: exposure/response prevention, reward programs validation and redirection, the use of metaphor to get around some of the entrenched, rule-governed thought processes, an emphasis on mindful living and values-driven action.

As I've discussed, the parent-child anxiety dance is often maintained by the negative reinforcement inherent in the process, especially the contingencies around escape and avoidance, and to a lesser extent, control. To change this pattern parents must learn to resist giving into the old habits, the old behavior patterns. At least initially, this change will be met with dismay and resistance on the part of the child. There may even be an increase in anxiety as the old rules are found to no longer apply and the benefit of the new contingencies have not yet been obtained.

Our next chapter addresses the need for parents to recognize when to *lean into* a situation and when to *hang back*. Leaning in may take the form of taking control of a situation in the service of moving life forward; Elena takes over shoe tying in the morning in order to reduce Mycroft's frustration and to get everyone out the door on time. Leaning in can also be the parent setting a limit on the child's behavior—Salma tells Brayden that being anxious is not an excuse for rudeness—or insisting that they give the "rolling the die" experiment a decent chance to help.

Hanging back is a strategic disengagement: Sara tells Wyatt it's time to get out of bed once, and then does not tell him again. Or, Holly validates Grace's frustration but does not rush in right away to solve the problem for her but instead waits to see if Grace can come up with her own ideas.

Unfortunately, as we've seen in other aspects of the overall process, what tends to drive our leaning in and hanging back is often our hot emotions and ideas in the moment or other setting events, as opposed to what the situation actually calls for.

The clinician, too, must be mindfully aware of her own states and setting events in the moment and know when to appropriately lean in and when to hang back in the course of the therapy hour.

Summary of Key Ideas

- Cognitive behavioral treatments have enjoyed great success, but there are limitations to their effectiveness.
- A new family of transdiagnostic therapies, emphasizing mindfulness and acceptance, has emerged in the last thirty years.
- Mindfulness helps parents maintain attention on the important features of the situation and avoid having their response (reactions) come under the control of moods and setting events.
- Surrender without action is passivity. Acceptance is neither passivity nor resignation.
- Instead of trying to eliminate or control parents' thoughts and feelings about their child's thoughts and feelings, we can help parents cultivate a mindful approach to parenting that will improve the dance at the level of actual behavior.
- Mindful parenting is "parental aikido": smoothly, not always calmly, meeting the child's behavior and emotional state with a supple stance and redirecting that behavior toward a better outcome.
- With choices, in many instances one never "arrives" at some goal; these are ongoing commitments. They are journeys rather than destinations. On the other hand, "decisions" involve many proximal or near-term actions that support the choice, the bigger commitment.
- Metaphor is used in mindfulness and acceptance therapies to convey important concepts in ways that are flexible and generally applicable across a range of situations and behaviors.
- Child-directed play and other strategies for developing parent-child attunement can increase the sensitivity and flexibility of the parent-child dance.

Part Three

*Sustaining the Dance—
and the Dancers*

CHAPTER 8

Learning When to Push
and When to Yield

In this chapter, I want to discuss two somewhat complementary processes that you no doubt encounter in your work with anxious children and their parents. These are the parents' need to sometimes yield and to sometimes push when their child is in the throes of anxious behavior. Put another way, there are times when parents grant autonomy and there are times when they take control.

Recall that general components of parental caregiving behavior have been linked to the development and maintenance of childhood anxiety. These are control/intrusiveness as augmenting factors and warmth/acceptance as protective factors. Parental warmth would include active listening, reflecting or validating, a calm but attentive presence, praise, and encouragement. This is an accepting stance toward what the child is thinking or feeling in the moment, while at the same time not forgetting that the situation at hand contains expectations for everyone's behavior. These behavioral expectations are in the service of valued goals that may have been forgotten in the midst of all the stressful thoughts and feelings: "Weren't we trying to get homework started before all *this* took us completely off track?"

A warm and accepting parental stance is important for creating the "holding environment" (Winnecott, 1960): a psychological as well as physical space that is both safe and open to challenge and that allows a child to experience, tolerate, and work through negative thoughts and feelings. These experiences of success contribute to the development of self-regulation skills in the face of anxiety and new, more flexible and realistic schema with which to regard and respond to anxiety-provoking situations.

The opposite of *warmth* is any parental behavior that is critical, harsh rejecting, disrespectful, dismissive, or minimizing of the child's experience. This would also include parenting behaviors of excessive control and intrusiveness, which are more or less the same thing: *Intrusiveness* is defined as high parental control or low autonomy granting. Clearly, parents need to have a lot of control over the lives of their children. But an ongoing part of the developmental process is that parents cede control and grant increasing autonomy to their children as maturity and circumstances dictate. Dressing a three-year-old is age-appropriate and often necessary. Needing to dress a neurotypical nine-year-old each morning in order to get out of the house is probably excessive. Not permitting a twelve-year-old to go to a well-known friend's house for a sleepover for fear of something abusive occurring is probably being overprotective.

The impact on the child is manifold. Harsh and dismissing parental behaviors undermine the child's growing confidence, self-esteem, and self-efficacy, all of which will interfere with good decision making, willingness, and courage. Overprotective parenting gives the child the clear message that the world is an extraordinarily dangerous place, while intrusive and overcontroling behaviors tell the child she is considered by the parent to be incapable taking care of herself (self-efficacy). The sad irony is that the parent unwittingly creates the situation he most fears: important self-efficacy experiences and skills are not acquired and the child is then especially vulnerable and at risk for harm because she lacks the skills, internal resources, and resilience to weather what life throws her way. Anxiety, for both parent and child, is perpetuated. A vital and expansive life is precluded.

In many ways *learning to let go* is the terrible heart of effectively parenting an anxious child. It is also one of the most basic and necessary parenting tasks—allowing the child the "freedom" to take risks, while both parent and child feel and work through the accompanying anxiety. The goal of therapy is to provide support and understanding to the parent so that he might feel and think all the expectable anxiety and worry that comes with granting one's child her autonomy while not letting these thoughts and feelings unnecessarily constrain the child's learning about the world and herself. It's a tricky business, and a clinician needs skill and tact to address it.

TOLERANCE: LEANING IN, HANGING BACK

Look up *tolerance* in the dictionary. You will likely find several definitions involving various ideas. There is "building up physiological resistance or unresponsiveness," as in tolerance to a parasitic organism or to a drug. We have "to allow something to be done without hindrance" as in religious tolerance. Commonly, we think of "tolerating" something as a kind of "gritting one's teeth and pushing on through," as one might tolerate a trip to the dentist. In most dictionaries, further down in the list of definitions you will find one that comes from engineering. In this context, tolerance is one of "allowable deviation," or the optimal distance between moving parts in a machine. The moving parts in your car's engine or your wristwatch were designed and manufactured to slide past each other with just the right amount of clearance or tolerance. If there is too little clearance between moving parts, they will rub together causing friction, heat, and possibly damage. If there is too much space or distance between moving parts, they may bang around. Damage may result, or perhaps you simply have a noisy and inefficient machine.

I find this last definition to be applicable to parenting. A new dance, one that replaces the habitual reactions of mutually encouraged avoidance and control, will involve the parent knowing how to create the right distance between himself and the child in any given moment. This could mean physical distance, or it could mean emotional or psychological distance.

When talking to parents about this kind of tolerance I hasten to state that I'm not talking about being *distant* or uncaring. I'm referring to a quality of one's transactions that is only partially captured by physical dimensions. I am thinking in terms of what the parent is trying to reach in those anxious moments. What I hope he is trying to achieve is some balance between offering support on the one hand and encouraging autonomy on the other: not leaning in too much and micromanaging, not leaning too far back and being disengaged. Surrender *and* action.

For example, every parent has experienced the frustration of their child trying to learn something—zipping up a jacket or tying her shoes. Under the best of circumstances, as everyone is getting ready to leave the house, a parent would hang back and let his child fumble with the jacket zipper in the service of her learning how to do it. However, we are often in a great hurry with little cushion for fumbling and practicing. The parent will feel an irresistible urge to lean in and say, "We're in a hurry; let me do that" and zip up the jacket himself.

I tell parents that it would in fact be so much easier and more efficient for us to do it all for our children; from zipping her coat to doing her chores and even her homework, and be done with the struggles associated with all these tasks. However, every parent recognizes that the child must learn to do these things herself, and that this valued achievement will involve a certain amount of fumbling, frustration, and impatience for everyone. Perhaps even some anxiety.

Tolerant parenting can involve a wide range of responses that can be categorized as leaning in, hanging back, or holding steady. It is helpful if parents can notice when they have the urge to do one of these and then notice what's driving that urge. Is it being driven by a frantic attempt to escape or change the parent's or the child's thoughts or feelings? Is it pressure to check yet another thing off the insatiable "to do" list? Or is it an orientation to what is real at that moment and to what support and direction the parent may offer his anxious child at that moment?

WHAT INFLUENCES PARENTAL TOLERANCE?

Recall my description from the last chapter of how setting events and other contextual factors can influence a parent's moment-to-moment decision making. This can be a problem if the parent's decisions regarding what to do next are "under the control" of current moods and previous events that may have little real connection to current events. This distraction or "attention deficit" on the part of the parent leads to parental dance moves that are out of sync with the child and with the needs of the present situation. This can look like a poorly tuned lean in when hanging back is actually called for, and hanging back when the parent actually needs to lean in. In short, what drives parental tolerance at times, perhaps many times, are factors that are not in sync with the actual needs of the situation or the valued goals of either parent or child. These factors can include everything from a dim but emotionally laden memory from the parent's own childhood to a current work-related stressor or an almost infinite number of other setting events:

ELENA: Mycroft just gets so frantic whenever he can't do something exactly right. There's no reasoning with him. My schedule is so tight. If a glass of juice gets spilled at breakfast, then getting it cleaned up puts us up against another time limit and there's no cushion. Then if he can't find the exact shirt he wants because it's in the laundry or the damn shoe tying business . . .

CLINICIAN: I can hear how you then can feel frantic. What makes the morning schedule so tight?

ELENA: I like to get to the office early, by 8:00, to check emails and phone messages so that I can be aware of anything that's frothing and needs my attention before the morning staff meeting at 9:00.

CLINICIAN: You're feeling pressure to be on top of things, to be prepared for whatever comes up.

ELENA: Yes, there's a lot of pressure. Most of it's self-imposed, I know. And I rarely need the whole hour to check everything. Usually there's nothing really I didn't already know about. But then I go downstairs to the lobby of my office building and get a latte and relax until I need to go upstairs closer to 8:45 when everyone else comes flying in. (*laughs*)

CLINICIAN: Sounds like those few minutes with your latte are an oasis amid the pressure and hectic pace. I can see why you can't wait to get to them.

ELENA: Sounds selfish on my part; fussing and hurrying Mycroft so that I can sit with an overpriced coffee for a few minutes.

CLINICIAN: It sounds like time well spent. You've found something that grounds you. No pun intended. Okay, maybe a little. But there is a conflict built into the process as it is currently; Mycroft's needs, work pressures, your time to collect and settle yourself before the work day truly begins, all in apparent competition for your attention and time. I'm wondering where things could shift a bit.

ELENA: I've thought of all the workarounds; shoes with Velcro closures, getting up ten minutes earlier, two of every article of clothing, checking messages from home. But the thought always shows up that a competent mother and a competent associate would be able to manage all this and there's obviously something wrong with me that I can't. There, I said it out loud.

CLINICIAN: Loud and clear. Tell me more about that thought.

ELENA: A competent person would be in control of all these situations, and clearly I'm not in control.

CLINICIAN: The idea that you're not in control is interesting, given how successful you are, from an outside perspective. But it certainly *feels* out of control and you feel compelled to try harder at control moves, the leaning in, with minimal satisfaction. I think all those ideas you mentioned—the Velcro shoes, having two favorite shirts, all that—are good ideas and are likely helpful. They won't, they can't, completely relieve you or Mycroft of all the stress of getting out of the house in the morning. But they can ease the stress by helping the routine be more efficient. But it seems to me that a great deal of your stress is coming from some ideas you have about how things ought to be, should be, and that you're failing because you can't attain these ideals. That's a burden and a distraction. It would be important to understand these thoughts and feelings better, so I'd like talk more about them.

THE MINIVAN METAPHOR

Parental thoughts in the form of "shoulds," outdated rules, self-criticisms, and so on can interfere with mindful attention to the current situation and subsequent responding. Eradicating these thoughts and accompanying emotions can be a fool's errand. Instead, parents and their children can develop the mindful habit of observing these private events and letting them pass on through awareness without having to react to them.

To help with this letting go or "stepping back," I use a variation of the classic acceptance and commitment therapy "bus metaphor" (Stoddard & Afari, 2014). It is an excellent vehicle (sorry) for exploring a parent's habitual thoughts and feelings and giving him a means for accepting their presence without letting them, personified as backseat drivers, unnecessarily influence how and where the minivan is driven. The metaphor might be conveyed this way:

> Imagine you're driving the family minivan. This is something you do every day. You're a good driver; experienced, attentive, and competent. You have your destination and you're heading there. When driving the family there are near-term goals or destinations such as "getting everyone to school and work on time." And, on a moment-to-moment basis there are many little tasks that make up "driving": steering, accelerating, braking. There are many moment-to-moment allocations of attention: the speedometer, the side mirror, drinking from your travel mug, attending to the traffic in front of you.
>
> In this metaphor for life there are other goals or destinations— for example, "to be a good and capable parent." Destination may not be the right word, because you never quite fully arrive at "being a good parent" or "being a good friend" or the like because there's always more to do and to work on. But these are valued goals that we work toward. Remember the distinction I made between "choices" and "decisions." The choice would be "being a

good parent." The decisions that go with that choice might change from one minute to the next just as moment-to-moment decisions are made while driving, all in the service of getting to your destination safely and efficiently.

However, there are "passengers" riding along with you in life's minivan, *and they can be very opinionated*. Every day from the "back seat" comes an almost constant barrage of comments, criticisms, demands, directions, threats, and just plain nonsense. All of this commentary is designed to alert you to any and all possible dangers that lie on the road ahead and to tell you, with sometimes contradictory advice, how to manage these particular situations and your driving in general. I'm wondering who some of these passengers are and what they tend to say? Let's take your work destination as an example.

When asked to consider some of one's regular "passengers" and their commentary, parents typically describe the content of old "tapes" that play whenever stress simmers: the self-doubts, the criticisms, the anxieties. Perhaps some passengers are readily identified as the parent's own parent or a critical, unsupportive individual from the past. Perhaps there's a passenger or two offering encouragement, but this is rare and often rather weak compared to the energy and determination of the critical passengers. Mostly our passengers are critical and pushy. But if we take their advice it is often at the cost of our vitality and making the most of the journey. Their advice often entails excessive avoidance or unhelpful control. Here's how the metaphor can be continued:

So, if you follow their advice or cave in to their threats you may eventually get to your destination. But what does your experience tell you? You are painfully aware of the U-turns, detours, and time spent idling at the side of the road that resulted from buying into what your various thoughts and feelings (the passengers) told you.

Now, the answer is not to try and silence or even to ignore the passengers and all their complaints and demands. Trying to *not* think something, as we've seen, only *increases* the clamoring. And you've probably discovered that you just can't kick a passenger out of the minivan; some of them have been there all your life. And threatening to "pull this minivan over" only interrupts your journey. The passengers will be vocal, although the content will change depending on where you're heading: work, parenting, taking time for yourself. But the comments and criticisms and "advice" are all rather the same—avoidance, control, sinking into discouragement, resentment, all of it. No, when the passengers clamor for your attention and obedience to their demands, what the situation actually calls for is returning your attention to the actions of driving to your destination, trusting your skills and the knowledge gained from your experiences. Observe. Breathe. Expand. Respond.

It's all about what we're paying attention to. You know from experience that when you drive there are parts of the immediate environment that you *glance at*—the dashboard instruments and the mirrors, for example. You keep your main focus ahead of you, looking out through the windshield. In a similar way, you can *glance at* your thoughts and feelings while keeping your eye on getting to your goal. If the gas gauge alerts you that you're low on fuel, you stop for gas at your earliest convenience. In the meantime you wouldn't continue to stare at the gauge and wonder how it came to be that you're low on gas or imagine all the terrible places you might run out of gas. Maybe you would, but it wouldn't be helpful.

Similarly, as you drive through town you notice many other streets, people, buildings, sirens, car horns, and so on. You may give only a passing thought to some of these sights or sounds while others (the siren) will alert and orient you. You may have a particular thought such as, "There's that restaurant I heard about. We should go there sometime." But then your attention would return to your driving. Again, it is the destination, the basic rules of the road, and a few fairly rare issues related to safety, that determine how you drive the minivan.

This idea of maintaining focus on the important tasks at hand while being aware of extraneous or competing events is important not just for the child's primary dance partner, but for other individuals who might be affected by or pulled into the dance. This is a difficult struggle for Dan.

CLINICIAN: When Wyatt and Sara get into it in the morning I'm guessing you have some fairly predictable thoughts and emotions that show up, maybe even before it all starts because you can probably see it coming from a mile away at this point.

DAN: Yeah, I wake up dreading what's coming.

CLINICIAN: What are you telling yourself as you try to focus on what you need to do to get the day going?

DAN: That I'd rather be somewhere else. I tell myself I'm not going to get involved this time. But I always end up getting involved.

CLINICIAN: What's the thought or emotion that shows up right before you get involved?

DAN: I think, "I never would have treated my mother this way. My father would have knocked me through the wall." Then I get angry, just blind angry.

CLINICIAN: And yet you don't knock Wyatt through the wall, as strong and awful as those emotions are in the moment. Something's allowing you to stay in control of yourself in spite of the thoughts and feelings that are present, vying for your attention. But we haven't yet found what you can actually *do* that will work to get Wyatt to school without all this crazy dancing. For now though, as a temporary measure while things are so hot, while we're trying to understand this better, maybe the best thing to do is to do nothing. We'll find out how you can teach Wyatt these important lessons about how we treat other people. Right now though we don't know exactly what that's going to look like. It probably won't look exactly like how things worked in your family growing up. And in the short run, maybe even for quite some time, these angry thoughts and emotions are going to show up. You're going to have treat them like backseat drivers, and you're going to have to continue to not act on them, as hard as that will be.

ONE TYPE OF TOLERANCE: DON'T JUST DO SOMETHING, STAND THERE

Often the best thing a parent can do, as an interim step in changing the dance or as an ongoing response, is to do nothing at all. At the very least, doing nothing is *not doing* the habitual dance. It is an act of awareness and self-control that contributes to the unraveling of the dance and its eventual replacement with some other, more helpful behaviors.

There is delightful and useful expression I first heard from a psychiatrist I once worked with, Dr. Dea Eisner: "Don't Just Do something, Stand There," or DJDSTST. Unless the house is on fire or the child is dashing out in front of traffic, a parent can afford to pause for a few seconds or longer to take a deep breath, collect his thoughts, and come up with what the situation calls for him to say and do, if anything. Going through the SOBER procedure is a mini-DJDSTST until the parent gets to the "response" step. Even then, the best response in the moment might be to not respond at all.

"Don't Just Do Something, Stand There" is an effective parental move when a more overt response would feel intrusive or provocative to the child and yet walking away would not be providing a good "holding environment" and might only serve to increase the child's anxiety and sense of loss of control. For example, when Mycroft or Grace are having a *pantrum* (a cross between a panic attack and a tantrum) leaning in with the threat of a consequence or even a validation might enflame the situation because the child is unable to make use of the parent's language in that overwrought state. On the other hand, Elena or Holly walking away might throw the child into a state of panic. Best to just stand there, close by, out of range of flailing limbs, and breathe until it feels okay to redirect.

GRAYBAR'S SECOND LAW OF HUMAN BEHAVIOR

Recall Graybar's First Law: "All behavior is a message, and a behavior won't begin to change until the message has been received." Well, Graybar has a Second Law: "He who cares least has the most power." Or, as I sometimes rephrase it, "The more you care, the more you must be willing to bear." Many times parents must care more about some situations than the child does—oral hygiene, school assignment due dates, table manners, learning to get along with people you don't like, among many others. This is because the adults can see the longer-term implications of such things and so lean on their children to brush their teeth, take their school assignment deadlines seriously, and practice good manners and social skills because they, the parents, know these are all good investments in the child's future. Parents are willing, mostly, to bear the weight of the nagging and reminding and scaffolding required. At the same time parents are working at creating more "caring" on the part of the child and more independence in these areas of responsibility. All throughout the childrearing years parents make countless decisions about when to lean in and when to hang back: "Whose science project is this, anyway?!" Or, "Does my child want more friends or do I want my child to have more friends?"

At a certain point, with certain situations, it is important that parents be able to recognize when they have stepped over an invisible line and find themselves caring more about some situation or outcome than their child does. Again, the parent may decide that shouldering the caring is necessary and good. At other times he will decide that the conflict and stress created by this "caring imbalance" are not balanced out by a likely positive outcome. The danger is in the parent's not seeing this caring as a choice he has made, not "owning" the caring and thus allowing resentment, frustration, and impatience to become a mental habit in these situations.

THE STRANGE, BUT NOT UNUSUAL, CASE OF JIMMY AND THE HOT POTATO

Jimmy is a thirteen-year-old boy who is in middle school. He is not doing any schoolwork, or at most, the bare minimum gets done but then only with considerable parental reminding, nagging, cajoling and threatening. His parents are quite frantic about Jimmy's profound lack of concern as his grades hover in the D+ range in all his classes. When asked about his grades and schoolwork in general, Jimmy shrugs and says that school is "boring" and that he has "no motivation"; besides, grades only start to really count when you're in high school, at which time he will be more motivated and will put in the work. To paraphrase St. Augustine, "Oh Lord, help me to be motivated to do schoolwork, but not yet."

Jimmy is doing some serious avoiding of the schoolwork that would make him anxious if he were to even think about it. But it's not just schoolwork: Chores, family activities, and even time with friends are met (or not met) with a great deal of inertia. Jimmy prefers a few solitary activities—mostly playing video games, drawing, or reading—that he has always been good at. Attempts at getting him activated and engaged are met with anger and sullen withdrawal.

Many preadolescent boys have an exquisite sensitivity to any perceived threat to their fragile self-esteem. It is much like a return to the black-and-white, all-or-none thinking of typical four-year-old. Any outcome less than perfection, any acquiescence to the unreasonable demands of the adults around you, is a searing humiliation and evidence of one's weakness and dependence. The best defense against all these feelings of anxiety, shame, weakness, and dependence is to avoid doing anything that isn't a sure bet to turn out fine. Failing that, the next best defense is to become highly indignant in reaction to the smallest intrusion. It's a fun age.

So, there are times when a child may be *not anxious enough* in the eyes of a parent. For example, there is a test or major project coming up (college applications is a classic) and the young person appears not especially concerned and is not applying herself to the task. The parent becomes anxious and frantic and a dance begins, one marked by reciprocal intrusiveness and avoidance, control, and resistance.

I describe this phenomenon to parents in terms of displacement of anxiety from the child onto the parent. The psychoanalysts refer to this unconscious process as "projective identification." I simply call it the Hot Potato: the child is unable to feel or even be aware of the anxiety inherent in the situation because to do so would be overwhelming. So, she expels her anxious distress onto the parent, who is more than willing to take the anxiety, feel it, and (re)act on it. Unfortunately, this puts the parent in the position of caring more about an outcome than the child does and often doing most of the heavy lifting to see the endeavor through. The child, meanwhile, does not learn to recognize and use anxiety as a signal that some action should be taken and does not learn to act (respond) effectively *while* experiencing some anxiety or stress generally. Plus, the science project's not getting done or it's thrown together the night before it's due amid great anguish. Recognizing this variation on the anxiety dance, the parent must gently but firmly *give the potato back to the child.*

What *giving back the potato* will look like will depend somewhat on the age of the child and how emotionally charged the situation might be. Basically, it is just another form of *increasing awareness* that I have described previously as a necessary first step in changing any habitual and largely unconscious process. For an older child who has some decent self-regulation skills a parent might say, "I suppose if you let yourself think about *your* project you might start to feel pretty anxious about it. That would feel bad, I know, but I really need you to think about *your* project just enough to start working on it so that we don't have a lot of panic the night before it's due. Once you get started and find you need my help, just let me know."

For a younger child, the parent may simply wonder aloud about the child's thoughts and feelings. For example, the child has been excited about a playdate but then balks at the last minute, saying she doesn't want to go. "I wonder what you're thinking right now?

I'll bet you have two ideas—you want to see Beth and you have some worry ideas too. That's okay, sometimes we have two ideas at the same time. Let's go see Beth. She'll be so happy to see you." And the parent is heading the child toward the door chatting lightly about some completely different topic.

Unless the parent is aware of some significant concerns (for example, Beth's little brother is known to trash their playdates and some pre-playdate proactive problem solving is warranted), the parent would want to move quickly to the "taking values-driven action" step and not linger over the anticipatory thoughts and feelings. Most parents and children have the experience that these worry ideas and feelings tend to evaporate once everyone's transitioned into the next thing—playdate, school, summer camp.

SAVING FACE THROUGH BOMB THROWING

Brayden does something similar to the Hot Potato, except that it's more like throwing a bomb. A functional analysis with his parents, Salma and Geoff, suggests that Brayden's rude, demeaning, and sarcastic behavior tends to occur in situations where he may be feeling insecure or feels he has little control. There are two specific contexts. First, there are unstructured social situations such as eating in the lunch room at school or riding the bus on a field trip where the busy, back-and-forth verbal jostling of his peers is hard for Brayden, on the edge of the group, to keep up with, as the rapidly shifting content and in-jokes whirl around. He feels excitement but also impatience and frustration that he's not the center of attention. Suddenly, he tosses a verbal bomb into the middle of the group—something crude and barely on topic. The other students will just look at him for a moment and then return to their verbal tribal dance. At that point Brayden may either escalate to the point of a teacher's intervention or slink away in sullen anger.

There's not much Brayden's parents can do about these situations since they are not there. If and when they hear about the incident they might validate Brayden's impatience and frustration feelings and perhaps offer suggestions for how he might better join in the group. At that point, Brayden will likely claim that he doesn't care. But Salma and Geoff's validation and articulation of the very feeling words ("frustrated," "impatient," "jealous") might help Brayden recognize these emotions the next time they show up, and this inner language might insert itself between impulse and action.

The second context for Brayden's anxiety-driven rudeness is very relevant to the parent-child dance. These are the situations that call for one parent or the other, usually Salma, to give Brayden directions to do something—reminding him of a chore, an activity of daily living such as brushing teeth or taking a shower, or unexpectedly asking him to lend a helping hand. Like Jimmy, Brayden's overwrought early-adolescent mind is quick to regard these reminders and requests as unreasonable and tyrannical assaults on his autonomy and control. Before the humiliation can even begin to register as an experience, he reaches for the weapon that is always nearest at hand: "I now summon Dark and Caustic Wit!" Again, the parents' best move in the moment is often a minimalist one: Validate the likely emotional undercurrent and then either lean in and insist on compliance or hang back and not turn it into a power struggle. Which the parent chooses will depend on his or her current levels of both caring and energy and the number of days since Brayden's last shower, which relates to caring.

GOOD LEANING IN: POSITIVE BEHAVIORAL SUPPORT

In their chapter on mindful parenting, Smith and Dishion (2014) describe the benefits of "positive behavioral support," a class of parenting behaviors that includes warmth, effective attention to and tracking of the child's behavior ("monitoring"), and positive reinforcement. The positive reinforcement or praise given by the parent is specifically directed at the child's *efforts,* and not so much the products of her actions: "You got started right away and really worked hard." Positive behavioral supports includes having expectations for the child's behavior and giving positive attention to the child's efforts to meet those expectations. It is encouraging courageous behavior and recognizing this behavior as an achievement in itself.

These authors cite studies showing that a lack of positive behavioral support is associated with child behavior problems and with the development of depression in older children. Further, an intervention that sought to increase parental positive behavioral support resulted in a decrease in adolescent depression (Connell & Dishion, 2008). Interestingly, Shaw and colleagues (2009) found that interventions that increased positive parenting reduced depression symptoms *in the caregiver.*

Consider the dynamics between Celeste and Freya. A functional analysis of their pattern revealed a set of Freya's behaviors that Celeste described as "moping." This behavior included hanging around the house on weekends with no plans or desire to do anything, lots of deep sighs, and staring into space for long periods of time. "She's just withdrawn," was Celeste's summary description. But further inquiry revealed that Freya always seemed to do her "withdrawn" behavior in whatever room Celeste happened to be in, moving as necessary to have her sighs be within earshot.:

CLINICIAN: So, when Freya is doing this moping stuff around the house, and interestingly, is making sure that you're a witness to it . . . how do you respond?

CELESTE: I give her lots of suggestions for things she could be doing instead; there's always her chores, schoolwork, she could call a friend. But she rejects them all.

CLINICIAN: I'm sure that's frustrating and even confusing; why would she not want to do something that might make herself feel better? It's curious. But let me back up. Maybe I should have asked this question first . . . What's going on for you in terms of thoughts and feelings when Freya is moping and withdrawn?

CELESTE: It doesn't help my mood.

CLINICIAN: I'm sure that's true. Can you tell me more about that?

CELESTE (*tearing up*): I start feeling helpless. I can't help Freya. I can't help my husband. I can't protect my son. But I'm not moping around. I have to function. Someone has to hold this family together.

CLINICIAN: There's a lot of helplessness in your house these days. Sadness and loss, too. It's here in the room right now. (*pausing*) There's this idea that came to me and I want to know what you think about it. I'm wondering if Freya's moping comes from her own feelings of helplessness and sorrow. I wonder if she seeks you out when she feels that way so that you can *share* those feelings with you. It might help her feel less alone. Maybe she's trying to help you feel less alone in these feelings you both share. Clearly Freya's resisting your suggestions for moving on from that place. Maybe the place to start instead is by gently recognizing the feelings in the room at the moment, letting them just be there. This could give her the message that you are strong enough to bear these emotions and so is she.

HEALTHY LIMIT SETTING

Structure, rules, expectations, and adult monitoring all serve to keep a child's behavior within safe boundaries and to minimize opportunities for true disasters to occur. The stability and security afforded by healthy limit setting helps create the *holding environment* in which edgy feelings and ideas can be experienced, not as bona fide threats, but as transient mental and physical events with no more power to disrupt or direct our lives than what we give them. This is an example of mindfulness in the sense that the parent and child, together, can be aware of certain thoughts and feelings (anxiety) but hold this experience lightly and within the larger context of stability and security.

Children might never admit it, but they appreciate structure and even limits on their behavior. They will certainly push against the limits until they find the unyielding contours. Lack of certainty, consistency, or clarity about rules and expectations is anxiety-provoking in itself. For children whose anxiety can manifest as inappropriate control behaviors, defiance, and even aggression (to varying degrees, Mycroft, Grace, and Wyatt), it can be fruitful to put effort into establishing and articulating clear and consistent rules, limits, and corresponding expected behaviors.

Healthy limits can have a beneficial effect on the parent. If there is reasonable consistency between the parents because the rules and expectations have been clarified, then one significant source of parental stress has been reduced. Salma reported that the "rolling the die" plan for limiting everyone's repeating words was helping and in ways she would not have anticipated before plunging in and seeing what would happen. She said, "After doing it for a few days, and I commend Brayden for his cooperation with it, I began to notice that I was less tense generally. And even when it came time to roll the die and do some repeating, it felt different. There wasn't that 'neverendedness' quality to it, if that's even a word, that these 'dances' as you call them so often had. There's a boundary there now. Like a guard rail on a curvy road. You still have to drive carefully, but just knowing it's there makes the drive feel safer and less tense. Less tense is good."

Channeling Wyatt

I sometimes think of good parenting as creating a channel for the child's behavior, like the banks of a river guide the flow of water, as opposed to a floodplain. This may be a somewhat more dynamic or active way of thinking about a *holding environment*. Good limit setting is not just damming up unwanted behavior. It certainly isn't about repressing anxious thoughts or feelings. Good limit setting should provide a channel, a way *toward* what the parent really needs to see happen in the moment. Recall the brief description of a possible reward program for Wyatt. It would be written in terms of *expected behaviors*—what we want to see Wyatt *doing* with certain criteria such as time limits, such as "getting out of bed within ten minutes of the alarm going off."

If Wyatt does not comply with the expectations, he would simply not obtain his reward. The rewards could be set up in such a way that life would be very boring as a result of not following expectations. However, recall "He who cares least has the most power." If Wyatt cares about not appearing to care (stay with me), then he may, on principle, feel compelled to not comply with the program. To comply too readily would be a loss of face. Dan and Sara would need some inoculation around this possibility (more like certainty) so that they might be able to recognize the frustration that comes up when Wyatt feels compelled to denigrate the plan and refuses to make it work. They would be instructed to not change any aspects of the program without discussion with the clinician first. This will help prevent angry "upping the ante" by the parents in the heat of the moment and piling on punishments or other drastic and desperate moves. Maybe they'll be lucky and it will all go well from the start.

WHEN THE CLINICIAN MUST HANG BACK

If parents are known to be compulsive problem solvers, clinicians can be worse. After all, we are in this business because we want to be helpful to people. And we can be. We have the technology. But there are times when we must recognize that we are succumbing to the contagion of the parent's frantic need to have the child's anxiety *fixed now*. We must recognize when we are caring more about the situation than the child is or even one or another parent is. We must be able to recognize when we've accepted a hot potato.

In the next chapter I will spend some time talking about clinician resilience, or how we can maintain a healthy stance toward our work and avoid becoming depleted by the inevitable stresses of this work. At this time I would just state that it is often best to err on the side of not responding than to speak in the service of filling a silence or rescuing a client, or oneself, from awkward thoughts or feelings. We most definitely provide a holding environment in which feelings and thoughts are regarded as potentially useful but essentially powerless physiological and cognitive events that will pass on through if we allow them to and that exert no more influence on us than we allow them to. In other words, the clinician must be mindful of his or her own tendencies toward avoidance or control when things heat up or grow cold in session.

WHEN THE CLINICIAN NEEDS TO LEAN IN

Having said that, there are certainly times when the clinician must lean in and set boundaries, reestablish the frame, or just plain tell people what needs to happen. I find that there are two situations that invite me to lean into the therapeutic moment. First, there are issues related to the therapeutic frame, which I discussed earlier. The frame can be stretched in any number of ways, some more problematic to the conduct of therapy than others. When the frame is disrupted, it is time to lean in, gently but firmly.

The client's not paying his bills is a problem we clinicians are often reluctant to confront. Few of us received any graduate coursework or training in the business of running a therapy practice, and money tends to be an uncomfortable topic. Nonetheless, we sometimes need to address financial issues with clients. Clearly setting out the fee schedule and payment expectations at the beginning of the assessment is not only a good idea, it is required by most professional practice guidelines. At some later point in the therapy these expectations may need to be revisited. For some of us this can be very anxiety provoking, yet it is an "opportunity" to practice our own willingness and courage. If we don't confront these and other issues, we run the risk of becoming resentful and depleted. Then the therapy suffers, which is in no one's interest.

Obviously, these situations must be addressed with tact and an appreciation for the complexities of family life. Changing the dance puts pressure on the family system. It is a disruption, even a threat, to the established way of doing things. All manner of resistances may emerge that disrupt the frame and undermine your efforts. On the other hand, there are certain conditions that allow you to be helpful to a family: They need to show up, you need to give them your best

attention and skills, they need to follow through with recommendations, you need to get paid, and so on. You find a way to bring these
matters into the room for an empathic *and* principled discussion to
see if resistances and roadblocks can be effectively addressed. If not,
it may be time to refer them out.

SKIRTING DANGEROUSLY CLOSE TO COUPLES' THERAPY

One area of possible frame bending is when marital issues start
showing up with regularity. Doing this work, discussing parenting practices, can't help but get you into marital territory to some
degree. For Elena, as a single mother, this is less an issue than it is
for working with Dan and Sara or with Salma and Geoff. By training,
experience, and temperament I am not a marital therapist. I don't
want to be practicing outside of my area of competence, even if the
boundaries are not exactly distinct between what I do, as described
in this book, and "real" marital therapy.

If I sense that the parents and I are skirting dangerously close
to doing couples' or marital therapy, I will say something along the
lines of, "This is clearly an issue of great importance [*whatever the
issue they're bringing in might be*] and it has come up more than
once now. To the extent that it affects your parenting, it's relevant to
our work and I want to make sure it factors into our discussions and
strategies. But I also think it deserves more time and attention than
we can give it in here with all we have to cover. And more important,
it deserves the attention of someone with more experience in this
issue than I have. So, I'd like to suggest that you see someone spe-
cializing in couples' work and really see what can be done with it."

A LOOK AHEAD

For parents, walking that fine line between leaning in and hanging
back is hard work—stressful, exhausting, depleting. Parents must
engage in the self-care strategies and habits that will allow them to

sustain the efforts over time. And for clinicians working with anxious families, this is hard work as well—stressful, exhausting, depleting. As such, all *clinicians* must engage in the self-care strategies and habits that will allow them to sustain the efforts over time.

That is the topic of our final chapter: parent and clinician resilience. I hope to make the argument that parent (and clinician) self-care is vital to the long-term success of your treatment efforts. And yet this is a topic that is rarely covered in the literature, at least with parents of anxious children. This is not covered well in graduate training either.

I will describe important components of a personal and professional life that support resilience. These include community, energy, strength, and commitment.

Summary of Key Ideas

- Parents need to exercise a lot of control over the lives of their children, but somehow without the quality of parental control or low autonomy granting that suggest intrusiveness.
- It is a basic and necessary parenting task to support the child's taking reasonable risks in order to work through all the expectable anxiety and worry, for both parent and child.
- A parent's tolerance, leaning in or hanging back, can often be under the control of the parent's moods, memories, and verbal rules instead of under the control of the child's behavior and what the situation actually calls for in the way of a parent response.
- Tolerance may take the form of Don't Just Do Something, Stand There.
- Many times parents must care about a situation more than the child does. The danger lies in the parent's not "owning" this caring and allowing resentment and frustration to obscure what is reasonable in the way of expectations for the child's behavior.
- Sometimes the child seems to not be anxious enough. Often one or another parent is more than willing to take on that anxiety for the child.
- Good leaning in can take the form of positive behavioral support and healthy limit setting.
- Clinicians, too, must be able to lean in and hang back as needed.

CHAPTER 9

Fostering Self-Care
and Resilience

This final chapter covers two related topics far too infrequently addressed in the clinical literature: parent self-care and resilience. One can find ample chapters and articles on promoting *child* resilience (e.g., Klimes-Dougan & Kendziora, 2005). And clinical work with disruptive and aggressive children has recognized the need to enhance parent resilience, given the stress these parents are experiencing (Cavell, 2000; Prinz & Miller, 1991). Yet the stress of parenting children with internalizing disorders is given scant attention.

Parenting an anxious child can be stressful and exhausting. This is especially so for the majority of parents who themselves experience significant anxiety. Their child's anguish evokes their own anguish. Their child's anxiety-related anger and defiance can trigger confusion, hesitation, and even traumatic memories from a parent's own difficult past. In this chapter I present strategies for talking about and promoting parent resilience and self-care. These are vital components of an overall treatment program that will support everyone's efforts toward understanding, communication, coping, and change. Further, as I mentioned in previous chapters, stresses and other setting events can erode hard-won positive changes in the family process. Resilience, by definition, allows parents to carry on and manage well. In fact, one of my favorite definitions is simply "struggling well."

As I've described, and you know from experience, changing unhelpful family behavior patterns is often quite challenging and takes a toll on all the dancers. Although I haven't mentioned this until now, you should consider yourself another dancer in this grand behavioral ball. As noted in the previous chapter, there are times when you, as the clinician, are an integral part of the process and must make choices and decisions related to leaning in or hanging back. And as it is with the parents, what ideally drives *your* in-session responses (as opposed to reactions) in any given moment will be as clear-eyed a focus on what's best for the child and parent as one can summon at 3:20 on a Thursday afternoon when you're feeling depleted and you're having the thought that you're the only one in the room who really wants things to get better. Being human, we have our own thoughts and feelings to acknowledge, accept, make room for, and not react to. I will use this chapter to touch upon a topic near and dear to my own heart: *clinician* self-care and resilience.

DEFINITIONS OF RESILIENCE

Typically we think of resilience as coping and persevering in the face of adversity. It is "bouncing back" from an adverse event and restoring equilibrium. Froma Walsh (2006) talks about resilience as "bouncing forward": when stressful life circumstances ask for an adaptive shift in thinking and doing. One can perhaps come out of the experience stronger, more skillful, or more deeply connected to one's values, family, or community. I like this way of looking at resilience. It suggests that we can emerge from difficult circumstances with new and better coping skills as well as an enhanced sense of effectiveness and confidence. That, after all, is what parents want for their children as they face the many challenges of growing up. Communication and coping skills, and the confidence that comes with them, are the best "tools" we can give children.

WHY TALK TO PARENTS ABOUT RESILIENCE?

Parent resilience or parental self-care is important to our work for several reasons. First, the work of changing the dance is challenging, tiring, and stressful in itself. There is invariably resistance to change, even among the most motivated and well-intentioned family members you work with. At the very least, habits are hard to change and the change process requires increased awareness and effortful control to shift attention. Any parent is going to need a great deal of stamina and perseverance in order to maintain her efforts at changing the parent-child anxiety dance. This includes taking care of oneself physically as well as mentally and even spiritually, however the parent wants to define that. Previously, I talked about the psychological factors, in the form of distal stressors, that affect parent consistency. These same factors erode parent resilience. Should discouragement or other stressors take control of parent decision making, parent and child are likely to regress to the old patterns. Efforts to shore up parent resilience will help the family make progress in the near term (e.g., managing exposure experiences) and in the long term (sustaining change in the face of stressors and new content).

Second, resilience can be framed as an *outcome goal* for the parent, the child, or both. For many families "increased resilience" could be a succinct description of the new dance you're trying to bring about: the capacity to tolerate distress in the service of getting to a valued goal and the skills to get you there. In facilitating this outcome, as I'll describe later, the clinician uses the same basic change process that the parent is using to help the child grow and persevere. The clinician validates the challenge of doing this work and expands awareness/redirects attention from a focus on the current difficulties to the valued goal of increased resilience, inner strength, hardiness, buoyancy, or any other term the family resonates with. Through this modeling and experience, the parent can then encourage the child's resilience in a variety of situations, regardless of particular content associated with that situation. Examples will follow later.

The goal of increased resilience itself further supports taking action toward other valued goals. As such, resilience becomes a process goal: "I will persevere, or stay on track, in spite of these compelling thoughts and feelings that threaten to derail my journey."

Recall in Chapter 4 that we often must deal with the activator conditions *as they are*. If we can eliminate or avoid triggers without making life less vital or effective, we can eliminate or reduce some of the anxiety the child will feel and perhaps then some of the anxious behavior. This is wonderful, but not always possible. As I sometimes tell clients, "Things must be able to change without things needing to change." In other words, the acceptance of the activator conditions, *including* everyone's anxious thoughts and feelings in the moment, are a prerequisite for changing behavior.

So, we can decrease a person's exposure to stressors and provocative situations, or we can increase his resilience, his ability to cope and adapt when stressors, external or internal, show up. The approach of increasing adaptability and resilience is often the more feasible, the more realistic strategy. At least in the short run, parents can expect that treatment efforts will not result in massive decreases in their child's distressing anxious behaviors. In fact, in many cases, the anxious behaviors will increase temporarily as the child adjusts to the new "rules" about how the parent responds. In behavioral terms, as mentioned in Chapter 4, this increase in behavior following a change in the contingencies is called an "extinction burst" or "Things get worse before they get better." We must bring this possibility into the room ahead of time to inoculate the parent against discouragement when, not if, things gets worse before they get better.

WHAT MAKES FOR RESILIENCE?

We know, through decades of research, what contributes to child resilience, the ability of children to do well following or in the midst of adversity. Three broad categories of predictive correlates of resilience have been identified: (1) Individual characteristics of the child,

(2) supportive family milieu, and (3) availability of external community supports (Klimes-Dougan, & Kendziora, 2005).

I am going to suggest, and this is purely conjecture because this is an area that is poorly studied, that these same factors of individual characteristics, supportive milieu, and supportive community contribute to parent resilience as well. Clearly, some of these factors are more malleable than others. But if we can be aware of what supports resilience, if the parents we work with can be aware of what supports their own resilience, then efforts can be made to "support the supports." For example, if a parent is refreshed and restored through time away from the family to pursue valued interests, then one would help arrange proactive support from a partner, friends, or a family member to make that time away happen *on a regular basis,* and not just in response (reaction) to when the parent is feeling overwhelmed.

Individual Characteristics of the Person

Here we revisit temperament. Certain temperamental characteristics observable in early childhood appear to be correlated with resilience in later childhood. These include the tendency to *approach* novel situations, as opposed to *withdraw,* along with moderately high activity level, alertness, responsiveness, and sociability. These are the qualities of the so-called "easy" baby and are likely to elicit positive attention from caregivers. Other factors associated with resilience include curiosity, good frustration tolerance and impulse control, and good reasoning and problem-solving skills. Also described is the combination of autonomous behavior with the ability to ask for help. This is an example of *interdependence,* which is so important for living in a society—even the relatively small society of a family.

Beyond temperament we find that enjoyable, nonacademic activities such as hobbies appear to be a protective factor. Rigid gender stereotypes are a risk factor for stress and poor resilience; boys who can express themselves emotionally and are socially perceptive and girls who are autonomous and confident tend to be more resilient.

If these are qualities of the individual and factors that support resilience in the child, could they not also contribute to resilience in an adult, such as the parent of an anxious child? As described in Chapter 2, temperament is not destiny. Tendencies can be recognized, and strategies for overriding one's tendencies can be developed and practiced. That is what we are asking the child to do. That is where parent mindfulness comes in handy:

CLINICIAN: You know, there was probably a time, millennia ago, when humans were terrified by all sorts of natural events— thunderstorms, fire, eclipses, even the phases of the moon must have been weird and disturbing to the earliest humans. And then, probably over a long period of time, people began to notice the patterns. 'Hey, this moon-disappearing-and-then-returning thing; it's actually kind of regular. We can even predict when it's going to happen next.' They made the same discoveries with eclipses and how fire behaves, and eventually many phenomena were understood and became less frightening because people *turned their fear into curiosity.*

Recall the SOBER acronym that we talked about. There are many ways to think about the "expand" step. One idea is to think about *curiosity.* Often our first reaction to a distressing situation is something pulled off the survival shelf: "Just get me through this." That can be appropriate when it's a real crisis or someone's in real danger. But oftentimes, even though you're caught up in the fight-or-flight reaction, you might actually take a different approach and take a moment to be curious about what's going on with your child. "What exactly is going on with my child right now? Why now?"

You could even be curious about your own reaction in the moment; "I wonder why this is bothering me so much more today than it did yesterday?" You may come up with answers, you may not. But it is a different tone, a new attitude, as in a "tendency or orientation, especially of the mind." Your mind is not so oriented to threat management; the tendency is instead toward understanding. Curiosity also helps with impulse control by buying you a little time to consider your next move.

Family Factors that Contribute to Resilience

One of the most important factors contributing to a child's resilience is the presence of a close bond between caregiver and child (Klimes-Dougan, & Kendziora, 2005). Such relationships are marked by responsiveness, warmth, caring, effective limit setting, and mutual respect. Such a relationship creates security, self-worth, and effective communication processes (a good dance) that allows problems to be solved and conditions to be managed without undue arousal and impatience. It creates that *holding environment* in which strong emotions and ideas can be held with security and understanding. It is reasonable to assume that a *parent's* resilience will also be influenced, for better or for worse, by the quality of her personal relationships. The therapeutic work described in Chapter 3 on communication is in part meant to encourage the kinds of close, caring, warm, and responsive relationships that will foster parent resilience. In addition to encouraging a warm and positive relationship between the parent and child, we hope to enhance other important relationships in the parent's life—with the spouse, partner, or co-parent, with supportive relatives and friends. It makes sense that, if these relationship are mutually supportive, parents will be more effective and resilient in the face of the difficulties encountered in any family.

The relationship between clinician and parent is a vital source of this warmth, caring, and support as well. For some parents this professional relationship may be their most important lifeline as they navigate the difficult waters of parenting an anxious child. Psychotherapists tend to be a mild and humble species and we sometimes, I think, underestimate our importance in the lives of the people we work with.

The Importance of a Supportive Community

The psychologist Timothy Cavell (2000) makes the important observation that the parent-child relationship is inherently vertical; the socialization process flows outward and down from parent to child. While the parent may obtain love, joy, satisfaction, even inspiration flowing up from her child, their relationship is by definition not that of equals, and there shouldn't be an expectation that it will be mutually satisfying or that the parent can expect the child to be responsible for, or even capable of, "taking care" of the parent. This is especially true with a high-demand, anxious, regressed child. If the nurturing is flowing more from child to parent than from parent to child, there's an unsustainable problem with the process.

A parent must be able to find care and renewal from sources outside the parent-child relationship. This could flow from one's spouse or partner, a friend, or even materials such as inspirational or educational books, films, or presentations. Certainly a clinician can be such as resource and support. But finding support from multiple persons in one's natural environment will only further parent resilience.

A KEY COMPONENT OF PARENTAL RESILIENCE: SELF-CARE

Parent self-care is related to resilience and has been defined as the "parents' ability to promote their own strengths and well-being so that they can continue the job of parenting" (Cavell, 2006, p. 194). It involves the many ways parents nourish their own well-being in order to carry on the business of being an effective, responsive parent. Parent self-care is therefore vital to parent resilience. But to consistently engage in self-care activities, a parent must build "me" time, sacred and protected "me" time, into her schedule. In the life of any family there are always many valid reasons to *not* take time for friends, tend the garden, or get to the gym.

Some parents believe that they can obtain sufficient nurturance from their careers. Having a satisfying career is wonderful and can be helpful in providing needed security, self-esteem, and self-efficacy. The risk is that one's job might become a refuge *from* the family, rather than a means of supporting the family and providing a positive ground from which the parent can return home able to be a better parent. Also, most jobs and careers have their associated challenges and stresses. It's important for parents to be vigilant to work stress bleeding into family life, or to the reverse, where stress at home begins to negatively affect performance or satisfaction at work. Many adults believe they can keep these various aspects of their lives, work and family, compartmentalized; but this is difficult to do:

> CLINICIAN: I want to spend a few minutes talking about how you manage to stay afloat with all the stress of getting Wyatt going every morning and all the other situations that seem harder than they ought to be. What revitalizes you or helps you to recharge your batteries?
>
> DAN: My work is my stress-relief valve. I go to work and solve financial problems—where's the money going, where did the money go? It's interesting but straightforward and I'm good at it. It's when I come home and can't do anything right. I don't understand what the problem is much of the time. That's when I wonder what I'm even doing there. I don't even try any more.
>
> SARA: I'm just the opposite. I live to be a mother to my children. People tell me I need to take time for myself, and I do, while the kids are in school. But I can't wait for them to walk in the door. Other parents seem to need more time away from their children. That's okay for them. But my kids will always know that I gave them everything I had.

Such descriptions, while they sound values-driven and are framed positively, make me nervous and concerned that parents such as Dan will not have the resilience to effectively engage the inevitable family stressors because these events will be seen as alien ("I don't understand what the problem is much of the time") and intractable, which can lead to a cycle of withdrawal (avoidance) and a continued diminishing of the parent's skills and effectiveness, real and imagined. For Sara, and for Celeste who also has boundary issues with her child, the reliance on the child for sustenance will ultimately be draining and unsatisfying. This can lead to periodic bursts of resentment by the parent when the child is not seen as meeting the parent's needs.

RESISTANCE TO SELF-CARE

I think of the instructions the flight attendant gives prior to take off: "Please secure your own oxygen mask first before assisting others with theirs." Prior to becoming a father, I would hear these instructions and think, "When I'm a parent I will put my child's oxygen mask on first, before I put on mine, because that is the kind of selfless parent I shall be." The very next time I flew after becoming a parent, and my infant son wasn't even on the plane with me, I heard this announcement for the umpteenth time and immediately thought, "Well, of course I'm going to put my mask on first! If I pass out I can't trust that anyone else is going to take care of my kid. Besides, his young brain can take a little hypoxia better than mine can."

No, I did not actually think that last part. But the idea, the revelation, that I needed to take care of myself in order to take care of my child struck me with a forceful certainty that surprised me and suggested some switch had been flipped in my psyche as the result of becoming a parent months earlier. Self-care is not selfishness in the least.

But many parents seem to resist taking care of themselves. Most will certainly acknowledge the importance of self-care, but the "yes, but"s quickly come out: time constraints, lack of social and recreational opportunities, financial constraints, lack of support in the form of alternative caregivers, to name just a few of the impediments. At times it seems that some parents may have a not-quite-conscious idea that taking care of oneself is somehow actually *detracting* from their role, their mission, their sacred duty of parenting with all their heart and soul. In other cases, parents may feel so frustrated and discouraged by their parenting that they stop trying to invest in self-care and resilience as a means of supporting responsive parenting. Instead, they might view work or other activities far afield of their parenting role as their only "escape." The brief exchange between clinician and Wyatt's parents illustrates both these situations. And, there is a real and important connection between parent self-care and effective parenting. Every parent you work with may nod and say he or she understand that this must be true. But it may be help-ful to spend some time discussing how and why, specifically, parent self-care is related to the anxiety dance.

Do It For the Kids

If parents resist the notion of self-care and other strategies for promoting resilience for any number of reasons, there is one ratio-nale you can pull out. Most parents would agree that their *child's* resilience is a valued goal, and they would be remiss as parents if they did not encourage and support resilience enhancement for the child. Well, you can say to the parent, the child is going to learn these self-care habits and other behaviors and supports for resilience *through your example*. It is the parent's responsibility to model and directly teach self care and resilience. Within that framework a parent might be more willing to scour her schedule for self-care time and devote more attention to nurturing community support, strength, energy, and commitment (see below).

The Connection Between Parent Self-Care and Effective Parenting

Cavell (2000) describes three goals, or direct benefits, of parent self-care: energy, strength, and commitment. Acquiring and nurtur-ing energy, strength, and commitment in turn contribute to parent resilience, which in turn supports an effective and sustainable par-enting program.

Not that resilience will make everything smooth and stress-free. In fact, struggling well creates new experiences, for both parent and child, of acting in effective and adaptive ways *even in the presence* of strong, "negative" thoughts and feelings. Much like the previously described benefits of exposure/response prevention, these expe-riences of struggling well allow parent and child to be willing to explore new challenges and encourage yet more responsive behav-iors when similar challenging situations arise in the future. A virtu-ous cycle of willingness, experience, cognitive reappraisal, and more willingness is launched. The cycle is maintained through the parent's energy, strength, and commitment.

Energy

Energy is the term Cavell uses to denote a parent's capacity to sustain her efforts "from moment to moment, day to day, week to week," and so on (Cavell, 2000, p. 195). Every parent is going to expend a tremendous amount of energy on the tasks of parenting. Oftentimes this is an expenditure of physical energy—keeping up with a toddler, driving children all over town, housekeeping tasks, and the list goes on. At other times, mental or psychological energy is required. The parent's own facilitated listening to the child is a prime example of an expenditure of mental energy.

Some tasks, depending on the child, tend to be more draining then others—vaccinations, swimming lessons, school drop-off, going off to camp or a sleep over, trying new foods, long-term school projects, to name a few. Managing a child's anxiety and fear can be among the most depleting of parenting experiences. Some days, there's little left in the tank by the time homework or bedtime rolls around. It is important for parents to understand their own energy needs and the factors that affect their ability to maintain a supple (strong but flexible) stance and to maintain some level of consistency across time. Questions to ask a parent include: What *drains* your energy? What are the warning signs that tell you when you're running low on energy, either physical or mental? What *refuels* you? For single parents, such as Elena, the demands are great and the support is often thin:

> CLINICIAN: I can't imagine how tiring it must be doing all this parenting virtually on your own. Let's think about what contributes to your endurance and what undermines it.
>
> ELENA: Some days I'm just sleepwalking it seems. What helps my endurance? When it goes well and when I can focus on it going well. When the pajamas are on and the teeth are brushed and Mycroft is snuggled against me and we're reading a book; it just makes it all worth it and I forget how tired I am or how angry

I was a few minutes earlier. But in the back of my mind I'm already anticipating the struggle that's going to come when I tell him we're done reading and it's time for lights out.

CLINICIAN: Those thoughts will creep in. The whispers of the passengers in the back seat. What do you do then?

ELENA: I know that if I focus on those thoughts I'll get stressed, it will ruin whatever fleeting and precious sweetness is going on in the moment, and it's already using up what little energy I have so that the "lights out battle" will certainly go badly.

CLINICIAN: Yes, that's a great observation. It's so important to make the shift back to the present, to *be* present to the loving, calm sweetness and not stay focused on the struggle and frustration of even a few minutes earlier or start getting worked up about an imagined future. You may even notice that our moments of struggle are often made especially challenging by the fact that we are not just dealing with the present-moment challenge, but our minds are adding to our stress by dredging up past events or anticipating future trouble. Those are drains on our energy and are often so unhelpful to managing the present situation, whether it's a problem or a condition.

Strength

Strength, from Cavell's perspective, refers to a parent's stock of effective strategies and tactics for managing the life of one's family as well as the parent's *willingness* to use those tools in the face of competing demands. This might mean that a parent must make an unpopular decision if she feels it's the right one in the moment. This second component of strength, that of willingness, is important. Often parents have the requisite tools to parent effectively, but they find themselves unsure and hesitant in the face of various factors such as low energy, poor cooperation from other key players in the life of the child, and other distracting, depleting setting events such as those I described in relation to the work of Wahler and Dumas (1989). The result can be inconsistency and wavering when the situation calls for resolve and commitment.

Clinicians should explore with parents the kinds of events, ideas, or feelings that tend to undermine the person's confidence and willingness to be the parent she knows she needs to be in the moment. This may uncover basic conflicts between "old" rules or internal working models going back decades and the necessities and salient features of the present situation. For example, as described in the last chapter, a parent's best move in the moment might be to do nothing at all: *Don't just do something, stand there.* This may be challenging if the child's anxiety is always regarded as a problem to be solved (control) or if the child is seen as vulnerable and incapable of managing the provocative situation (leading to avoidance or escape). A parent may hold a long-standing, perhaps multigenerational, idea or rule that a child's rudeness or defiance must always be swiftly condemned if the parent is to not be perceived as weak or permissive. This can lead to power struggles, along with missed opportunities to uncover what else may be going on with the child in the moment and create a teachable moment. As I've describe previously, the goal of your in-session questions would be to elicit descriptions of challenging situations and to make everyone's *inner* conflicts, thoughts, and feelings more conscious. The clinician can honor the former importance or usefulness of the old rules ("It sounds like, in your family growing up, that rule was important for your survivial"), and then orient the parent to what *this* parent-child dyad needs at *this* time.

Like parental energy, replenishing a parent's strength comes from the activities she engages in as well as from positive transactions with other adults. Assuming of course that other adults aren't undermining the parent's commitment and resolve, having a community of fellow parents can help the parent of an anxious child obtain perspective and encouragement. As I often tell parents, "They [children] don't come with manuals." Plus, we live in a society where young adults move from one city to another for their education or work opportunities. Children are born, and the potential wisdom of extended families and multiple generations of childrearing is unavailable or at least not easily accessible. Having a community of parents for mutual support can be an antidote to feelings of isolation and self-doubt which in turn can lead to vacillation and inconsistency in parenting.

Commitment

Commitment is both a goal—to maintain one's commitment to responsive parenting—and a strategy for achieving goals: Having a commitment organizes and prioritizes one's decision making. This gets back to the idea of *choices* and *decisions:*Where are we going and what are the next steps that will get us moving in that direction? Additionally, a commitment to parenting means that a parent not only holds the values and goals necessary to guide her parenting behavior but also *believes* that she personally can manifest those values and reach those goals. In that latter sense, this aspect of commitment is akin to having faith in oneself. How does a parent acquire faith in his ability to parent? The same way the child develops his own self-efficacy: through experience. This is the same feedback loop we see in exposure therapy. Having a valued goal inspires a leap of faith, courageous behavior, which allows a new experience of competence and satisfaction that in turn creates new internal working models of oneself and the world. The new and more conscious models of self and the world can be summoned and used the next time that challenging situation is met.

So, it is useful to periodically return to the topic of values and goals in order to remind parents why they are doing this hard work. Doing so can help reorient everyone to the treatment goals and shore up sagging parent efforts and cooperation:

SALMA: The rudeness has got to stop! I can't say anything to Brayden without him trying to make some sarcastic comment or putdown. I wish you would stop encouraging him in this. It's spilling over into school again. I'm the one getting the emails from the vice-principal. I hate always having to be the bad guy, but somebody has to set some boundaries here.

GEOFF: Okay, I'll let Brayden know that he can only do that with me and to be respectful to you. I don't know what's going on at school, but I'm sure it's overblown. We pay them good money to manage him there.

CLINICIAN [*before Salma can respond (react!)*]: We've talked before about this rudeness and sarcastic behavior and how it may at times be a cover for feelings of anxiety, self-doubt, and loss of control. Do we still think this is the process at work, at least some of the time?

(*Parents nod in agreement*)

CLINICIAN: And it seems these behaviors have become a knee-jerk reaction to any adult or peer interaction where Brayden does not feel completely in control and the anxiety and humiliation threaten to break through. It's become quite automatic through years of practice and we can't let him practice these behaviors any more, under any circumstances, with anyone. That's the only way we can break this habit. Can we agree on that?

(*Parents nod*)

CLINICIAN: I think it's best to go back to the validation/redirection moves that you've *both* found helpful so far. It will be important that *both* of you take every opportunity to help Brayden understand what's likely going on with him in those moments, insist that he communicate respectfully and effectively, and together find some better ways of coping with the situation. And, you *both* need to let him know that these expectations extend beyond any one family member and out into his social world generally. Can we do that?

PARENTS; USE OF THE VALUED LIVING QUESTIONNAIRE

Recall the Valued Living Questionnaire from Chapter 7. It can be a useful instrument for helping parents organize their thinking around valued goals that would promote self-care and enhance resilience. To the child/adolescent version found in Appendix D one could add the domain of partner/marital values and goals. Identifying and committing to resilience-supporting goals for the week ahead will help build self-care habits and, as mentioned, model for the child this commitment to self-care for the sake of the entire family.

Often, one parent goal that needs encouraging is taking time away from the children. This time should be regularly scheduled so that it is just a given, and not time snatched from the mainstream of life on a haphazard basis, *fleeing* from the children in frustration, anger, or resentment. This "away time" should be a minimum of two hours, as a solid block, each week. Most clinicians will meet with some resistance from parents when proposing this goal. There will be agreement that it should be done, but also many reasons why it can't be done. Insist. Persist.

A FEW WORDS ABOUT CLINICIAN RESILIENCE AND SELF-CARE

It's really, really, important.

Promoting Clinician Resilience

This is hard work that we do. Sigmund Freud referred to psychotherapy as the "impossible profession" because it is so inherently difficult and frustrating. As my own therapist was fond of saying, "We are in the misery business." A bit of hyperbole, but the work we do is stressful as often as it is rewarding, sometimes simultaneously. In behavioral therapy terms, we are often on a "lean reinforcement schedule"; we do not often see spectacular results from our efforts. Sometimes we take solace in knowing that we are planting seeds that may blossom miles down the road, to mix a metaphor. Stress is common among mental health professionals and can affect not just our own well-being but our therapeutic effectiveness by reducing our attention and concentration, negatively influencing our decision making, and compromising the therapeutic relationship in any number of ways.

If you work in a solo practice there is perhaps the added stress of isolation. You may deprive yourself of regular consultation with peers or just "bouncing ideas off" another professional in order to achieve some perspective and additional insight or perhaps just affirm that you've made the best possible call in a particular situation.

When stress is chronic there is risk for *burnout*. Burnout is a recognized syndrome that is a response to chronic interpersonal job-related stress. It consists of physical and emotional exhaustion, irritability, and discouragement, as well as a sense of low personal accomplishment (Spickard, Gabbe, & Christensen, 2002). Among physicians, not surprisingly, burnout is associated with poor patient care (Shapiro, Astin, Bishop, & Cordova, 2005). It should not be different for psychotherapists and our clients. A vicious cycle can occur in which a sense of ineffectiveness leads to depletion and discouragement, which negatively influences effectiveness, and so on.

Risk Factors for Professional Burnout

Certain factors have been shown to be associated with increased risk for burnout in the health professions (Blust, 2009). These include being early in one's career, lack of a life partner, a passive or defensive approach to stress, and a lack of sense of control over one's professional life. It would make sense that a lack of experience and confidence, combined with a sense of isolation, would place a clinician at risk for burnout. Similarly, avoiding recognizing and addressing the signs of professional burnout will lead to slipping further into the syndrome.

With regard to the last factor, a lack of control over one's professional life, it's unclear as of this writing what changes health-care reform will bring to the professional life of psychotherapists. But it seems likely that the days of the truly independent practitioner are numbered. Integrated care and affiliating with providers from other disciplines will help clinicians feel less isolated, which will help prevent burnout. But many of us, and future clinicians certainly, are likely to be working in settings where we have less control over our schedules, the number and types of clients we see, and even the therapy we conduct. These factors will likely contribute to stress and burnout if we're not alert and responsive to these issues.

Take Your Own Pulse First

There is little argument that resilience is vital to our effectiveness as clinicians and to our own well-being generally. The first step in dealing with stress and avoiding the syndrome of burnout is to monitor your own state for signs that you are becoming stressed, exhausted, and depleted. New medical students, dealing with their first crises and needing to be The Doctor, are commonly advised to "Take your own pulse first."

While everyone is different, and the symptoms of burnout may differ from one clinician to the next, there are a number of telltale signs that a professional is slipping toward depletion, exhaustion, and burnout. Like the symptoms of a clinical diagnosis, these factors are typically found along continua; there are mild to severe manifestations of all of them. For example, every clinician is going to find her mind wandering somewhat during a session. That said, some signs of burnout may be more "pathognomonic" than others. Here are just a few important signs:

- Difficulty concentrating on what the client is saying in session
- Fatigue and feeling drained or apathetic
- Missing or being late for appointments
- Avoiding returning calls or neglecting collateral tasks such as writing reports
- Feelings of resentment or bitterness toward the client or the work generally
- Excessive alcohol or drug use outside of work, and especially if one is "self-medicating" during work
- Vicarious trauma from clients' stories
- Finding that thoughts and images from work come home and interfere with relaxing, enjoying time with family and friends, or sleeping

Dealing with Burnout Before It Happens

All of the strategies I've described for developing and maintaining resilience in the parent apply to us as well. Let's start by thinking about the individual characteristics associated with resilience in individuals. Even if we ourselves do not naturally possess a moderately high activity level, alertness, responsiveness, and sociability (i.e., we're not "easy babies"), can we find ways to cultivate these qualities? At the very least, can we be aware of, and work against, any natural tendencies to inertia, dullness, and social isolation? Similarly, can we work to develop and nurture our curiosity, frustration tolerance, impulse control, and reasoning and problem-solving skills through hobbies, learning to play a musical instrument, running in 5k races and working up to marathons, or taking on challenges outside of our professional life? For example, we might join and be active in a professional association or community group. Can we combine autonomous behavior with the ability to ask for help?

Working with anxious children and their parents is stressful because *anxiety is contagious*. It is easy to resonate with the child's or parent's anxiety, to feel and take on the parent's frantic need to *do something now*. We so readily take this on without considering (a) whether that's what the situation calls for, and (b) the effect this course of action might have on our own well-being and ability to be an effective clinician over the course of treatment.

Recall some of the concepts I have discussed in relation to parent coping and responsiveness. There was the SOBER acronym. Many times we feel the need to rush in and be the rescuer of the child and parent when what we need to do is stop, observe what's going on (including our own automatic thoughts and emotions), breathe, and expand our view of the situation to ensure that our next response will be just that: a response and not a reaction.

In keeping with *clinician* responsiveness, we have the notion of "tolerance," knowing when to lean in and when to step back based on what the situation actually calls for rather than going with our own immediate urges. We may feel the urge to validate, empathize, make an interpretation, provide advice, or set a limit. Any of those thera-peutic moves might be exactly what is called for. Or not. Similarly, the clinician may retreat or refrain from saying something that, in fact, should be said in the moment because of any number of clear or vague reasons. Often, if an opportunity is missed to make a point, the chance will come back around.

Mindfulness and Evenly Hovering Attention

As with the parents we work with and their ability to navigate anxiety-rich family situations, we as clinicians can benefit from mindfulness practice in our regular lives and especially in session. Sigmund Freud talked about the clinician maintaining what he called an "evenly hovering attention" during the therapy hour. I interpret this as the clinician maintaining attention to what the client is say-ing, without becoming complacent but also without going too far, too quickly, in one's mind toward conclusions or interpretations. It means not indulging the urge to say something wise or clever for the sake of sounding wise and clever. It also means keeping a mindful eye on one's feelings, as they can provide useful information as well as an opportunity to validate or mirror the client's experience in the room, in the moment. This is powerful stuff and, like the facilitated listening we're asking the parents to do, it is exhausting.

Connecting with Others

While mental health-care or behavioral health-care delivery will surely go through major changes in the next decade, at this time there are quite a few clinicians still in solo practices. This can be lonely and stressful, depleting one's resilience. Plus, it's unwise to practice entirely alone without the names and numbers (on speed dial) of a couple of trusted, experienced clinicians one can call on for a quick consult or to check to see if something is hiding in your blind spot. Getting consultation from a trusted and experienced peer is a clinician's first and immediate move if you think you're in a questionable ethical situation or simply have concerns about your assessment or treatment plan. Gnawing doubts and second-guessing can have a corrosive effect on confidence, mood, attention, and even physical health. Take care of it and move on.

I encourage early-career clinicians to network, to make connections with clinicians who know your clinical area and then provide consultation to each other as needed. Join a consult group centered on a type of presenting problem (e.g., child anxiety) or a particular therapy (e.g., acceptance and commitment therapy). Having a solid theoretical stance to work from (it almost doesn't matter which one) increases a clinician's confidence and allows for efficient decision making.

Get to know local clinicians who have experience and skills that you don't have so that you can make helpful referrals when a set of problems comes to you that is outside your area of expertise. Attend workshops and conferences and expand your knowledge and skills base.

All of these strategies will help a clinician feel more confident, vital, secure, and connected within a larger therapy community. To this I would simply add that all the self-care strategies that help parents be more resilient will also help with clinician resilience: good sleep hygiene, exercise, good eating habits, and minimal if any use of intoxicants.

A LOOK AHEAD

My sincere hope is that you have come this far with me because the preceding pages have been interesting, thought provoking, and of possible utility in your work with the parents of anxious children. Let me try to summarize some of the key points that have been covered.

A Transdiagnostic Approach

The therapeutic stance taken in this book has been more *process* oriented than *symptom* oriented. By focusing on common processes in our treatment, we can apply general strategies to a host of particular diagnostic categories and shift the focus of treatment away from an overemphasis on symptom reduction and toward increasing good functioning regardless of the moment's emotional or cognitive states. Chief among the processes found in childhood anxiety are avoidance, along with excessive and ineffective control behaviors.

Temperament

Temperament and other aspects of human biology can predispose one child over another to meet the world with behavioral inhibition, negative affect and emotions, and difficulties with attentional control. These predispositions can set the stage for a pattern of avoidance and control.

The Role of Parents in Childhood Anxiety

Certain parenting behaviors and styles have been linked with childhood anxiety. These include excessive control, intrusiveness, and overprotection. On the other hand, parenting behaviors that convey warmth, encourage age-appropriate autonomy, and support courageous behaviors are associated with confident and competent children.

The Parent-Child Anxiety Dance

Held together by the power of mutual negative reinforcement, parent and child will develop a highly predictable and largely automatic set of behaviors in response to certain challenging situations. More so than the "symptoms" of anxiety themselves (worries, physical sensations of the fight-or-flight reaction), it is this dance that is in fact the presenting problem.

Avoidance and Control

What makes the anxiety dance problematic is that the resulting behaviors, the end point of the dance, so often consist of either escape from the anxiety-provoking situation, avoidance of such situations, or unhelpful efforts at controlling the situation (e.g., compulsive behaviors, safety behaviors such as hand washing).

Communication.

Effective communication among family members is critical for (1) replacing physical manifestations of the anxious upset with more helpful verbal communication, (2) modeling and teaching the child how to use language as inner speech to promote self-regulation and distress tolerance, and (3) to help orient the child and parent away from simple avoidance and control strategies and toward values-driven actions.

Changing the Choreography

There's a saying attributed to a number of people, "Things are the way they are because they got that way." The dance got that way over time. It is learned behavior. It can be unlearned. That is the basis of most cognitive behavioral therapy: unlearning old behavior patterns; both one's overt behavior in the world and the "inner" behavior of cognitions. The dance is changed through increased awareness, shifting attention, and redirecting attention and behavior toward valued goals in the moment. A goal in the moment might be just coping and getting through it. Validation techniques are an important component of increasing awareness.

Cognitive Behavioral Therapy

Cognitive behavioral therapies, mostly in the form of exposure/response prevention, can be quite helpful in treating anxieties of all kinds. The client is given an opportunity for growth in the form of new experiences and in changing one's ideas (internal working models) about the world and oneself through the process of cognitive reappraisal. Parents play an important role in the implementation and eventual success of these treatments

Mindfulness- and Acceptance-Based Therapies

More recent therapy models have emerged from the CBT tradition that use mindfulness practice and emphasize radical (as in "root") acceptance of what is in the moment as a necessary starting place from which change becomes possible. The goal of these trans-diagnostic therapies is less reducing or eliminating symptoms and instead moving behavior in the direction of life goals.

Leaning In and Hanging Back

A new and more effective parent-child dance will involve processes of leaning in (giving attention, providing support, setting healthy limits) and hanging back (waiting, granting autonomy, "Don't Just Do Something, Stand There"). It is most helpful if the parent's decision to lean in or hang back is based on what the immediate situation calls for in the way of a response, and not so much on the parent's own turmoil in that moment. It is a supreme challenge for some parents to let go of their own control agenda. For others, it is the work of not avoiding, of leaning in and experiencing life as it is in the moment, that is most difficult.

Resilience

Finally, parent (and clinician) resilience is an important, if neglected, component of a successful treatment plan for child anxiety. Developing self-care plans for the parents, for the child, and for yourself as the clinician can support everyone's efforts in the work of psychotherapy.

IN CLOSING

So, we leave these families still struggling to find their way. Mycroft and Grace, Wyatt and Brayden, Freya and Jimmy. There have been changes in how the problems of anxiety are regarded by some of the parents, if not by the children themselves. Not yet, at least. Some changes to the choreography are happening, still tenuous in some cases. Overall there's an increased awareness of what each person is doing in relation to his or her own thoughts and feelings and of how that behavior is affecting important others. It's a good, if fragile beginning.

Given that anxiety is an unavoidable fact of life, or at the very least is avoided only at a certain cost, it is unlikely that we will obtain true "cures" among the anxious clients we see. Instead, we can be satisfied with equipping these young people and their parents with the information, strategies, skills, and experiences to "struggle well." I often tell parents that real progress doesn't always look the way we might expect it. Recall the figure in Chapter 7 showing the changes in duration, intensity, and frequency, with decreasing duration likely happening first, and intensity being the last variable to change. At other times I describe this work as much like gardening. You plant seeds and tend them. The little shoots do not come up in an orderly fashion. There's one here, tiny and fragile. Then another over here. Ah, patches of green emerge and then eventually spread and fill in until there's more green foliage than bare dirt. It's a process that requires patience and faith. May you have both in abundance.

Summary of Key Ideas

- Parent resilience and self-care is not commonly discussed in the child anxiety literature, but it is a vitally important component of a successful treatment program.
- Definitions of *resilience* include "struggling well" and "bouncing forward."
- Parent and clinician resilience is important throughout the treatment process, but it is especially important to emphasize good self-care at the difficult beginning phases of therapy when things aren't changing that much and discouragement can occur.
- Resilience is correlated with certain characteristics of the individual (curiosity, sociability, and others), with a supportive family milieu, and with the availability of external community supports.
- Relationships marked by responsiveness, warmth, caring, effective limit setting, and mutual respect are associated with resilience.
- Parent and clinician self-care are vital to resilience through enhancing one's strength, energy, and commitment.
- Secure your own oxygen mask first before offering assistance to others.
- Take your own pulse first.

Validation Handout

VALIDATION

Graybar's First Law of Human Behavior:

"All behavior is a message, and a behavior won't begin to change until the person knows the message has been received."

Validation (also known as "mirroring" or "reflecting")

- Closes the communication loop: "message received"
- Provides accurate and nuanced emotional vocabulary
  - "Frustrated" instead of "angry"
  - "Nervous" instead of "scared"
- Replaces ineffective *reassurance* in many situations
- *Connects* certain thoughts and feelings with certain situations
  - Frustration with a challenging homework problem
  - Jealousy at another child's birthday party
- *Disconnects* thoughts and feelings from old behavior patterns and *redirects* child toward a better behavior
  - You can be angry and not hit; use your words.
  - You can be nervous and still do what's expected; *be brave.*
- Can include describing the interpersonal process or dance—both currently and what's possible. I like to include a "time stamp" such as "now" or "here" that suggests this unhappy state of thinking and feeling is both situation specific and temporary.

- "You're having those scary ideas right now and you want me to go upstairs with you now. I can do that in a few minutes."
- Promotes "mentalizing": the awareness of, and curiosity about, one's own thoughts and feelings and those of others. Curiosity is a new and different relationship to the thought or feeling instead of automatically regarding it as true and a problem.
  - "Huh, I wonder why that thought is showing up now?"
- Young children, and all of us under stress, will regard thoughts as literal and true. This leads to big upsets when others have different ideas or the child's expectations aren't met. Validation directs thinking toward the idea of "ideas": mere thoughts that may or may not match with reality or come true in the future.
  - "Ah, you had the idea there were popsicles in the freezer."
  - "Oh, you were expecting to go straight home and now you're angry because we need to go by the store."
- Validation says nothing about your agreeing with that thought or feeling or the "appropriateness" of your child's state at the time.

Validation Techniques

- It's best to leave out the "I understand" as in "I understand you're upset." It's unnecessary and kids will go right to "You *don't* understand!" and now you're arguing about whether or not you truly understand.
- Use emotional vocabulary that is as specific as possible, adjusted for the child's age. Instead of "upset," use a more specific or nuanced word as described above; "nervous," "jealous," "frustrated," "contrary." This is part of stepping back from and being interested in and curious about feelings and "ideas" instead of being pushed around by them. Introduce your child to new emotion words such as "dudgeon." Look it up.
- Use simple and specific "Ah" statements:
  - "Ah, you're feeling *frustrated*."
  - "Ah, you're having one of those 'I can't do it' thoughts and you want my help."

- Use "I wonder" statements if you're not sure what's going on with your child or your want a more subtle or less intrusive approach at that moment.
  - "I wonder if you're thinking you won't know anyone there, and that thought is inviting you to be nervous."
- Offer "refusal rights" with older kids
  - "I could be wrong, but you look like you're feeling nervous right now."
- Always keep validation very, very brief. It's not a lecture. It's a simple and specific "message received."

Whole Body Validation

- 80 percent of human communication is *nonverbal,* and people will believe your nonverbals over your verbals.
- So, resist taking on the *opposite* emotional state of your child in the moment—e.g., super-calm when he is angry or perky when he is sad. That is both invalidating and annoying.
- Instead, when you validate be okay with showing some emotion in line with what your child is feeling at the moment so that he knows you really get it. After all, the heart of validation is your expressing *empathy* for your child in that moment. Facial expression and tone of voice will help you do that in a meaningful way.
- Please note, *validation won't turn off your child's behavior like flipping a switch,* but it can be an important first step in winding down an emotional episode and getting to some reasonable communication, problem solving or coping.

Child-Directed Play Handout

CHILD-DIRECTED PLAY

DEFINITION: Child-directed play, or CDP, is a one-on-one play interaction between a parent and a child in which the child directs and leads the play in any way he or she wishes (unless there is harmful or destructive activity, see below).

RECOMMENDED AGE OF CHILD: Primarily for children ages two to seven but can be modified for interactions with children through adolescence.

Objectives of CDP

1. To enhance the child's sense of appropriate control, self-regulation, and self-confidence.
2. To provide an opportunity for the child's access to focused, uninterrupted adult attention and close contact, without having to rely on negative or provocative behaviors to do so.
3. To improve the attunement or "dance" between the parent and child and the child's sense of confidence and security in that relationship. This allows for more subtle and effective interactions in the future.

Adult Behaviors to Do

Follow the child's play and other behaviors

- Locate yourself physically close to the child. If he is on the floor, you will be on the floor. Within reason, move with the child.
- Watch the child's play activities closely.

Describe what you observe

- Verbally describe *some* of what your child is doing with the play materials. Be specific. Be brief. For example, "You put the red block on the blue block"; "There goes the car"; "Here it comes!" Show enthusiasm!

Imitate some of what your child does

- Physically repeat something your child does with the play materials; put one block on another, make your car go, and so on.
- Verbally repeat something your child has said: "Look out, the car is coming"; "That flower is going to be red," and so on. You can also imitate nonverbal sounds and vocalizations: "Woo hoo!" "Vrroom."

Praise occasionally

- This is not a time to be lavishing your child with praise. It is in fact a neutral time when the child is valued simply because he exists. For this period time, at least, his worth is completely unconditional and unearned.
- *So, use praise sparingly.* If you are going to praise, focus on some quality of your child, rather than the object he has made. For example, if he makes a nice tower with the blocks you would say, "You're a great tower builder" rather than, "That's a great tower."
- You can praise some action, such as "You're being very careful with the paints." But this, too, should be done sparingly.

Adult Behaviors to Avoid

Commands

- Avoid giving commands regarding your child's behavior or the toys—e.g., "Let's play with the house" or "don't get out the blocks yet." (Handling misbehavior is described below.)

Changing the direction of the play

- Don't change direction of the play. This is for your child to decide and maintain or change as he wishes. Refrain from giving your child your play ideas.

Teaching

- CDP is not a time to quiz your child, rehearse skills, or teach new facts or concepts. Allow your child to play with the toys or materials in any way that is not harmful. Remember—there is no "right" way to play.

Questions

- Questions can be a subtle way of attempting to take control of the play or to teach: "What color is that block?" "Do you want to play with the shark?"

Handling Misbehavior

- Children rarely misbehave during CDP once they figure out it is their special and undemanding play time. In the event of destructive, annoying, or physically aggressive behaviors, stop the play, briefly explain why you've stopped it (the child's specific behavior), and tell your child that the play cannot continue if the behavior continues. Describe the behavior you expect (gentle, respectful, etc.). If the problem behavior continues, stop the CDP until the next scheduled time. At that time you can *briefly* restate the rules about expected behavior.

PLEASE NOTE: *CDP is sacred time.* It should not be used as a reward nor taken away as a punishment. If your child is misbehaving close to the time you are scheduled to do CDP, remind him that your special time together is coming up and you hope he will be calm and ready to enjoy it. If your child chooses not to do CDP with you, matter-of-factly accept that choice and move on. CDP will be available to him next as scheduled.

Handling Your Own Reactions

- As the adult in the CDP interaction you may notice any of a number of unwelcomed responses that are *very common*—your mind wandering, confusion, boredom, irritation, to name a few.
- When this happens, focus on a deep and steady breath or two and then gently bring your attention back to what the child is doing at the moment. The kind of mindful attention CDP calls for is often hard work. It is also a skill that will become easier and more natural with practice.

Implementing Child-Directed Play at Home

Setting

- Pick a quiet place where you will not be disturbed by siblings, TV, phone, pets, and so on.

When/how long/how often

- Do CDP two to three times per week for 10 to 15 minutes per session.
- It's best to do CDP on as regular a schedule as possible—e.g., Tuesday and Thursday evenings from 7:00 to 7:15.
- Set a timer so that your child will know how much time is left in the play.
- Make sure the CDP time does not conflict with or compete with your child's favorite TV show or other valued activity.

Types of toys

- Toys that the child already knows and likes are often best.
- Competitive games are to be avoided as are any games or toys that are highly structured (e.g., lots of rules to follow). Computer and video games, even two-player games, are to be avoided. Ideally, you want activities that create possibility and the use of imagination.
- Reading books or playing sports are not ideal for child-directed play.

How to present CDP to your child

- Explain to your child that this is his "special time" with you and you alone.
- Tell him of the time limit.
- Show him the choice of toys or materials you've picked out *and have ready ahead of time.*
- If the child says "No" to your offer or the choice of toys, don't argue or push. Offer again the next day. You can do some negotiating about the toys available as long as you stay within the above guidelines. Remind your child that he has many other opportunities to play computer games or other activities not suitable for CDP.

Breathing Exercises Handout

BREATHING EXERCISES

Finding Your Breath

1. Start by breathing naturally through your nose. Find a comfortable rhythm and pace. Your eyes can be open or closed.

2. Now feel the sensation of the breath as it travels in and out of your nose. Notice how you can put your attention right there, at your nostrils. With each slow inhalation, notice how the air you take in is cool against the skin around the edges of your nostrils. Notice how, on the out-breath, the air is now warmer, heated by the body. Notice how this warmth makes the sensation of the outgoing air even more subtle against the skin.

3. Keep breathing. Notice how you can detect ever more subtle variations in the quality of the breath: air speed and pressure, temperature, smoothness, little whistling noises, and so on. You will notice the other sensations going on both inside and outside your body. If you find your mind wandering off, gently bring your attention back to your nostrils and your breathing.

4. Feel free to continue as long as you like. Five or ten in-out cycles, done with attention, is sufficient practice and perhaps all a young child may be able to do at one time.

Whistling, Pinwheels, and Blow Cups

Whistling a tune is practicing breath control. You can play with pin-wheels and blow cups, the pipe-shaped objects with a little basket and ball that you blow into and keep the ball suspended above the basket.

Basic "Belly" or Diaphragmatic Breathing

Belly breathing is a great tool for quickly gaining control over the body and steadying the mind when it is alarmed. Belly breathing can be done anywhere, at any time, and it is inconspicuous.

1. Sit in a chair comfortably but with your back straight and feet on the floor.
2. Find your bellybutton, poke it with your finger, and then place your other hand on your belly just above where finger is.
3. Breathe in. As you do so, imagine that you are blowing up a balloon that is expanding against your hand. Continue to inflate this bal-loon with your breath until the inhalation is complete.
4. Breathe out, deflating the balloon until your belly collapses a little underneath your hand.
5. Repeat.

Eight or ten breaths is sufficient practice for one sitting. Practice a couple of times a day—first thing in the morning and at bedtime work well.

Another good way to practice belly breathing is lying on your back. You might do this right after your child gets into bed at night:

1. Have your child lie on his back.
2. Place his hand or a small, light object (e.g., a rubber duck) on the belly just above the belly button.
3. Ask him to belly breathe. As your child breathes in, the duck rises up as if on a wave that's passing beneath it. As he exhales, the duck sinks back down.

The Darth Vader Breath

This is my name for what is known in yoga as "ujjayi" (pronounced oo-ji-ee) breathing. You make this sound every time you say "hat" or "how." This involves a slight narrowing at the high back of the throat just behind and below the nose. This will create that soft rushing "h" sound while breathing in and out. It would be a growl if you got the bottom of the throat involved and a snoring sound if it's too high in the nose. Some describe this sound as ocean waves rolling in and out again.

1. While slightly narrowing the high back of your throat, breathe in.
2. Continue narrowing the back of your throat and breathe out.
3. Repeat for four or five cycles of inhaling and exhaling.

Narrowing the throat in this way restricts the flow of air just a little, slows down the breath, and allows for a long, even inhalation and exhalation. Like sipping liquid through a straw, ujjayi breathing makes it hard to "gulp" air. Additionally the sound it makes, like Darth Vader breathing, makes you more conscious of your breath and what it's doing: slow, fast, steady, halting. Practice will help you and your child develop a long, steady, and smooth breathing pattern that will be incompatible with the fight-or-flight response.

The Up-and-Over Breath

This is a simple but very engaging technique. As you breathe in, imagine a wave of water rising up from your low belly, washing up over your chest, your face, and your forehead. As you reach the fullness of the in-breath, this wave goes over the top of your head and, as you breathe out, cascades down the back of your head, neck, and back. The cycle starts again with your next in-breath. If you like, you can think of a rising, cresting, and descending current of air or wind, a stream of light, or whatever image you prefer. This breathing technique is simple and encourages long, steady, even breaths. It is a soothing and relaxing sensation.

The Ferris-Wheel Breath

This is sometimes called the "square breath" in yoga, although in reality it's more like a rectangle. I want you to imagine a Ferris wheel, the kind you might find at a county fair. Imagine it turning in a slow circle, down one side, up the other. Imagine that you are riding it and it stops—and there you are in the car at the very top, paused in your arc. Now the Ferris wheel starts again and you descend. Now, for the Ferris-Wheel Breath, do the following:

1. Breathe in naturally, counting about once per second. You may get to a count of three, four, or five when the inhalation is complete. How long the breath is isn't important.
2. Breathe out, counting again—one, two, three, four. Do this a few times, breathing in and out naturally, counting as you go.
3. Now breathe in to the top of your inhalation and then pause while you count one, two, and so on—again about one count per second.
4. Exhale fully. At the bottom of the exhalation, pause and count again—one, two, and so on.
5. Repeat Steps 3 and 4 for four or five cycles of inhaling and exhaling.

Like the Ferris wheel pausing in its cycling, your breath will rise, pause, descend, pause, rise again, pause, and so on. This pause should not be a straining or gripping action or even really "holding" your breath. The goal is to establish rhythm, control, and mindful awareness of your breath.

Introduce this image to your child and practice the Ferris-Wheel Breath a few minutes each day as you would practice the other techniques. Look for opportunities to gently suggest using the Ferris-Wheel Breath when you notice your child is anxious or upset in some way.

Lion's Breath

1. Take a long, deep breath.
2. Open your mouth wide.

3. Make your eyes big.
4. Let you tongue hang out.
5. ROAR!!

The Alien Breath

This is a very interesting experience. You are going to breathe in the manner of an alien from a planet where creatures breathe not through their mouths and noses but through the palms of their hands and the soles of their feet.

1. Sit comfortably or lie down and breathe naturally. Hands and feet can be positioned in any way that is comfortable. You can be wearing footwear.
2. Find your breath—Breathe through your nose and notice the tingly coolness of the air as it passes through your nostrils during the inhalation. Notice the subtle and warm feeling of the air as you exhale through your nose. Notice those sensations now as you breathe in and out.
3. After a few breaths, use your mind to picture the palms of your hands.
4. Breathe in. Use your imagination to feel a sensation of movement across your palms from outside to inside. "Feel" the air, cool and tingly, pass through your palms and into your hands, and travel up your arms and into your lungs.
5. Breathe out. Use your imagination to feel a sensation of movement from inside to outside. Feel the air leave your lungs, travel down your arms, and out through the palms of your hands, warm and subtle.

Now, in the same way, try breathing through the soles of your feet.

1. Breathe in. Feel the cool air enter the bottoms of your feet, travel up your legs, and into your chest.
2. Breathe out. With your exhalation, push the air all the way down and out the soles of your feet, the breath warm now from having traveled through your body.

For variation, you can breathe in through your hands and breathe out through your feet, or the reverse. Have fun with it. This imaginative breathing is subtle and may be difficult for some younger children to grasp. It can be quite intriguing to older children. Alien breathing takes the mind out of the head and creates some distance from the habitual chatter in the brain. This can be especially helpful when you or your child is having difficulty "turning the mind off" in order to fall asleep.

Valued Living Questionnaire

Importance
1–10

1. Family   _____   Goals _____

_____

2. Friends/
   Social Life   _____   Goals _____

_____

3. Work   _____   Goals _____

_____

4. School   _____   Goals _____

_____

5. Recreation/Fun   _____   Goals _____

_____

6. Spirituality   _____   Goals _____

_____

7. Citizenship/
   Community   _____   Goals _____

_____

8. Physical Self-care
   (diet, exercise, sleep) _____   Goals _____

_____

APPENDIX E

Resources for Parents

Coyne, L. W., & Murrell, A. R. (2009). *The joy of parenting.* Oakland, CA: New Harbinger Publications.

Guare, R., Dawson, P., & Guare. C. (2013). *Smart but scattered for teens.* New York, NY: Guilford.

Harris, B. (2003). *When your kids push your buttons and what you can do about it.* New York, NY: Werner Books.

Harvey, P., & Penzo, J. (2009). *Parenting a child who has intense emotions: Dialectical behavior therapy skills to help your child regulate emotional outbursts and aggressive behaviors.* Oakland, CA: New Harbinger Publications.

Kastner, L. S. (2013). *Wise minded parenting.* Seattle, WA: ParentMap.

McCurry, C. (2009). *Parenting your anxious child with mindfulness and acceptance.* Oakland, CA: New Harbinger Publications.

Mogel, W. (2001). *The blessing of a skinned knee.* New York, NY: Scribner.

Mogel, W. (2010). *The blessing of a B minus.* New York, NY: Scribner.

Race, K. (2014). *Mindful Parenting: Simple and Powerful Solutions for Raising Creative, Engaged, Happy Kids in Today's Hectic World.* New York: St. Martin's Griffin.

Wilson, K. G., & Dufrene, T. (2010). *Things might go terribly, horribly wrong: A guide to life liberated from anxiety.* Oakland, CA: New Harbinger Publications.

Wilson, R. & Lyons, L. (2013). *Anxious kids, anxious parents.* Deerfield Beach, FL: Health Communications.

References

Achenbach, T. M. (1991). *Manual for the Child Behavior Check-list/4-18*. Burlington, VT: University of Vermont.

Allen, J. G., Fonagy, P., & Bateman, A. W. (2008). *Mentalizing in clinical practice*. Arlington, VA: American Psychiatric Publishing.

American Psychiatric Association. (2013). *Diagnostic and statistical manual of mental disorders, 5th edition*. Washington, D.C.: American Psychiatric Publishing.

Anderson, E. R., Smith, A. J., Christophersen, E. R. (2011). A creative approach to teaching anxiety management skills in children. *The Behavior Therapist, 34*, 3-7.

Appleton, P. (Ed.). (2008). *Children's anxiety: A contextual approach*. New York: Routeledge.

Arditte, K. A., & Joormann, J. (2014). Cognitive biases in child psychopathology. In J. Ehrenreich-May & B. C. Chu (Eds.) *Transdiagnostic treatments for children and adolescents: Principles and practice* (pp. 59-83). New York: Guilford Press.

Armbruster, P., & Fallon, T. (1994). Clinical, sociodemographic, and systems risk factors for attrition in a children's mental health clinic. *American Journal of Orthopsychiatry, 64*, 577-585. doi: 10.1037/h0079571

Bailey, C. E. (Ed.) (2005). *Children in therapy: Using the family as a resource*. New York: W. W. Norton.

Bar-Haim, Y., Lamy, D., Pergamin, L., Bakermans-Kranenburg, M. J., & Van IJzendoom, M. H. (2007). Threat-related attentional bias in anxious and non-anxious individuals: A meta-analytic study. *Psychological Bulletin, 133*, 1-24. doi: 10.1037/0033-2909.133.1.1

Barlow, D. H., Allen, L. A., & Choate, M. L. (2004). Toward a unified treatment for emotional disorders. *Behavior Therapy, 35*, 205-230. doi: 10.1016/S0005-7894(04)80036-4

Barmish, A. J., & Kendall, P.C. (2005). Should parents be co-clients in cognitive-behavioral therapy for anxious youth? *Journal of Clinical Child and Adolescent Psychology, 34*, 569-581. doi: 10.1207/s15374424jccp3403_12

Barrett, P., & Farrell, L. (2007). Behavioral family intervention for childhood anxiety. In Briesmeister, J. M. & Schaefer, C. E. (Eds.), *Handbook of parent training* (3rd Ed.) (pp. 133-163). New York: John Wiley and Sons.

Barrett, P. M., Rapee, R. M., Dadds, M. M., & Ryan, S. M. (1996). Family enhancement of cognitive style in anxious and aggressive children. *Journal of Abnormal Child Psychology, 24*, 187-203. doi:10.1007/BF01441484

Baumrind, D. (1968). Authoritarian vs. authoritative parental control. *Adolescence, 3*, 255-272.

Barrett, P. M., Rapee, R. M., Dadds, M. M., & Ryan, S. M. (1996). Family enhancement of cognitive style in anxious and aggressive children. *Journal of Abnormal Child Psychology, 24*, 187-203. doi:10.1007/BF01441484

Beidel, D. C., & Turner, S. M. (2005). *Childhood anxiety disorders: A guide to research and treatment.* Hove, U.K.: Routledge.

Blackledge, J. T., & Hayes, S. C. (2006). Using Acceptance and Commitment Training in the Support of Parents of Children Diagnosed with Autism. *Child & Family Behavior Therapy, 28*, 1-18. doi: 10.1300/J019v28n01_01

Blust, L. (2009). Health professional burnout: Part 1. *Journal of Palliative Medicine, 12*, 639-640. doi:10.1089/jpm.2009.9594

Bowen, S., Chawla, N., & Marlatt, G. A. (2010). Mindfulness-based relapse prevention for addictive behaviors: A clinician's guide. New York: Guilford.

Bradley, R., Greene, J., Russ, E., Dutra, L., & Weston, D. (2005).

A multidimensional meta-analysis of psychotherapy of PTSD. *American Journal of Psychiatry, 162,* 214-227. doi: 10.1176/appi.ajp.162.2.214

Burke, C. A. (2009). Mindfulness-based approaches with children and adolescents: A preliminary review of current research in an emergent field. *Journal of Child and Family Studies, 19,* 133-144. doi:10.1007/s10826-009-9282-x

Capps, L., Sigman, M., Sena, R., & Henker, B. (1996). Fear, anxiety, and perceived control in children of agoraphobic parents. *Journal of Child Psychology and Psychiatry, 37,* 445-452. doi: 10.1111/j.1469-7610.1996.tb01425.x

Carmody, J. (2009). Evolving conceptions of mindfulness in clinical settings. *Journal of Cognitive Psychotherapy: An International Quarterly, 23,* 270-280. doi: 10.1891/0889-8391.23.3.270

Cartwright-Hatton, S. (2010). *From timid to tiger: A treatment manual for parenting the anxious child.* New York: Wiley-Blackwell.

Cavell, T. A. (2000). *Working with parents of aggressive children: A practitioner's guide.* Washington, D.C.: American Psychological Association.

Cheron, D. M., Ehrenreich, J. T., & Pincus, D. B. (2009). Assessment of parental experiential avoidance in a clinical sample of children with anxiety disorders. *Child Psychiatry and Human Development, 40,* 383-403. doi: 10.1007/s10578-009-0135-z

Chorpita, B. F. (2007). *Modular cognitive behavioral therapy for childhood anxiety disorders.* New York: Guilford Press.

Chorpita, B. F., & Southam-Gerow, M. (2006). Fears and anxieties. In E. J. Mash & R. A. Barkley (Eds.), *Treatment of child disorders* (3rd Ed.) (pp. 271-335). New York: Guilford Press.

Connell, A. M., & Dishion, T. J. (2008). Reducing depression among at-risk early adolescents: Three-year effects of a family-centered intervention embedded within schools. *Journal of Family Psychology, 22,* 574-585. doi: 10.1037/0893-3200.22.3.574

Cordova, J. V., Jacobson, N. S., & Christensen, A. (1998). Acceptance versus change interventions in behavioral couple therapy: Impact on couples' in-session communication. *Journal of Marital and Family Counseling, 24*, 437-455. doi: 10.1111/j.1752-0606.1998. tb01099.x

Cosgrove, V. E., Rhee, S. H. , Gelhorn, H. L., Boeldt, D., Corley, R. C., Ehringer, M. A. (2011). Structure and etiology of co-occurring internalizing and externalizing disorders in adolescents. *Journal of Abnormal Child Psychology, 39*, 109-123. doi: 10.1007/s10802-010-9444-8

Costello, E. J., & Angold, A. A. (1995). Epidemiology. In J. S. March (Ed.), *Anxiety disorders in children and adolescents* (pp. 109-124). New York: Guilford Press.

Cowart, M. J. W., & Ollendick, T. H. (2010). Attentional biases in children: Implications for treatment. In Hadwin, J. A., & Field, A. P. (Eds.). *Informational Processing Biases and Anxiety: A developmental perspective* (pp. 297-319). New York: John Wiley & Sons.

Cowden, P. A. (2010). Social anxiety in children with disabilities. *Journal of Instructional Psychology, 37*, 301-305

Coyne, L.W., McHugh, L., & Martinez, E.R. (2011). Acceptance and commitment therapy (ACT): advances and applications with children, adolescents, and families. *Child and Adolescent Psychiatric Clinics of North America. 20*, 379-99. doi: 10.1016/j.chc.2011.01.010

Craske, M. G. (2012). Transdiagnostic treatment for anxiety and depression. *Anxiety and Depression, 29*, 749-753. doi: 10.1002/da.21992

Dadds, M. R., & Roth, J. H. (2001). Family process in the development of anxiety disorders, In M. W. Vasey and M. R. Dadds, (Eds.), *The Developmental Psychopathology of Anxiety* (pp. 278-303). New York: Oxford University Press.

Dumas, J. E. (2005). Mindfulness-based parent training: Strategies to lessen the grip of automaticity in families with disruptive children. *Journal of Clinical Child and Adolescent Psychology, 34*, 779-791. doi: 10.1207/s15374424jccp3404_20

Duncan, L. G., Coatsworth, J. D., & Greenberg, M. T. (2009). A model of mindful parenting: Implications for parent-child relationships and prevention research. *Clinical Child and Family Psychology Review, 12,* 255-270. doi: 10.1007/s10567-009-0046-3

Ehrenreich, J. T., Buzzella, B.A., Trosper, S. E., Bennett, S. M., Wright, L. A., & Barlow, D. H. (2008). Unified protocol for the treatment of emotional disorders in youth. Unpublished treatment manual, University of Miami and Boston University.

Ehrenreich-May, J. & Bilek, E. (2009). *Emotional detectives treatment protocol.* Unpublished manuscript.

Ehrenreich-May, J., & Chu, B. C. (Eds.). (2014). *Transdiagnostic treatments for children and adolescents: Principles and practice.* New York: Guilford Press.

Eifert, G. H., & Forsyth, J. P. (2005). *Acceptance & commitment therapy for anxiety disorders.* Oakland, CA: New Harbinger Publications.

Eyberg, S. M., & Boggs, S. R. (1998). Parent-child interaction therapy: A psychosocial intervention for the treatment of young conduct-disordered children. In J. Briesmeister & C. E. Schafer (Eds.), *Handbook of parent training: Parents as cotherapists for children's behavior problems* (pp. 61-97). Hoboken, NJ: Wiley.

Eyberg, S. M., & Graham-Pole, J. R. (2005). Mindfulness and behavioral parent training: Commentary. *Journal of Clinical Child and Adolescent Psychology, 34,* 792-794. doi: 10.1207/s15374424jccp3404_21

Foa, E. B., & Kozak, M. J. (1986). Emotional processing of fear: Exposure to corrective information. *Psychological Bulletin, 99,* 20-35. doi: 10.1037/0033-2909.99.1.20

Fonagy, P., Steele, M., Steele, H., Leigh, T., Kennedy, R., Mattoon, G., & Target, M. (1995). Attachment, the reflective self, and borderline states: The predictive specificity of the Adult Attachment Interview and pathological emotional development. In S. Goldberg, R. Muir, & J. Kerr (Eds.), *Attachment theory: Social, developmental and clinical perspectives.* New York: Analytic Press.

Forehand, R., (2005). *Helping the Noncompliant Child, Second Edition: Family-Based Treatment for Oppositional Behavior.* New York: Guilford Press.

Galatzer-Levy, I. R., & Bryant, R. A. (2013). 636,120 Ways to Have Posttraumatic Stress Disorder. *Perspectives on Psychological Science, 8*, 651-662. doi: 10.1177/1745691613504115

Garber, J. & Weersing, V. R. (2010). Comorbidity of anxiety and depression in youth: Implications for treatment and prevention. *Clinical Psychology: Science and Practice, 17*, 293-306.

Ginsburg, G. S., & Schlossberg, M. C. (2002). Family-based treatment of childhood anxiety disorders. *International Review of Psychiatry, 14*, 143-154. doi 10.1080/09540260220132662

Gobrial, E., & Raghavan, R. (2012). Prevalence of anxiety disorder in children and young people with intellectual disabilities and autism. *Advances in Mental Health and Intellectual Disabilities, 6*, 130-140.

Greenspan, S., & Wieder, S. (2006). *Infant and early childhood mental health.* Washington, D.C.: American Psychiatric Publishing, Inc.

Greco, L. A., & Hayes, S. C. (Eds.). (2008). *Acceptance and mindfulness treatments for children and adolescents: A practitioner's guide.* Oakland, CA: New Harbinger Publications.

Hadwin, J. A., & Field, A. P. (Eds.) (2010). *Information processing biases and anxiety: A developmental perspective.* New York: Wiley-Blackwell.

Hawley, K. M., & Weisz, J. R. (2005). Youth versus parent working alliance in usual clinical care: Distinctive associations with retention, satisfaction, and treatment outcome. *Journal of Clinical Child and Adolescent Psychology, 34*, 117-128. doi: 10.1207/s15374424jccp3401_11

Hayes, S. C., Strosahl, K. D., & Wilson, K. G. (2012). *Acceptance and Commitment Therapy,* (2nd Ed.). New York, Guilford.

Higgins-Klein, D. (2013). *Mindfulness-based play therapy: Theory and practice.* New York: W. W. Norton.

Hirshfeld-Becker, D. R., Masek, B., Henin, A., Raezer Blakely, L., Rettew, D. C., Dufton, L., . . . & Biederman, J. (2008).Cognitive-behavioral intervention with young anxious children. *Harvard Review of Psychiatry, 16*, 113-125. doi: 10.1080/1067322080 2073956

Jacobson, N. S., Christensen, A., Prince, S. E., Cordova, J., & Eldridge, K. (2000). Integrative behavioral couple therapy: An acceptance-based, promising new treatment for couple discord. *Journal of Consulting and Clinical Psychology, 68,* 351-355. doi: 10.1037/0022-006X.68.2.351

Kabat-Zinn, J. (1994). *Wherever you go, there you are.* New York: Hyperion.

Kabat-Zinn, M., & Kabat-Zinn, J. (1997). *Everyday blessings: The inner work of mindful parenting.* New York: Hyperion.

Kagan, J. (1994a). *Galen's prophecy.* Boulder, CO: Westview.

Kagan, J. (1994b). Inhibited and uninhibited temperaments. In W. B. Carey & S. C. McDevitt (Eds.), *Prevention and early intervention: Individual differences as risk factors for the mental health of children* (p. 35-41). New York: Brunner/Mazel.

Kagan, J., & Snidman, N. (2004). *The long shadow of temperament.* Cambridge, MA: Belnap.

Kanter, J. W., Manos, R. C., Bowe, W. M., Baruch, D. E., Busch, A. M., Rusch, L. C., (2010). What is behavioral activation?: A review of the empirical literature. *Clinical Psychology Review, 30,* 608-620. doi: 10.1016/j.cpr.2010.04.001

Keating, T. (2006). *Open mind, open heart.* New York: Continuum.

Kendall, P. C. (1994). Treating anxiety disorders in children: results of a randomized clinical trial. *Journal of Consulting and Clinical Psychology, 62,* 100-110. doi: 10.1037/0022-006X.62.1.100

Kendall, P. C., O'Neil Rodriguez, K. A., Villabo, M. A., Martinsen, K. D., Stark, K. D., & Benneyer, K. (2014). Cognitive-behavioral therapy with children and adolescents. In Ehrenreich-May, J., & Chu, B. C. (Eds.). *Transdiagnostic treatments for children and adolescents: Principles and practice* (pp. 161-182). New York: Guilford Press.

Kessler, R. C., Gruber, M., Hettema, J. M., Hwang, I., Sampson, N., & Yonkers, K. A. (2008). Co-morbid major depression and generalized anxiety disorders in the national comorbidity survey follow-up. *Psychological Medicine, 38,* 365-374. doi: 10.1017/S0033291707002012

Kiff, C. J., Lengua, L. J., & Zalewski, M. (2011). Nature and nurture: Parenting in the context of child temperament. *Clinical Child and Family Psychology Review, 14*, 251-301. doi: 10.1007/ s10567-011-0093-4

Klimes-Dougan, B., & Kendziora, K. T. (2005). Resilience in children. In C. E. Bailey (Ed). *Children in therapy: Using the family as a resource* (pp. 407-427). New York: W. W. Norton & Co.

Knox, L. S., Albano, A. M., & Barlow, D. H. (1996). Parental involvement in the treatment of childhood obsessive compulsive disorder: A multiple-baseline examination incorporating parents. *Behavior Therapy, 27*, 93-115. doi: 10.1016/S0005-7894(96)80038-4

Langer, E. J. (1990). *Mindfulness*. Cambridge, MA: Da Capo Press.

Lieb, R., Wittchen, H., Hofler, M., Fuetsch, M., Stein, M. & Merikangas, K. (2000). Parental psychopathology, parenting styles, and the risk of social phobia in offspring: a prospective, longitudinal community study. *Archives of General Psychiatry, 57*, 859–866. doi:10.1001/archpsyc.57.9.859

Lonigan, C. J., & Phillips, B. M. (2001). Temperamental influences on the development of anxiety disorders. In Vasey, M.W. and Dadds, M.R. (Eds), *The developmental psychopathology of anxiety* (pp. 60-91). Oxford: Oxford University Press.

Marlatt, G. A., & Kristeller, J. L. (1999). Mindfulness and meditation. In Miller, W. R. (Ed.) *Integrating spirituality into treatment: Resources for practitioners* (pp. 67-84). Washington, D.C.: American Psychological Association.

Marmorstien, N. R. (2007). Relationships between anxiety and externalizing disorders in youth: the influences of age and gender. *Journal of Anxiety Disorders, 21*, 420-432. doi: 10.1016/j. janxdis.2006.06.004

Maslow, A. H. (1966). *The psychology of science: A reconnaissance*. New York: Harper.

Maughan, B., Rowe, R., Messer, J., Goodman, R., and Meltzer, H. (2004). Conduct disorders and oppositional defiant disorder in a national sample: developmental epidemiology. *Journal of Child Psychology and Psychiatry, 45*, 609-621. doi: 10.1111/ j.1469-7610.2004.00250.x

McCauley, E., Schloredt, K., Gudmundsen, G., Martell, C., & Dimidjian, S. (2011). Expanding behavioral activation to depressed adolescents: Lessons learned in treatment development. *Cognitive and Behavioral Practice, 18*, 371-383. doi: 10.1016/j.cbpra.2010.07.006

McLeod, B. D., Wood, J. J., & Weisz, J. (2007). Examining the association between parenting and childhood anxiety: A meta-analysis. *Clinical Psychology Review, 27*, 155-172. doi:org.offcampus.lib.washington.edu/10.1016/j.cpr.2007.03.001

McMahon, R. J., & Forehand, R. (2003). *Helping the noncompliant child: A clinician's guide to effective parent training.* (2nd edition). New York: Guilford.

McNeil, C. B., & Hembree-Kigin, T. L. (2010). *Parent-child interaction therapy.* New York: Springer.

Michelson, S. F., Lee, J. K., Orsillo, S. M., & Roemer, L. (2011). The role of values-consistent behavior in generalized anxiety disorder. *Depression and Anxiety, 28*, 358-366. doi: 10.1002/da.20793

Mills, J. C., & Crowley, R. J. (1986). Therapeutic metaphors for children and the child within. New York: Brunner/Mazel.

Murrell, A. R., & Scherbarth, A. J. (2011). State of the research and literature address: ACT with children, adolescents, and parents. *The International Journal of Behavioral Consultation and Therapy, 7*, 15-22. doi: 10.1037/h0100921

Olatunji, B. O., Deacon, B. J., & Abramowitz, J. S. (2009). The cruelest cure? Ethical issues in the implementation of exposure-based treatments. *Cognitive and Behavioral Practice, 16*, 172-180. doi: 10.1016/j.cbpra.2008.07.003

Osborne, T. L. (2012, October). *Exposure therapy of anxiety disorders: Bridging the gap between science and practice.* Workshop presented at the Washington State Psychological Association Fall Convention, Seattle, WA.

Norcross, J. C., & Guy, J. D. (2007). *Leaving it at the office: A guide to therapist self-care.* New York: Guilford Press.

Norton, P. J. & Barrera, T. L. (2012). Transdiagnostic versus diagnosis-specific CBT for anxiety disorders: A preliminary randomized controlled noninferiority trial. *Anxiety and Depression*, 29, 874-882. doi: 10.1002/da.21974

Patterson, G. R., & Forgatch, M. S. (1985). Therapist behavior as a determinant for client noncompliance: A paradox for the behavior modifier. *Journal of Consulting and Clinical Psychology, 53,* 846-81. doi: 10.1037/0022-006X.53.6.846

Pine, D. S. (2010). Editorial: Lessons learned on the quest to understand developmental psychopathology. *Journal of Child Psychology and Psychiatry, 51,* 533–534. doi: 10.1111/j.1469-7610.2009.02218.x

Pine, F. (1987). *Developmental theory and clinical process.* New Haven: Yale University Press.

Prinz, R. J., & Miller, G. E. (1991). Issues in understanding and treating child conduct problems in disadvantaged populations. *Journal of Clinical Child Psychology, 20,* 379-385. doi:10.1207/s15374424jccp2004_6

Puliafico, A. C., & Kendall, P. C. (2006). Threat-related attentional biases in anxious youth: A Review. *Clinical Child and Family Psychology Review, 9,* 162-189. doi: 10.1007/s10567-006-0009-x

Puliafico, A. C., Comer, J. S., & Pincus, D. B. (2012). Adapting parent-child interaction therapy to treat anxiety disorders in young children. *Child and Adolescent Psychiatric Clinics of North America, 21,* 607-619. doi: 10.1016/j.chc.2012.05.005

Random House College Dictionary, Revised Edition. (1980). New York: Random House.

Rettew, D. (2013). *Child temperament: New thinking about the boundary between traits and illness.* New York: W. W. Norton.

Rettew, D. C., Stanger, C., McKee, L., Doyle, A., Hudziak, J. J., & Boomsa, D. I. (2006). Interactions between child and parent temperament and child behavior problems. *Comprehensive Psychiatry, 47,* 412-420.

Roemer, L., & Orsillo, S. M. (2005). An acceptance-based behavior therapy for generalized anxiety disorder. In S. M. Orsillo & L. Roemer (Eds.) *Acceptance and mindfulness-based approaches to anxiety: Conceptualization and treatment* (pp. 213-240). New York: Springer. doi: 10.1007/0-387-25989-9_1

Rothbart M. K. (2011). *Becoming who we are: Temperament and personality development.* New York: Guilford.

Rothbart, M. K., & Bates, J. E. (1998). Temperament. In W. Damon

& Eisenberg, N. (Eds.) *Handbook of child psychology, 5th ed., vol. 3, Social, emotional, and personality development* (pp. 99-166). New York: John Wiley and Sons.

Sameroff, A. (2009). *The transactional model of development.* Washington, D.C.: American Psychological Association Press.

Schwartz, C. E., Snidman, N., & Kagan, J. (1999). Adolescent social anxiety as an outcome of inhibited temperament in childhood. *Journal of the American Academy of Child and Adolescent Psychiatry, 38,* 1008-1015.

Semple, R. J. & Lee, J. (2011). Mindfulness-based cognitive therapy for anxious children. Oakland, CA: New Harbinger Publications.

Shapiro, S. L., Astin, J. A., Bishop, S. R., & Cordova, M. (2005). Mindfulness-based stress reduction for health care professionals: Results from a randomized trial. *International Journal of Stress Management, 12,* 164-176. doi: 10.1037/1072-5245.12.2.164

Shaw, D. S., Connell, A., Dishion, T. J., Wilson, M. N., & Gardner, F. E. M. (2009). Improvements in maternal depression as a mediator of intervention effects on early childhood problem behavior. *Development and Psychopathology, 21,* 417-439. doi: 10.1017/S0954579409000236

Silverman, W. K., Kurtines, W. M., Jaccard, J., & Pina, A. A. (2009). Directionality of change in youth anxiety treatment involving parents: An initial examination. *Journal of Consulting and Clinical Psychology, 77,* 474-485. doi: 10.1037/a0015761

Singh, N. N., Lancioni, G. E., Winton, A. S. W., Singh, J., Curtis, W. J., Wahler, R. G., & McAleavey, K. M. (2007). Mindful parenting decreases aggression and increases social behavior in children with developmental disabilities. *Behavior Modification, 31,* 749-771. doi: 10.1177/0145445507300924

Smith, J. D., & Dishion, T. J. (2014). Mindful parenting in the development and maintenance of youth psychopathology. In J. Ehrenreich-May & B. C. Chu (Eds.) *Transdiagnostic treatments for children and adolescents: Principles and practice* (pp. 138-158). New York: Guilford Press.

Spicard, A., Gabbe, S., & Christensen, J. (2002). Mid-career burnout in generalist and specialist physicians. *JAMA, 288,* 1447-1450. doi: 10.1001/jama.288.12.1447

Stark, K. D., Humphrey, L. L., Laurent, J., Livingston, R. & Christopher, J. (1993). Cognitive, behavioral, and familial factors in the differentiation of depressive and anxiety disorders during childhood. *Journal of Consulting and Clinical Psychology, 61*, 878–886. d.o.i: 10.1037/0022-006X.61.5.878

Stoddard, J. A., & Afari, N. (2014). *The big book of ACT metaphors: A practitioner's guide to experiential exercises and metaphors in acceptance and commitment therapy*. Oakland, CA: New Harbinger Publications.

Thapar, A., & McGuffin, P. (1995). Are anxiety symptoms in childhood heritable? *Journal of Child Psychology and Psychiatry, 36*, 439-447. doi: 10.1111/j.1469-7610.1995.tb01301.x

Thomas, A., Chess, S., Birch, H., G., Hertzig, M. E., & Korn, S. (1963). *Behavioral individuality in early childhood*. New York: New York University Press.

Thomas, A., & Chess, S. (1977). *Temperament and development*. New York: Brunner/Mazel.

Tichener, E. B. (1916). *A text-book of psychology*. New York: McMillan.

Vasey, M. W. and McLeod, C. (2001). Information-processing factors in childhood anxiety: A review and development perspective. In Vasey, M.W. and Dadds, M.R. (Eds), *The developmental psychopathology of anxiety* (pp. 253-277). Oxford: Oxford University Press

Virring, A., Lambek, R., Jennum, P.J., Møller, L. R., & Thomsen, P.H. Sleep problems and daily functioning in children with ADHD: An investigation of the role of impairment, ADHD presentations, and psychiatric comorbidity. *Journal of Attention Disorders*, 2014 Jul 11. [Epub ahead of print] doi: 10.1177/1087054714542001

Wahler, R. G., & Dumas, J. E. (1989). Attentional problems in dysfunctional mother-child interactions: An interbehavioral model. *Psychological Bulletin, 105*, 116-130. doi: 10.1037/0033-2909.105.1.116

Wahler, R. G. & Meginnis, K. L. (1997). Strengthening child compliance through positive parenting practices: What works? *Journal of Clinical Child Psychology, 26*, 433-440. doi: 10.1207/s15374424jccp2604_12

Wahler, R. G., Rowinski, K., & Williams, K. (2008). Mindful parenting: An inductive search process. In L. A. Greco & S. C. Hayes (Eds.). (2008). *Acceptance and mindfulness treatments for children and adolescents: A practitioner's guide.* Oakland, CA: New Harbinger Publications.

Wallis, A., Roeger, L., Milan, S., Walmsley, C., & Allison, S. (2012). Behavioural activation for the treatment of rural adolescents with depression. *Australian Journal of Rural Health, 20,* 95–96. doi: 10.1111/j.1440-1584.2012.01261.x

Walsh, F. (2006). *Strengthening family resilience, 2nd Ed.* New York: Guilford.

Wegner, H. (2011). Setting free the bears: Escape from thought suppression. *American Psychologist, 66,* 671-680. doi: 10.1037/a0024985

Wilson, K.G. (2009). *Mindfulness for two.* Oakland, CA: New Harbinger Publications.

Wilson, K. G., Sandoz, E. K., Kitchens, J., & Roberts, R. (2010). The valued living questionnaire: Defining and measuring valued action within a behavioral framework. *The Psychological Record, 60,* 249–272.

Winnicott, D. W. (1960). The Theory of the Parent-Infant Relationship. *International Journal of Psychoanalysis, 41,* 585-595.

Wood, J. J. & McLeod, B. D. (2008). *Child anxiety disorders: A family-based treatment manual for practitioners.* New York: W. W. Norton.

World Health Organisation. (1992). ICD-10 Classifications of Mental and Behavioural Disorder: Clinical Descriptions and Diagnostic Guidelines. Geneva. World Health Organisation.

Yoon, S. Y. R., Jain, U., Shapiro, C. (2012). Sleep in attention-deficit/hyperactivity disorder in children and adults: Past, present, and future. *Sleep Medicine Reviews, 16,* 371-388. doi: 10.1016/j.smrv.2011.07.001

Young, S. E., & Hewitt, J. K. (2011). Structure and Etiology of Co-occurring Internalizing and Externalizing Disorders in Adolescents. *Journal of Abnormal Child Psychology, 39,* 109-123. doi: 10.1007/s10802-010-9444-8

Index

Note: Italicized page locators indicate figures.